GREAT AMERICAN DREAMS

Other books by Robert G. Kaiser

Russia: The People and the Power

Cold Winter, Cold War

GREAT AMERICAN DREAMS

A Portrait of the Way We Are

ROBERT G. KAISER
and JON LOWELL

HARPER & ROW, PUBLISHERS

New York, Hagerstown,
San Francisco,
1817

London

FIRST EDITION

Designer: C. Linda Dingler

Library of Congress Cataloging in Publication Data

Kaiser, Robert G 1943–
  Great American dreams.
  1. United States—Popular culture. 2. National characteristics, American. I. Lowell, Jon, joint author. II. Title.
E169.12.K23   973   78–20169
ISBN 0–06–012237–0

---

79 80 81 82 83 10 9 8 7 6 5 4 3 2 1

For
Hannah
and
Amy

CONTENTS

GREAT AMERICAN DREAMS

1

THE BEGINNING

This is a book about America now. It contains an argument about what is going on in the United States at the end of the 1970s, and it contains evidence, too—the voices of Americans talking about things that interest them. We have come to think of this volume as something like a documentary film in words. It is not a conventional book.

Our method was to record interviews with scores of people who seemed to fit into the category of Americans we wanted to describe. We hoped we could find in the dreams and reflections of these people some important evidence about the state of the nation.

In many ways we found just what we were looking for, but we also found much that we had never expected. Jack Gordon, for example. Gordon is the inventor of a machine that pits any citizen willing to risk 50 cents against a live chicken in a game of tick-tack-toe. A live chicken. And the chicken always wins. The chicken beat Lowell.

Well, America is like that, and so is this book. We know from our own experience that different readers will react in widely differing ways to the voices within. We offer no irrefutable scientific evidence, no rigorous statistical analysis, no new polls or surveys, no right answers. We do offer some theories about the country today and the people in it, but they are theories born of reporters' instincts, based on what we've seen but not provable in court or in a computer. Mostly we offer food for thought: life stories and anecdotes that are meant to set the mind to work reflecting on how a culture exists, how its members survive or thrive.

Most of the interviews in this book were conducted in Las Vegas, Nevada, and therein lies a tale. The two of us met in Las Vegas, where we had been sent by *Newsweek* (Lowell) and the Washington *Post* (Kaiser) to cover one of the infrequent conventions of the International Brotherhood of Teamsters. Neither of us had spent much time in that emporium of culture before, and we were both stunned by it. Not because it was so weird—and it is weird if you look for the buzzard-eyed blackjack dealers and fools losing thousands and old women pulling the handles of slot machines at all hours—but because it was so perfectly American. Las Vegas is the most popular resort in the United States (about 11 million visitors a year). It is a mecca of sorts, and a mirror of popular style and taste. Las Vegas is the home of the clean deal—you get what you pay for, not what you were born to or educated to or elected to. Status, excitement, sex appeal—all can be purchased with cash, nothing more required. Americans like that.

Las Vegas seemed to us a picture window on an enormous American subculture, perhaps the dominant American subculture. We used Joseph Kraft's name for it then, Middle America, and that still seems to be the best label, though the phrase has political connotations that are often irrelevant to real Middle Americans.

Our Middle America is a category that coincides with the 50 percent of the population that considers itself "middle class." (A poll conducted for the government produced that result.) This is not the wealthiest 5 percent, and not the poorest third or so. Merely the act of separating this category from the entire population is statistically revealing; it gives us a "typical" enough collection of Americans, but a thoroughly unrepresentative one too. These Americans do not often suffer the best-known social ills like unemployment or illiteracy. Their ranks include a disproportionately small number of non-whites. They feel no kinship with the upper classes, a distant "them" who march to an almost foreign drumbeat.

These Middle Americans have been the beneficiaries of the fantastic growth in personal prosperity of the last quarter century. Many of them have taken advantage of the extraordinary possibilities for upward social and economic mobility available to Americans since the end of World War II. They pay more these days for a car than many of their parents paid for a house. Not long ago father and his lunchpail rode to work on a trolley car; now husband and wife may leave for separate jobs in separate cars. In a culture whose truck drivers can

earn more than bank vice presidents, whose coal miners' wages exceed
$20,000 a year, the traditional social categories no longer make sense.
From auto worker's blue collar to dentist's white jacket we have created
a two-car, boat-in-the-garage, cabin-at-the-lake class that defies old
measures of social rank. Many of these people exploited the sudden
growth of higher education in America, an unprecedented phenomenon
that now permits half the college-age population in the country to
attend some kind of college. (In West Germany the comparable statistic
is 20 percent; in Japan, 25 percent.)

These are the people for whom America works. They repay their
America with the fiercest loyalty and patriotism. They repay with
faith in the original American Dream.

Though they don't yet realize their influence, these Americans
define the popular culture of our time. They are the heart of the
mass market whose satisfaction is the stated objective of television,
the central element of the popular culture. Their preferences produced
urban sprawl, the highway culture and the decline of the old central
cities. These Americans sustain the national mania for sports, the
fast-food chains, Ford and General Motors. They made millionaires
of the makers of citizen band radios and striped tennis sneakers.

Compared to their parents, these Americans live extremely well,
and they know it. To a degree that may be unfashionable to acknowl-
edge, they seem to be having one hell of a time.

And, of course, these Middle Americans shape our public life too.
No election can be won without a lot of their votes. There can be
no national consensus that is not their consensus. They are us.

We began talking about these subjects at our first meeting in Las
Vegas, while we watched Teamster stewards cheer their elected leaders
on cue. We came to think we could use Las Vegas as the locale for
an intense series of interviews with these Middle Americans, and with
other Americans who claim to know what pleases the mass. But we
weren't entirely confident we could find the right people, or that they
would talk into our tape recorders if we did find them.

We moved to Las Vegas for a summer and sublet an apartment.
It was a blue apartment—all blue, from blue shag carpet to blue toilet
paper to blue-and-silver-patterned wallpaper—that we thought might
have been designed as the Nevada affiliate of a New Orleans bordello.

We rented it from a gentleman with a Sicilian name who accurately described himself by telephone as looking like a bear. We moved in and began talking to people of all stripes and stations.

Our hypothesis was that if we could get people to tell us what they dream about, what they are afraid of, what their lives consist of, we could use what they told us to draw a portrait—literally an impressionistic portrait—of Middle America at the end of the 1970s.

We found a rich variety of friendly, open, curious people who were willing to cooperate with our inquiry. If we had tried walking up to people in any other country on the planet and asked to interview them about their private lives and thoughts, we'd have received more punches in the nose than cooperation. Americans are different. One we found, Dr. Edward Frankel, who runs cosmetic plastic surgery clinics in Los Angeles, insisted that we promise in writing to mention his name and services in return for an interview (there you are, Dr. Frankel). Most others seemed intrigued with the idea of contributing to a book.

After some weeks in Las Vegas, after long hours of interviewing and talking between ourselves, one of Las Vegas's cultural traditions took on the quality of a metaphor for our endeavors. That cultural tradition was "The Perfect, $4.50, All-You-Can-Eat, Champagne Brunch Buffet," a glutton's delight spread out on long tables, dish after dish to sate any appetite. (It is offered in Las Vegas hotels to attract potential customers to the gambling tables.)

The champagne brunch buffet seemed to us to symbolize a style of life that is now accessible to 100 million or more Americans. The morally strong might be able to dismiss it as simple hedonism, but it is more complicated than that. The ability to sample all the different dishes on the mammoth buffet table is the freedom of the age. Don't like where or how you live? Move. Bored? Buy a camper, or get a divorce. Tired of being bald? Buy new hair. Nervous about a flat chest? Buy new breasts. Play hard. Borrow money. Stay *young*.

Staying young in this culture means more than keeping one's figure and fighting wrinkles. The customers at the giant buffet table often fight just as hard to hold on to the fantasies of youth—the dreams one dreams at an age when all dreams are permissible. In cultures that revere the elderly, the aging process produces something valued called maturity, but many Americans find that a discomforting idea.

These are people for whom giving up one's early fantasies simply means giving up. Growing old gracefully is not an American virtue; growing old is an American phobia. Let's not think about it. (Happily, most of the time most people don't have to think about it.)

So back to the buffet. Despite any number of recessions, riots, national scandals and an awful war, the great bulk of the American nation truly does enjoy unprecedented possibilities in life. We have been coming to this for a long time, since the 1950s probably, when "middle class" Americans began to test the limits of a prosperity unlike anything known in any other country at any other time. The society has undergone profound changes in these years: families have shrunk (the most common size for an American family today is *two* persons), women have gone to work, divorce and what used to be called "living in sin" have become commonplace, automobiles have become universal, so have credit cards.

Americans from backgrounds that would have put them in the peasantry in the Old World discovered that you didn't need references to buy a Cadillac or take a vacation in Florida. In fact, because the Great American Dream still lived, you could actually move to Florida or some other place where it never snowed and become a new breed of American pioneer, reinventing yourself and your style of life in the process.

The variety and the opportunities scare some people and appall others, but seem to appeal to most. Many are awed by the possibilities in their own lives, and quite a few people brooded openly with us about whether their children could ever have it so good.

The idea that a large proportion of Americans think that their lives are pretty terrific is a missing element in most contemporary social or political analysis, but it is a fact. An important fact, too, if one is to understand American society and American politics. Politicians and pundits who find "conservatism" in the electorate are often projecting their own interests and thoughts onto people who generally don't share them. Americans are not much taken with politics; any honest reading of the statistics on who votes (barely half the voting-age population in 1976, barely one-third in 1978) confirms that. Middle America doesn't need new programs, new government activism—or it doesn't perceive the need. Middle Americans enjoy being left to their own devices. The "conservatism" so many politicians claim to see is really something much simpler than politics; it is *contentment* with the way things have been going, and reluctance to allow much change.

That contentment will be audible in the voices in this book. So will joy and vanity, hope and ambition, ruthlessness and bigotry, curiosity and smugness. We found great sadness too. We found families with the full array of boats, cars and opportunities who felt a complete absence of what they understood to be family life. We found deep conflicts between desire and responsibility.

There is an obvious contradiction between the infectious excitement of happy Americans and the fact that a lot of Americans don't catch the infection. The sociological implications of our general theory of a contented half of America are not especially cheering. They suggest divisions between those who hold the middle ground and those still looking up that appear profound, perhaps permanent.

But if Jack Gordon could train chickens to win at tick-tack-toe, anything can happen. Hold on.

2

THE GREAT AMERICAN BUFFET

"Everybody Helps Themselves"

The Perfect, $4.50, All-You-Can-Eat, Champagne Brunch Buffet that is served every Saturday and Sunday in the MGM Grand Hotel consists of the following:

Cold Dishes

Assorted Fresh Fruit
Sliced Melon
Peaches
Pears
Tangerines
Waldorf Salad
Cole Slaw
Potato Salad

Sliced Tomatoes
Cottage Cheese
Cream Cheese
American Cheese
Swiss Cheese
Macaroni Salad
Fruit Jello Mold

Kadota Figs
Prunes
Salmon (or Lox) Mousse
Ambrosia Salad
Ham
Turkey
Assorted Rolls

Hot Dishes

Scrambled Eggs
Baked Ham
Bacon
Sausage Patties
Corned Beef Hash
Fried Chicken

Sea Food Newburg
Rice Pilaff
Swiss Steak
Pepper Steak
Pork Chops
Cheese Blintzes

Chicago Round
Steamship Round
String Beans
O'Gratin [sic] Potatoes
Belgium Waffles

Pastries and Desserts

Small Danish Pastries
Blueberry Muffins
Bran Muffins
Coffee Cakes (Prune,
  Cheese, Apple)
Strawberry Shortcake

Pumpkin Pie
Spice Cake
Strawberry Cheesecake
Pineapple Cheesecake
Vanilla Pudding

Apple Pie
Cherry Pie
Fudge Cake
German Chocolate Cake
Coconut Cake

Beverages

All the coffee, tea, milk or "MGM Champagne" you can drink.*

* "MGM Champagne" is a generic term covering a California sparkling wine bought by the hotel in five-gallon tanks. Leon Schelbert, food and beverage director of the hotel, said he was quite sure it came from the Paul Masson winery. Pierre F. Vireday, executive chef, didn't have any idea where it came from.

The man responsible for this array of temptations is Leon Schelbert, a German-Swiss by birth, but an American citizen for many years now, who is the food and beverage director of the MGM Grand Hotel. Schelbert is in his mid-forties, and still speaks with a thick German accent. He is trim and direct. Before coming to the MGM he was the executive chef at Caesar's Palace, the MGM's principal competitor, which also offers a champagne brunch buffet on Saturday and Sunday mornings. Schelbert is convinced that the MGM buffet is better:

The food is basically the same. A scrambled egg is a scrambled egg in both places. And you get the ham, bacon, sausage, corned beef hash, chicken liver, fried chicken, pot roast, uh, pork chops, uh, cheese blintzes, beef Stroganoff, seafood Newburg. Then you get the bagels, the cream cheese, the fresh fruit and the sliced cold cuts—that's the same. It's the way it's presented and the attitude of the people that are serving it. I am in the midst of a tremendous courtesy campaign. I'm totally sold on the courtesy campaign.

And of course there's the matter of presenting. Over at Caesar's they've got one line and they've got dish-out people behind it. When you have the dish-out people they don't always give you the amount that you want to eat. So we have changed it. We set up two lines where the people can go down both sides, so in fact we've got four lines and everybody helps themselves. And they get as much as they want to, come back as often as they want to. And we have found a tremendous response to this. We are using more food this way, but people leave happier. They help themselves to what they want, and— There is some waste, where we see that their eyes are bigger than their stomachs. But as a rule what they take they'll eat, and enjoy it.

As a European-born American, did Schelbert have any opinion as to the symbolism of the all-you-can-eat buffet for Americans? Do Americans like to eat too much?

Well, I would say Europeans are much more weight-conscious than Americans are. And I don't think it's because the Europeans don't like to eat any more. It's because in Europe appearance still means a hell of a lot more than over here. Over here the people do what they want to do and enjoy it, and if they get fat—well, the hell with everybody. And that's a fact, that's a fact.

People do what they want to do and enjoy it. Schelbert's observation, like the buffet he serves, provides a nice introduction to one of the cardinal elements of life in Middle America. Hedonism is the wrong word for it, because hedonism suggests pleasure for its own sake, pleasure above all else, and these Americans don't take it that far. But they come very close. They have unprecedented opportunities for gratification through consumption, opportunities not simply to eat or dress or live well, but to alter their lives—even their bodies.

These opportunities distinguish our time from any other. Modern America has democratized conspicuous consumption—not universally, but widely enough that the half or so of the population we are dealing with here can all partake to some degree. Moreover we have redefined the basic notion of consumer goods, so it now covers not only the traditional *things* like cars and refrigerators, but also intangible goods—for example, a divorce. These intangibles fall into a category Americans often call "freedom," by which it is meant the freedom to "do your own thing." Self-indulgence, a puritan would call it, but it is more like self-fulfillment to those who take part.

The desire to do one's "own thing," to satisfy whatever urges may arise that don't seem blatantly illegal or immoral, may be a by-product of the great American cult of youth and beauty. Pepsi-Cola did not invent the "Pepsi Generation" simply to sell cola to young people; that slogan is meant to appeal to everyone. We take great pains to stay youthful, look youthful, act youthful, often at great expense. But it goes beyond that. Now we have licensed the citizenry to cling to their youthful fantasies well into middle age or even beyond. Staying young means dreaming—and indulging—young dreams.

Kaiser talked about this with a young psychiatrist named David Silverman, a tall, dark man who wears sandals in the Las Vegas summer and smokes a large pipe. He came to Nevada to practice several years earlier because he was offered a good job there; it was not his first choice. But Los Angeles is nearby, he notes, and his kids like the desert and the warm weather. Silverman seems to be doing well. When he talked to Kaiser he was about to begin a new weekly television program on a Las Vegas station, an interview show that would deal with various human dilemmas.

Does Dr. Silverman often see in his patients a desire to preserve their youthfulness?

Yeah, but not in the same sense a cosmetic surgeon does. I encounter it more in the fantasy life of people. People grow up with certain fantasies they don't want to give up. They involve things they want to do later in life, expectations that aren't met. When they get into later life, whatever that is, and find out that these expectations haven't come about, they maybe can panic a little bit. This is something we see very often. So I don't see it the same way a cosmetic surgeon sees it, but we're dealing with the same kind of thing—an attempt to hold on to these fantasies.

It seems to me it's a luxury to be able to entertain these fantasies. I suspect in this country we can grow up with kind of omnipotent fantasies that can remain viable for a much longer period of time than in other cultures. Children growing up all over the world have the same kind of omnipotent fantasies, but elsewhere, where survival is what you have to deal with, these daydreams and fantasies turn to dust a lot earlier. You become involved with survival, family, just remaining intact with what you have, trying to eke out your own niche. In America it's quite different. Even people who don't have a lot of money still have time and still see conspicuous consumption all about them. Making a fast dollar is still easier in this country than elsewhere. Leisure time kind of promotes these daydreams. I suspect in other countries people deal with these issues earlier. We find ourselves waiting until middle age before we have to give up certain long-held dreams.

Of course Dr. Silverman tends to see people who aren't coping very well, who need his help. Most Americans do cope, even if vast numbers of them share this desire to preserve childhood fantasies that Dr. Silverman was talking about. One difference between those who become psychiatrists' patients and the rest may be that the rest find satisfaction in sampling the dishes on the great buffet table of Middle American life.

And that buffet table fairly buckles under the load of its own delights, rather like the buffet tables at the MGM Grand Hotel. It includes an immense variety of physical goods, from electronic TV games, stereo sets and CB radios, to snowmobiles, all sorts of "recreational vehicles," boats, airplanes, water beds, instant cameras, what have you; and also a new product range, including abortion and divorce, new hair for the bald and new breasts for the flat-chested, organized sex therapy, virtually unlimited geographic and class mobility, countless religious or spiritual options and many newly acceptable styles of life previously considered perverse, illegal, immoral or all three.

This variety of treats has been produced for the use of our era through a series of historical coincidences. (Perhaps they were not coincidences at all, but inevitable consequences of the evolution of American society.) For example, it is difficult to imagine American life developing as it has without the help of television, a medium that has not only given the great American masses a body of common experience, but also has introduced them all to ways of life, attitudes, options and urges that many had no way of discovering before television. The final stages of the automobilization of America also preceded our era, bringing with it the suburbanization of the population. This in turn gave us the "suburban housewife," a rich market for new gadgetry, new forms of food, new soap, wraps and traps.

The first exploitation of atomic energy, the rise of the computer, man's first ventures into space, the jet plane and other technical wonders of the age have all been both necessary preconditions to the creation of today's Middle American culture and also important contributors to a transformed psychological climate. Because we have been so much affected by these monuments to our own ingenuity, we have come to assume that we are living in a special time, far removed from even our parents' youth, beyond the reach of our grandparents' imaginations.

All of this adds up to an unspoken maxim of the age: There is no excuse for the old-fashioned. Bring on the new—styles, attitudes, whatever. Wallow not in old habits. Do your own thing.

Darrell, a white-haired man of about sixty who is the proprietor of Darrell's Hairdressers, offered this explanation of the way times have changed:

When I first got into the business we were sort of like the doctors were a few years ago. Now their image is changing too, as far as blind faith is concerned. But we used to have a client come in [to the beauty parlor] and sit down, and as long as you had a license and you were the hairstylist your word was god. Quite honestly, the Toni changed it all. When the Toni first came out everybody in our business said, "It's going to ruin us." Our business did slump, but what it eventually did was open up millions of women to the idea of professional beauty service.

For the first time in their lives they saw what curly hair would do for them. Women began to read more and more. They began to come in and tell us what they wanted, bring pictures in.

I was discussing this with a doctor friend the other night. He said, "Don't feel bad. Women will come in and say they want so many cc's of this and so many milligrams of that. They have diagnosed their case and they know exactly what I should prescribe for them."

You used to be able to forecast what the next trend would be. But today we have long hair, we have short hair, we have straight hair, we have curly hair. We have natural hair, we have colored hair, we have wigs. We have every conceivable shape, size, description. What makes anything right is, it's a state of mind.

The Toni did it to hairdressing, some other gimmick or gadget or revolution has done it to almost everything else one can think of. Our inventiveness has cut us off from our past.

Technology has also infected our efforts to deal with the ancient pains caused by human relationships. We have a wildly diverse collection of experts and hustlers to advise Americans on their relationships with fellow humans. We have computer dating, schematic sex manuals, authoritative scientific defenses of everything from naked aggression to total submission, and new laws in virtually every state simplifying marriage, abortion and divorce. We also have large new industries dedicated to the proposition that there is a physical answer to psychological dysfunction. They give us makeup in a million guises, vaginal deodorant and foolproof deodorant soap, hair tonics and toothpastes and skin conditioners and drugstoresful of related miracle substances. And when all else fails we have Librium, Valium, Quaaludes—chemical pacifiers for all kinds of inner turmoil.

We all know this list now. We are used to hearing these things damned or praised and constantly hawked before our eyes. We act as though they are all perfectly normal, which for Americans on the eve of 1980 they are.

We aren't the same people we used to be—a true observation about Americans at numerous stages in our history, no less true today. The best evidence may be what has happened to the family. Today 60 percent of all Americans live in families of three or fewer members. The most common size for an American family now is two people. Marriage has survived as an institution in American life, but it faces unprecedented competition. In Southern California now about half the marriages end in divorce, and the rate of divorce climbs steadily throughout the country. Dr. Silverman again:

I think there's been a change in family orientation—that the family needs to stay together only as long as they're really satisfying each other. When that stops the family falls apart. Whereas earlier, the family stayed together out of necessity, out of external necessity, because that was the only way the family could survive. Now those pressures are off and there isn't a whole lot holding the family together except the mutual satisfaction of being there.

This has certain advantages and disadvantages. The advantage is that if you made a mistake, you do have a chance to correct it later on. You don't, because of external necessity, have to stick it out. Because that's no good either. You wind up with a family that's full of bitterness, hostility and resentment.

I'm not sure the increase in the divorce rate is a terribly bad thing. Assuming a person can learn something from what he's been through. That's the theoretical goal. Most people don't. That's why people go from one family situation to another and recreate the same thing.

Neil Slocum makes much of his living from divorce; he is an attorney. In his forties now, Slocum became a lawyer as an adult, after many years in the Army. He is a straightforward person, a direct speaker and a firm believer that a good divorce lawyer should be divorced too. "It's very important to know the emotional situation." Slocum is twice divorced and thrice married.

It is quite likely in my opinion that eventually it'll get to the point where practically every marriage ends in divorce, and there will be only a few long marriages. And I think that's not necessarily a bad thing—I think that's just the trend.

I maintain that there are no more bad marriages now than there were, but in the old days—fifty years ago, even thirty years ago—women were tied to economics. There just wasn't any work for women and that has changed lately. And as women discover they are not economically tied, this releases them to realize they may not have to stay in a relationship that's bad if they think they can support themselves some other way, and the children. Many, many women do this now.

Now that we have more leisure time, we can look around and say, "Well, gee, I'm not interested in that person, because he or she doesn't have anywhere near the interests that I do." Women can exercise this independence now more than they ever could before. And it's still true, I think, that there are very few divorces in countries where women do not have that economic independence. Most of them are covered by this veneer of religion or custom or something like that.

Divorce as equal economic opportunity—exactly right. Another dish on the buffet table; try it, you might like it.

How would Slocum instruct young couples who wanted to get married, to help them avoid a bad marriage?

What I would like to do is convince people that marriage is not forever. The majority of marriages do not seem to be forever, they seem to have a duration—five, seven, whatever might be the number of years. And I would try to tell people that they should not expect it to be forever, they should just have less of an expectation for the marriage, and that way they would not feel so upset and shocked and guilty when the marriage did fail.

See, the problem is that people change every year. They say that the cells of our body change every seven years. If that's the case, our relationships change. The person that you are very comfortable with at twenty is totally wrong for you at forty, for example. If we could evade or avoid that guilt—that's the thing that I'd like to do, is get rid of that guilt. Which is the worst part of most divorces.

Slocum met his second wife in law school, where she was also a student. How was this marriage surviving?

Oh, jeez, I wish you wouldn't ask that, I don't know. [He is trying to make light of the question.]

I won't hold you to any prediction.

How soon is this book coming out? [A laugh.] No, uh, my wife and I are, I think, in some kind of a—a crisis, and we're trying to resolve it. But it's possible that we might not. I mean I'd like to make it. I think we will, but it's hard to say.

We both have a lot in common, which has helped us considerably. Because we met in law school. But my wife has suffered some reverses, which have really caused a great problem. For example, she has been unable to pass a bar examination. This has caused us just terrible problems. I mean, she has the degree and all.

Plus, in my own marriage as in most second or third marriages, it's the children. I have children by the first marriage, and that's always a problem, no matter what. No matter what you want to do, until the children grow up, you have to have contact with the other party, the first spouse. It would be nice if you could forget it, but you never can.

Aren't Americans particularly uncomfortable with the notion of permanent problems like that?

That's true. And it is—there's no question it's permanent.

The problem, that is, not the marriage. When Kaiser saw Slocum again some months later, his second marriage had broken up and a third one had begun.

Why do people get married at all if the likelihood of divorce is so great?

That's very simple. There's got to be some orderly way to do two things—to handle property with liability and responsibility, and mainly and most importantly there's got to be some means in society for providing children with name, security and so forth. That's one very strong reason for marriage—legitimization of children.

Is there a human factor too? I mean, is there still something comforting and protecting—

Oh, absolutely.

A spell has been broken in modern America (as it has in a number of industrialized European countries). People no longer feel responsible for their own marriages, nor do they see anything especially noble or grand about the establishment of a family, particularly after the fact. Once this idea starts to take hold, it is impossible to dispel. Now it is generally believed that even the children of an unsuccessful marriage will be better off if the parents get divorced; this is the best advice of the best counselors and psychiatrists. It may even be true.

The ultimate modern American divorce may be one in which *neither* spouse wants the children. "I've heard of that, but I never really have encountered it," Slocum says. In all of his divorces, someone has wanted the children. "I guess you could say that is reassuring."

As to the permanency of problems, this is the land of happy-ever-after, so only happiness is meant to be permanent. Thomas Jefferson promised every American an opportunity for "the pursuit of happiness," but in the intervening two hundred years the idea of the pursuit has fallen out of fashion. Many Middle Americans believe or hope that the happiness itself is their right, as much a right as life or liberty.

It is not marriage that is in jeopardy in modern America, but *permanent* marriage. The marriage business happens to be booming. Merle Richards, for example, is doing very nicely in the marriage trade:

I must have handled half a million couples by now. When we first started this thing [thirty-five years ago] we used to do five and six weddings a week. My Lord, now, during the week we do five or six weddings a day, and on weekends we do forty or fifty a day.

"This thing" Richards started was a Las Vegas wedding chapel, the Little Church of the West. It offers a clean deal: twenty-five dollars to hire the chapel, ten dollars and up for photos, five dollars and up for flowers, artificial or (more expensive) real, and five dollars for a tape of the ceremony. The client must contract independently with a minister; Richards has two on call. The staff of the Little Church is friendly, soft-spoken and efficient. Whether the mood of the wedding is perfunctory or festive remains the responsibility of the participants. Richards, now well into his sixties, is pleased:

We don't get as many movie stars as we used to. I guess a lot of them are living together. Mickey Rooney did five here. Then there's a guy from Arizona, better not tell you his name, who comes barging in here hollering, "Here I come with another one!" He isn't kidding either. People do the funniest things. You wouldn't think things like this go on. I never did until I got involved in it. You meet them when they're happy. It's a big day when they're getting married. Especially when it's the first time. That's one thing that attracted me to this business. You don't have any disgruntled customers, you know. They come in and they're happy and the fact they're happy and everybody's happy makes it an easy business to get along in. They don't come back to me to complain and they're happy while they're here.

Not only movie stars are living together, of course. Marriage was once a license to cohabit, but the license is no longer required. Now marriage is another dish in the buffet. Lowell talked to Mr. and Mrs. William Long moments after they were married in Richards's chapel:

Why did you decide to get married?
   Mr. Long [age twenty, thin and intense]: Well, we lived together for about six months. My parents kind of—well, they won't have anything to do with me right now. I don't know, I was raised in a Catholic family. I guess it got to my conscience. I figured if I loved her enough to live with her, I might as well go the whole way.

Going the whole way—how the meaning of that sort of phrase has changed!

The great American buffet includes lots of new dishes that people can try on an experimental basis. Saul Shuster provides one of them.
   Shuster is a small round balding man of about fifty. He is a photographer, and worked for many years doing publicity work for Hollywood studios and television. He was divorced from his wife in the early 1970s, and moved from Los Angeles to the beach resort at La Costa "to lick my wounds, so to speak." In La Costa, he says, he developed "a system where I can do serious portraiture for a tourist that only stays two and a half days," instead of the ten days commercial portrait photographers generally require. "Once I developed this, I decided that the best place in the world, the largest marketplace in the world for it would be obviously Las Vegas." So he rented space in the shopping arcade of the Dunes Hotel.
   His shop is a glassed-in area at a busy corner in the arcade, its walls covered with color photographs of babies, old men, children, and several nude women, including one dominant one, the most striking photograph on display. It is a picture of a marvelously proportioned blonde who is demurely holding her hair in a loose bun on top of her head and turning away from the camera while her breasts jut into the foreground.

How's business?
   Excellent, excellent. And—I don't know whether it's a shift in the morality of the country—we're doing quite a few nudes.

Just people who want to have their picture taken nude?
   Right, yeah.

Who is this blond gal? Is she a celebrity?

Nobody, nobody, nobody special—just a neat lady who decided to give her husband a nude portrait of herself last Christmas, to be hung in the bedroom. It comes down when their folks come to town. But this girl isn't at all stupid. She gets it back a hundred times. He looks at that on the wall, and—and off he goes, right? And the same applies to the lady in the chair over here. [He points to another nude on his wall.] Of course the only nudes you see hanging are those that I have written permission to display.

What's happened to make this possible—for middle class burghers to break through those old taboos? Do you have any theory about what's happened to us that makes that possible?

Yeah, I think so. The beautiful people today, uh, think nothing of shacking up. They don't care if their parents know it. As a matter of fact they inform their parents. Youngsters are doing it; you *know* they are. Whereas at one time this was absolutely taboo. So I think things are loosening up. And the dominant male sex role is quickly abating. Like, uh, Donohue on television—starts his program the other day with Masters and Johnson. The reason I know is I had a commercial on his program, and he starts the very, very first phrase—all right—"Tell us about clitoral stimulation." That was the opening line! Nine o'clock in the morning on television during summer vacation when all the kids are glued to the set. At one time you couldn't say anything like "bust," you know, until after Johnny Carson.

So I think everybody finds nudity acceptable, and women are now gyrating and groaning, where at one time it wasn't acceptable. I hate to admit this, but I remember the time when it wasn't acceptable. It was a service they performed. Not any more!

I had a lady in there [nods toward his studio behind the walls filled with photographs]—the procedure is a gentle one, quite seriously now. We start with some clothesed photographs, and then I can see the skin tones and shadows and lights and darks. I've been doing nudes now for a number of years and I would always excuse myself. I'd say, "I'll give you a little privacy to make yourself comfortable," and hand 'em a shawl to drape with, and then slowly we do away with the shawl. But lately, the last year or so, I'll say, "I'll leave and give you a little privacy," and they say, "If you don't care, I don't care." And off come the clothes. And these are, in my opinion, all very, very nice ladies.

I've—not that I'm counting—but I've done five schoolteachers, one married to a vice president in a bank. And the nude is a twenty-by-thirty, prominently displayed in the living room, and it comes down for nobody except his widowed mother. Her parents [he laughs]—she says her parents generally come in and sit in a chair immediately below, so they don't have to look at it. But they're not at all ashamed of it. They're proud of it, and she swears it has strengthened their marriage. And I can believe that. I think that, uh, when they share this thing, and share the responsibility—if she grabs his hand and says, "Right there is where I like it," I think it adds enormously to whatever is happening. And that is exactly what they're doing now. I mean Masters and Johnson just blatantly come right out with this information. And there are clinics now— I know there's one in Van Nuys where they teach women to masturbate. I'm sure I'm not telling you something you don't know.

The idea of pursuing a happier marriage through Saul Shuster's kind of photography is a fine example of how the great American buffet can please its customers. Many Americans are enthused by the thought that ephemeral notions like happiness or freedom can be transformed into tangible, acquirable things. We met any number of Americans, for example, who held a private definition of freedom that tied that idea to a physical object, usually a vehicle.

A twenty-one-year-old woman explained the significance of her only substantial possession, a red Corvette:

I throw my luggage on the luggage rack, take the tops off and put them behind the seat. It makes you feel like a bird soaring free. You have the air rushing against your face and you have the sun beaming down on you. It gives you a big sense of freedom, it's not like you're cooped up.

A fifty-year-old pilot who flies small planes for charter explained what he liked about flying: "The freedom of it. It's one of the last free things left."

Don Hedrick, the retired outlaw motorcycle rider who appears in Chapter 16, described the appeal of motorcycles:

It's a freedom thing. You're out in the air . . . We ride a motorcycle because we're out in the air with the wind blowing on us. . . . It's like a guy who flies an airplane. When he gets up in that airplane he's in a different world.

We also heard tangible definitions of happy-every-after, for instance from Mr. and Mrs. Tony Marnell. He is a successful young architect.

Tony: We have a dream, we have a goal.

Sandy, his wife: We're going to leave, and the only thing we're going to take is our children and our books.

Tony: That's all. Just the family and the literature. We have it all planned. [They laugh together.] Someday we're going to take whatever there is monetarily, and we're going to take all the people that have been around us, that worked for us and with us, and whatever is there we're just going to divide it up between everybody. And we're just going to take the literature and the kids and—who knows if at that time they'll be old enough, who knows when it'll come—and put them in the jet and tell the pilot to take us away. I'm trying now to buy a piece of property along the Italian-Swiss border, and we're going to build us a little glass house up there in the mountains. Very, very, very, very simple. And I think we'll just spend the rest of our time up there.

A little later in the same conversation, Tony talked about money: "Money is only freedom. That's all money is in our society. It just— It allows you X amount of freedom."

Speed away, fly away, hide away—freedom. This may not be exactly what Thomas Jefferson had in mind, but then he didn't live to sample the buffet.

Or perhaps these definitions of freedom are just adolescent musings—no matter how old the people who offered them.

3

CLIMBING UP

"I Believe in This Country"

Most of the 110 million or so people who inhabit Middle America are beneficiaries of "upward mobility"—they feel they are living better than their parents did, usually much better. The old palaver about the Great American Dream isn't palaver to them; it actually happened.

That is the import of the American boom that began at the end of World War II. The new American middle class has risen like a perfect soufflé. The speed of the ascent and the distance it covered have left many Americans slightly breathless. It would be difficult to exaggerate the degree to which ordinary people's lives have changed: from city apartments to homes in the suburbs; from the struggle for self-improvement to the realization of education and prosperity; from dreams dreamed to dreams fulfilled.

This is why the Horatio Alger mythology lives on in America. It isn't mythology at all for tens of millions of Americans—it still comes true. Of course it is pure myth for another large category of the population, including the people who could benefit most from Alger-like leaps forward. But they are not the subjects here.

The subjects here are people who have made America work for them, or whose parents or grandparents did, plus the strivers who intend to become the next generation of Horatio Algers. For them the idea of upward mobility—of getting ahead or doing better—is a central element of their lives, either a cardinal source of pride or an inspiration.

"If you work hard there is almost nothing you can't accomplish." We heard that line again and again with only slight variations in wording or syntax. This notion provides both justification for the accomplishments of those who have accomplishments, and an explanation to (or at least an explanation for) those who don't. "Anybody can get his if he works for it"—that is a Middle American slogan.

We heard dozens of Americans' private versions of the Horatio Alger story, but none so vivid or entertaining as Battista Locatelli's. The New York Central Railroad, the Pennsylvania Railroad, even the Penn-Central Railroad may all be bankrupt, but the American Dream is doing fine, thank you. Battista Locatelli is the proof.

Locatelli speaks English like a halting spaghetti commercial. He writes English hardly at all, and has "very little" formal education. Though without any experience in business, he opened Battista's Hole in the Wall Restaurant with a total capitalization of seventeen dollars. Seven years later he is a millionaire—owns his own airplane, and even owns some new hair on the once-bald top of his head.

You're how old?
Forty-six. I'll be forty-six in December.

How long have you had this place?
Seven year and four month to be exact.

When did you come to the United States?
About twenty-eight year ago. I work in a farm driving tractor, cultivating, you know, in California. I was born as American citizen in Italy. My family has been immigrating in and out of the United States since way back in 1800s. When I came to Santa Cruz, California, I got a job in the farming. Then I went to the Portland Cement plant. Then I worked in the slaughterhouse. From that I moved to Los Angeles. Tried to get into the show business as a singer. I had quite a beautiful natural voice. From there I went to restaurant busboy, waiter, then I went back into driving trucks and busses for Shell Oil Company and a private bus company in Los Angeles.

I wanted to be free to push my career, and these people at the bus company they would give me time to come and go as I please. It worked out very good for me, but I didn't quite make it. I sung at most of the major hotels, as a guest appearance, things like that. Then I just come to Las Vegas, cause I like the town, and give it a shot at the restaurant business. I can truly say from zero penny, zero knowledge, we probably have one of the most successful restaurants in the country. The Hole in the Wall of course isn't a hole in the wall any more. We do about four hundred dinners a night. Last Saturday we had Jerry Lewis. Not that it matter, but it's good public relations to have them.

How did you succeed in a business notorious for failures?

Well take one of the main things. I remember a thing that Caruso said. I read in a book. Caruso was the greatest tenor. There were many other tenors around. I can name a whole bunch of them. But he said, "Work, work and work." When he finished work, he replied, "More work."

I'll stay up at night, think of something, get all excited, come down the next day and make the little change. I'll ask questions about the food. Now my wife never cooked. She started out to be the cook. People would come in. They'd say, "Will you make me fettucine Alfredo?" We don't know how to do it. The customer say he know how to do it. I say, "Okay, come in the kitchen and show us how." People actually came in here and cooked their own dinner and were very happy to pay us to help us get going. We were humble. When I didn't know how to do, I told them. And we had people like Sergio Franchi come in and cook a dinner for us and help us out. He got behind the stove. Jerry Vale, Pat Cooper, so many of them. They took a liking. A little family. They called it the "Hole in the Wall" because it was a hole in the wall. We only sat fifteen or sixteen people. It was just a little tiny coffee shop. Then I got books, cookbooks. My wife and I would stay up and fall asleep with our heads on the floor. We started to make spaghetti sauce marinara, meat sauce, we would just destroy it. We didn't know how to. Then the big cook be coming in here, chefs from the Caesars [Caesar's Palace Hotel], and I'd say, "Hey, how do you make this sauce, how you do this, how you do that?" And they were so helpful. We were so grateful they would show us. Now we're known from coast to coast. Canada. People really make reservations weeks ahead from back East. We have a following that's unbelievable.

Battista spews all this out like a high-speed pasta roller. He seems to have a great time just talking.

He is handsome, with a high forehead under his transplanted sandy hair, and he has an athlete's physique.

How many hours a day do you work?

Now I tapered down a little bit. But I used to put in as much as twenty hours. Still I'm in and out now sixteen, seventeen, eighteen

hours. I get up very early, four or five in the morning. I jog, I walk a lot. I believe in physical fitness. I watch extremely what I it [eat]. I'm usually down here five in the morning. I believe in a superclean operation. We have no dirt in our kitchen. We want people to come in and see our kitchen. We close ten or ten-fifteen. We're only open about five hours, but, we have to work ten, twelve hours preparation. The daughters come in to make the manicotti, the pasta. We have people here eighteen hours a day.

What do you think of when you hear people say they can't find work?
I don't believe in that. I've never been out of work in this country. Because I was willing to do *anything* to provide my family with a living. I work as a garbage can man, collecting garbage. I clean streets. I cut lawns. You name it, I've done it. I've never, never been out of work. I believe in this country. You are willing to work, there is enough work for everybody. People say, "I'm a bookkeeper; I can't go out and clean the street." Why can't you go out and clean the street? Our family definitely believes in this. There is a lot of work to be done in this country. I worked in places where the boss say, "This is all I can pay." Hell, I was happy to take it. I worked for sixty-five cents an hour when I first came from Italy. I was happy to have the work. The government has given so much free we are becoming, how you say, freeloader. Not willing to get up in the morning. You see, by nine o'clock in the morning I believe the day has already went by. If you get up early, you're willing to work, there is work out there for you. I've never been out of work with that attitude.

How many children do you have?
Four. I was the eldest of twelve living. My father has four brothers, and the four brothers have fifty-six kids. No television in the old country those days [he laughs].

What do you think about families in this country?
I've raised my kids like my dad raised me. There was twelve of us, brothers and sisters. We never had really any problems. None of us has ever been in jail, or arrested, no kind. We never been involved with the law except to help the law. To do good things for the law. He loved us but he was always ready to hit us if we just stepped out of line.

I really believe that the Dr. Spock way of raising people is never going to work. People must have respect and discipline. Respect of other people's property, respect of everything. We have a huge family. Maybe fifteen hundred in this country alone. I tell you I'm proud to say we won't need the police force because we maintain ourselves, we respect other people's property.

I called the teacher up when my kids went to school and said, "I'll give it to you in writing. My kids get out of line beat the hell out of them." Teachers worry, especially if people have money or power. "I can't touch this kid." By doing that we're helping kids deteriorate. Not making them strong. And solid. In my family when we put food on the table there was no such thing as "I don't like this" and "I don't like this." Everybody ate what went on the table. It made a healthy family. Could it be we are so busy about ourselves we forget about our kids? We are blaming the kids for many things, but they are not to be blamed. The parents are to be blamed for what's happened to the kids. Not enough discipline, not enough love.

Are you interested in politics?

I would like to get involved in it, but I don't think I have enough schooling to. Politics today has too much technicality to it. It's not like the old days. You were a good man, you did your duty. You stuck behind your belief. Today is much more complicated.*

Do you go to church?

We don't go too much really to church. We help many various charity. We feel we do our work for God by giving respect to others, giving respect to what God has put on this planet. If we go up into the forest you won't see none of us leave a can or anything. We feel you do more by being a good citizen, all the time, than just going in there and saying forgive and going out and being a bad guy. How you say it in English? Not doing what you're preaching.

What do you find boring?

I don't find anything boring. I always find something to do. I just love life. I love what I'm doing. I love nature. If I find something not interesting I just close my eyes and look up at something of beauty around me. Even if it's just a big tree. I say, "You son of a gun. You been standing there all these years and I didn't see you." Maybe it sounds silly?

Did you ever think it would end up like this?

Never. Never. It's hard to believe.

---

* Here is a thought we met time and again—politics is out of reach, too much (or too little) to cope with. Locatelli's indifference is typical of the people we met, typical indeed of the American nation. More on this anon.

Would you rather be a singer than run a restaurant?

No. I rather run a restaurant.

What went wrong with your singing career?

Well, I think the timing was off. Presley came in. The Beatles came in. I concentrated too much on opera, and by the time I realized it, I wasn't going to make it in opera because of the finance you have to have behind, and all of the—how you say it in English?—you got to know somebody. Unless you have the machine behind you to really push you, it is a hard business. I'm not too sure how it is now, but it's probably the same. You've got to know somebody. It takes a lot of money. Maybe I wasn't really ready for it, maybe I didn't work enough with it. I was trying to raise a family, had a job with a truck or a bus. I was told the voice had makings.

You might get the idea from this that Battista gave up on the singing. He did not. He has a long-playing record of the songs he likes to sing from time to time in the restaurant—arias and Italian love songs. When Lowell did this interview, Battista gave him a copy of the record. When we went back for dinner a few weeks later, Battista gave both of us a copy of the record. When Kaiser sent a friend from Washington to see him a couple of months after that, Battista used the good offices of the friend to send Kaiser a copy of his record.

You consider yourself lucky?

I have to give it some luck, but the main things was lots of work. The whole family working, working, working. And we're successful. I'm not saying money is everything. But it helps happiness. It's good to have.

With all that working, even Battista has found time to sample the great American leisure industry. He has taken up flying.

How did you get started flying?

The people who own the Westward Ho [motel] came in and said, "Hey Battista, how would you like to go to Alaska? Take a couple of days off?" Well, I really don't like to take time off. People expect to see me here at night. My wife and the kids say, "Why don't you go, Daddy? We'll take care of it. We'll show you we can do it." They did a beautiful job.

Coming back on their Lear Jet, they say, "Battista, why don't you learn how to fly?" I said I don't know, it's pretty tough. But I'm pretty much of a positive thinker. They said, "You can do it." But I never went to school. I don't know how to write. Well, I read English, I write kind of a forty-fifty percent. I came back one night and I say you know, "I'm going to give it a shot." And in two and a half months I had my license. I just worked on it. Two, three hours every day. Practice, practice. Learn how to talk to the tower people. I bought a 210 Turbo Cessna. It cost over $100,000.

You sound like somebody who's always got a new goal?

Real estate. I've done very well in real estate. The money that came out of the Hole in the Wall. We have profit sharing. When I buy a piece of real estate I study the area. Growth. I go downtown in the city. I ask questions of people. What's happening here? What's happening there? I bought one piece of property, just to give you an idea, paid $247,000 for five acres. I bought it for five thousand down. For two acres I turn down one and a half million profit in four years.

Fifteen years ago did you think you'd be a millionaire?

No. It was always my dream, to be a millionaire, but I never thought it would happen so fast. I think I did it in about three years. I haven't changed. When I did it, I sang a song, jumped in the air, hugged the wife. I'm sure I did that. We just celebrated our twenty-fifth anniversary, so I got Momma a new Mercedes. She was very happy. She deserve every bit of it. We're as happy today as we were when we first met. Our relations, our sex life, everything. We combined our minds, keep the spark alive. As we grow older, its good for the man to do little things for the wife. "How nice you look, you hair," a little pat on the *culo*. It gives them a feeling of security.

Are you having fun?

I'm not having the fun of parties every night, going on. But, how you say, that doesn't turn me on. I'm having fun because I'm doing what I want. I can have fun driving down the street listening to the ballgame. I see beautiful pictures instead of something depressed or ugly.

4

THE NEW AMERICA

"Life's Fun . . . Considering the Alternative"

We never found one person whose story embodied all the characteristics and interests of Middle America that we thought deserved some attention, but we did find Sandy Ford. She is ordinary compared to Locatelli, but extraordinary in the degree to which her life and attitudes echoed many others we discovered.

Sandy Ford is a thoroughly likable, effervescent and energetic widow, age thirty-six. She is a buyer of "non-food products" for a large chain of supermarkets, a mother of four, a regular bowler (Monday nights) and a pleasure to talk to.

She is also a beneficiary (and victim) of upward mobility, a parent whose ambitions and fears for her children are typical of many, a classic American consumer, a familiar skeptic on the subject of politics and politicians and a stubborn optimist, despite her own bad luck.

Sometimes I think I miss the hungry years. We've all been through those periods when we think we're poor, and we're living from paycheck to paycheck, we're struggling, and we're trying to pay our bills. We'd like to eke out a little bit and put a couple of bucks away and then one day go down and blow it all on Chinese food—you know, once every two weeks, that's a big treat. I was talking to some friends the other day, and they said they have found that since they're better-to-do, wealthier, they miss those things. They could go and eat anywhere in town now if they want to, but it's not the same. It's not really a treat. It's strange what money does to you.

My kids think they're so poor. We have a friend that has a Cadillac. And when we were running the fireworks stand up here over the Fourth of July—we have a fireworks stand for Pop Warner football to raise money for the team—Tony and his wife stopped by in their green Cadillac. Jay and Michael [her two younger boys] were with me. They thought it would be really fun to sell fireworks, but they were getting hot, and it's not really as much fun as they thought. Tony says, "Let me take the kids, Sandy, and I'll run down and buy 'em a pizza and a cold drink." And they came back, and they're eyes are like this [she opened hers wide, and talked in an excited whisper]: "Hey, Mother, he's got a Cadillac car! You should see all the neat things in this Cadillac car!"

It amazes me to think that my children think they're poor. You know, I think, Golly, you guys, you're not really poor. You've got a swimming pool in the back yard and Jay's got a motorcycle. But they really think they're poor. A lot of that, I think, is associated with the loss of their father. They're not thinking in terms of money, they're thinking how lucky little Guy is that his daddy can take him to have pizza.

It's really nice to think that your kids can have a lot more opportunities than we did when we were children. There's nothing that they can't do, not a darned thing that they can't do if they really set their mind to it. Education is a lot better for children now. I think the new generation is just much better educated than we were. They have more fun, they really have more fun.

Where did you grow up?

Cody, Wyoming. Five thousand people. Icky. Yech.

How old are your kids?

I have Greg, that's my oldest boy, he's seventeen; then I have Jay and Michael. They're my football players, the little ones. Jay's twelve and Michael's eight. Vicky is fifteen. It's funny, she goes to the country club with friends, swims over there and has lunch. She says, "Oh, Mother, we've got a dance, I've got to have a dress." So we go out shopping. That's a lot of fun, you know, to buy your daughter a dress for a dance—fun, and fifty dollars. You know, I think about it, a few years ago fifty bucks was a lot of money. Fifty dollars was going to pay the rent for a month, right? Now I'm going out and paying fifty bucks on this kid to go to a dance? I can't believe it. I'm just grateful that I have it.

What did your husband do?

He worked for a cement company, as a foreman. That's why we came down here [to southern Nevada]. He worked construction in Wyoming, too. We figured we'd work maybe eight months a year before the weather set in really bad and you couldn't work. And we would save like heck in the summertime to try to get us by in the wintertime. That's what brought us down here, of course, was just the dream of having more money and being able to own our own home and just improving our standard of living. We never lived that bad before. I didn't think, you know, but when I think about it, it's funny how quickly you become accustomed to the luxuries of life that you never had before, and never missed.

Like a dishwasher. That's one thing I never wanted was a dishwasher. I never had one till we came down here, bought this house. Then we had one, right? Big deal, what's a dishwasher? I do the dishes by hand. Then one day somebody said, "Why don't you use the dishwasher, it's nice?" So I tried it a few times. Now the dishwasher is out of action overnight and I'm in a panic. Can you imagine me going back to washing dishes? Like I used to do all the time and thought nothing of? Now I've got a dishwasher, I should ruin my hands doing dishes? You just quickly get accustomed to having that.

You make more money down here. Like, when I go back home, I've got a couple of friends that have supermarkets up there and they pay their girls three and a quarter an hour. That's pretty good wages for Cody, Wyoming. And we're making six dollars an hour down here, plus all our union benefits like health and welfare. That's paid, and your retirement. So you really make good money. It's interesting what it does to you. Like I got my power bill, a hundred dollars. And I thought, This is strange, a hundred dollars. And you think, Oh, O.K. it's a hundred dollars. Next month it's going to be lower. But your whole attitude really changes. It's no big deal; it doesn't press you up against the wall to where you're pulling your hair out saying, "How in the hell am I going to pay a hundred-dollar power bill?" Because you figure, "Well, my check is going to be $250, so half of that will pay the power bill, and there's still going to be money left over."

Will your kids lives be different because of this? Because they never went through that—

Well, in a way it worries me. Right now I don't think that the children are as independent. They have a very casual attitude about money. They really don't realize what three dollars is, or five dollars. I'm not sure how it's going to change them. I don't think their desire is going to be as strong as mine was to achieve something. To really crawl up there on top. I really want to be on top, is my desire. I want to be secure, you know, and I have the drive that I think will enable me to get there. And the kids seem like—

Well, Jay. Jay had to have a motorcycle. "Oh, dear mother, I have to have this motorcycle."

"Jay, you know that motorcycle is a hundred dollars." We bought a used one.

"O.K., dear mother, but I'll be so grateful, I'll mow the lawn and do this and do that."

He's had it what, three months? He's lost interest in it. He's really not interested in that motorcycle. And I think, God, when I was a kid—I can remember like working since I was twelve years old. In the summertimes I would babysit every day for like twelve hours a day. And I can remember going to work at Blair Drug when I was fourteen years old. I really had the drive to have this tidy little sum of money so I could become independent and do my own thing. And I don't see that in my children. They really don't worry about it. They don't think, Maybe I should get a job, or, Maybe I should start saving money. Even my seventeen-year-old, when he worked he saved twenty-five dollars a week, but he doesn't have any really wild desire to do anything. That disturbs me a little.

If you allow yourself to daydream about your kids ten or fifteen years from now, what would be a good outcome for them?

I really sincerely hope that they'll be happy. Not wealthy, particularly—I guess that's my own sore feelings. I found that my husband and I worked so hard for so many years to have things, you know, that I have now by myself. And it makes me feel really kind of sad. I feel somehow I was cheated, like, "You've finally made it, and there's nobody here to share it with." That's what disturbs me a great deal. But I just hope the kids will be happy. I don't want 'em to have to worry about money, you know.

I think Jay will probably be a professional football player. Greg probably— I don't know; he may be living with me till he's forty-five or fifty [she laughs]. Vicki will be gone. I think they're all pretty good kids. But it's funny—I don't want my children to think that money is very easily come by. I want them to put a value on something. If Vicki wants a dress for fifty dollars, that's terrific—but I want her to realize the value of that dress. I'd go out and buy her a dress if that's what she really wants. I idolize my children. But just as long as she realizes that this dress is not to be worn and tossed in the back of the closet and never seen again— They should appreciate the good things of life.

Among the good things in life that Sandy has cared about are sports and cars, the two great American preoccupations. Every year she contributes $500 of her own money to sponsor a team in the local Pop Warner football league in memory of her husband. The kids run around in orange jerseys that say "Bill Ford" across the chest. Both her younger sons play on the team, and she is serious about the possibility that her Jay might someday play professional football. Sandy was asked why Americans are such sports-crazy people.

Because we like violence, because we're a violent people. That's part of it. And I think the other part is simply being competitive. Everybody loves a winner. We all want to be winners, right? And we want to be on the winning team. I think we drive that into our children, that it's important to be a winner. I think it's good to play team activities, to realize that you have to work as a team to get the whole thing going. I don't think there should be a lot of pressure put on these young children. It's no big deal. It's not like they're getting paid eighty thousand dollars to play this season. The coaches [in the Pop Warner league] can get nasty too, let me tell you. They get really serious about this, and are sometimes abusive to the children playing for them. I've seen that happen on a couple of teams. Of course the whole organization is also aware of it and they have replaced these coaches—you know, asked 'em to turn in their resignations. It's supposed to be a fun thing.

You know, football's really a pretty violent sport. Really it's very hostile. It's neat to get out there and stick it to 'em good, you know?

What about Americans' love affair with the automobile?

Sure, it's a status symbol. Well, myself, I can remember when I really thought being *in* meant owning a station wagon. To me that had to be something really neat, to have a station wagon and have all the kids pile in—you know. I don't like Suburbia, U.S.A., or whatever, but to me that was my goal. So I've had two of 'em. And I promptly learned that I hate station wagons. You've got seventeen hundred kids in the back seat screaming in your ear. And you not only have room for your four children but by gosh you can get at least seventeen other kids in that car. No thank you. I got rid of the station wagon. I've got me a little Oldsmobile now. That's not my hangup now; cars are not my hangup.

I don't know for sure where I got that idea about a station wagon. I've often thought about it. Evidently, you see, I must have known somebody that in my mind was very successful and was probably, um, just everything perfect. She must have been the perfect mother and she must have looked really sharp and her husband must have idolized her and everything just must have been perfect in this woman's life. And I think about it. Who was it that had a station wagon when I was a kid?

It was a long time ago. To me that station wagon— You know, it's somebody that's very settled—right?—they're not flighty and they're not into big cars. They're very stable, because they're content to drive a station wagon where somebody else is screaming for a Cadillac or a Rolls-Royce or a Mercedes or a Corvette—here's this nice stable station wagon. But as I said, I had one and learned that's not where it's at at all.

It's funny the things you get stuck in your head. I sort of wanted to get a Cadillac [she laughs]. Tell you the truth, this was a secret. I thought, Jeez, wouldn't I like to have a Cadillac, that would be spiffy, driving around in this Cadillac and people's eyebrows would raise and they'd say, "Look at that really neat Cadillac!" [She puts on a deep voice to say this. She likes to put on voices for these asides.] But I didn't get one. I thought, That's ridiculous. I don't even know what they are—twelve thousand dollars maybe? For a car? My whole year's wages I would put on a car? No way. I couldn't do that.

We usually asked people how they thought the country is doing these days. We originally thought that question would elicit a good deal of political commentary, but in fact it seldom did lead to politics. Most people responded in the general way the question was posed, without reference to issues of public policy or specific politicians. Sandy Ford was unusual in this regard. She took the question as a political one, and answered it that way. She was also unusual in the amount of time she spent personally trying to follow public affairs.

What about the country in general—do you feel good about America and where it is going?

Yeah, well, I'm kinda nervous right now. I'm not quite sure where America's going. I really have faith though that it's going to turn out right. I get a little disturbed, you know. I think that a lot of people don't— It's easy to say, "What can I do? I'm only one person. How could I possibly change what's going on?" But I think people are becoming more conscious, and they are going to be taking a more active part in their government and really trying to figure things out.

Why would that happen?

Because people aren't satisfied with the way things have been going. I'm a pretty little naïve person, but I'm horrified to think— Well, the Watergate for instance, that really kicked my props out. I don't have much faith left in politicians, that they would do such ugly things. You put all your trust in this fellow, and you think they're going to do a great job for the country, and they do a rotten thing like that. It really leaves me a little dumfounded.

I was very proud of Ford. I think he did a pretty decent job. I think he did about the best he could under the circumstances. Carter I'm not sure about. I haven't quite formed an opinion of him yet. I'm just not sure. He'll do the best he can. Most of the people thought he could, right? Who am I, a lonely Republican, to disagree? So I think it will turn out good.

I wonder, though—like the shortages and everything that they say. I really wonder if we have all those shortages, or if— I'm becoming paranoid now, and wonder like if they're always telling us the truth or if they're lying to us. I just can't help it.

How much do you pay attention to those things personally?

I read. I read my *Time* magazine every week, trying to keep abreast of what's going on. Sometimes it staggers me, and I don't understand it all. I wish I had more time. I've spent maybe an average of four hours a week just reading or watching the news on TV or specials or whatever. I have too many other things to do—like bowling. [A little laugh.] I think we should pay more attention to what's going on. A lot more attention.

I had a friend that was a U.S. senator. [This is a Wyoming Republican she knew years ago, but she asks specifically that his name not be mentioned, in light of what follows.] He said you cannot believe the rotten things that go on—there really are rotten things that go on back in Washington. You know, the manipulations. He said we don't own the government anyhow. They run it back there the way they want to.

There's a lot of manipulating that goes on in the Senate, you know. It seems like it's not very open to me, the way they control things. "I'm going to scratch your back, but in exchange for that you have to do this." That always amazes me. I don't understand why people can't just be open and honest, and let it go at that.

This is what I worry about, that we're not getting our share of good politicians because they're too concerned, once they get in there, about taking care of themselves. "The heck with the American people. What do I care about those jerks? We needed their votes, we got 'em, so let's take care of ourselves."

This is the kind of attitude I really have gotten lately about politicians— that they're not concerned with our welfare or what's beneficial to us. Maybe I'm wrong, I hope so. Public servants aren't what they used to be. They're usually out for whatever they can get as quickly as they can get it.

Do you think they were ever any different?

I really don't know. I think maybe—maybe a few of 'em I knew back in Cody, I knew Mayor Smith, and I knew Mayor Hindorf, and probably because I knew them maybe my eyes were shaded a little. But I think they were good men and honest men. I still don't really believe they got anything out of it. What, seven thousand dollars a year salary, something like that? But down here [in Nevada] politics is really big business. You can really pave your way into a castle if you handle it right. You know it kind of makes me sick? I kind of think kids get the wrong idea of trust when they see this [bribery of politicians]. And I believe that it happens, I really do.

Sandy Ford was widowed at thirty-three by a freak accident. Her husband was electrocuted on a construction site. Their son Jay saw it happen. Sandy has been struggling to become philosophic about this, to fit it into her life rather than succumb to the sense of loss.

Sandy is a sentimental person, probably more sentimental since Bill Ford died. Now she looks for simple reminders of the benefits of being alive, and she is not embarrassed to talk about them. Sandy has the gift of candor, a quality we heard often in Middle American voices. She can speak directly to an issue, even her own sentimentality, which embarrasses her a little. While she was talking about how the loss of her husband had affected herself and the children, Sandy's oldest son, Greg, seventeen, came out of his room into the dining alcove to complain.

"Hey, Mom," Greg said, "you're not telling him all *that* stuff, are you?"

"Sure," said Sandy Ford. "Why not?" She seemed to enjoy the prospect that her workaday concerns might somehow mean something in an unexpected new way, as grist for a book, of all things. She liked talking into the tape recorder.

You know what I like to do, for just kicks? Go up to the mall. You go up there, and you sit inside, you sit there on the bench and you look at all these people. And it's terrific, you know. You see *all* kinds of people. You see these luscious, luscious women on the arms of little old short pudgy guys. It's really a trip; I love it. I like to go out there and look at the people and wonder what they do, where they're from, and I wonder why they're here and I—you know—just wonder all these things. I do it at least once a month.

You know, all we have to live with is our fellow human beings. And, I have no idea what the world population is there now, but it's kind of neat to know that you really aren't as individual as you thought you were. You share the same fears that I do, and you share the same hopes, and we all really have a lot in common. Of course, I always relate it to myself. I guess maybe that my hangup is I always think, Gosh, that poor person, you know, I feel so sorry for him.

You know what I hate to do? I just can't stand to go to an airport and see all these people crying! It's funny. It happened when I took the kids out to the airport the other day, I put 'em on the plane to Omaha to see their grandparents. There sat a man and a woman and a little boy. The little boy was maybe four or five years old, and the woman and the child are leaving on the plane. The guy is standing there, and they're getting ready to walk on the plane, and it's very slow cause it's crowded, and he bends over and he hugs this little boy, and the little boy just— God, you were going to have to pry the kid's arm from around his daddy's neck. And he says to the little boy, "Goodbye, Scot." And little Scot's back is just like a spike; he is not going to turn around and look at his father. And I can just feel the tears coming [she is speaking with melodramatic sobs in her voice]—I'm not kidding—and I'm thinking, Oh, my God, how painful. That guy has the same emotions that I do. He's not very happy to be letting his child go off. And here my kids are sitting on the plane and I'm trying to be a big grown-up—"Well, they're just going to Omaha, that's no big deal." [Sandy mocks her own reassurances to herself at the time.]

[A long pause.] It's— Life's fun, though, you know. You wouldn't want to miss it for the world. Considering the alternative, right? It's just neat to be here, to be experiencing it. It's nice. You learn a lot. Some of it not so good, but you learn a lot.

Have you ever had what you thought was a really original idea, sort of "Ahhh, now I understand"?

Yeah, I've had ideas like that. I don't know if they're ideas. It's like, well, for instance, after my husband was killed. I was married when I was sixteen years old, and I lived with my husband for seventeen years, so he had me longer than my parents had me. And it was very painful for me to open my eyes and say, like, "I'm all alone in the world. Here I am thirty-three years old, and I'm a big girl. I've never been a big girl in my life." That was really scary. I had a hell of a time there.

Then finally it seemed—I can't explain this; probably it came just through struggles with myself—it seemed that "You really don't have to be afraid, Sandy. They're not going to come around and evict you. You're perfectly capable of making that house payment, you're perfectly capable of working." And finally I guess it like dawned on me that "Ahh, you see, Sandy, it's not so hard to be grown up and by yourself after all." To me that was an original idea, that I was perfectly capable of being by myself.

This led to a conversation about psychological strain, and then psychiatrists:

You know, it's funny, I took my little boy Jay, the twelve-year-old who was with his father when he was killed, and he was a witness to it. And it was very traumatic for Jay. So I took him to a psychiatrist. He wasn't doing anything really weird or kinky. In fact, he didn't talk about his father, like, from that day on he never mentioned him. That was it. He cut it out. So I took him to Dr. Hess, a child psychiatrist, who said it's just a process of grief, you know, it takes a long time.

And I said—stupid me, I could have kicked myself—I didn't think, and I said to him, "Would you think this would be a permanent-type damage?"

And he looked at me and said, "Sandy, certainly it will be permanent. His father is dead. That's pretty permanent. He will learn to live with it, and adjust to it, and eventually things will work out." That was a year ago, and things are stabilizing. But it was hard for the little fella, really super hard.

It took me a long time before finally it could sink into my head that he really wasn't coming home. I guess probably I kept all of his things— his clothes and all of his pipes. As you can see, I still have a lot of them. But it was very difficult for me to pack those things away. I guess it was nine months, and finally I thought, Well, I guess I might as well get rid of them. It was painful, it really was. So I can imagine what little Jay and little Michael—

You know, he will say he wants a daddy in the worst way. Oh, God, that kid wants a daddy. Every once in a while he'll be sitting watching TV and he'll say— A little tear will trickle down his cheek, and he'll say, "Mother, you just don't have any idea how hard it is to be a little boy growing up without a daddy."

And of course I get—chokey. "Yeah, you're right, Michael, I don't. Someday I'll find you a daddy, buy you a pony." He thinks that's neat.

Sandy Ford escaped from Cody, Wyoming, to unexpected affluence, and is now conscious of how her new standard of living has changed her attitudes. Her new respect for the dishwasher symbolizes the change.

She is scared about her kids, scared they're spoiled, scared they don't know the value of a dollar, scared they won't know how to compete the way she did, and yet she finds this hard to talk about directly. She "idolizes" her children, but they make her nervous. She is impressed by the opportunities they seem to her to have.

She loves her house in the suburbs with the pool in the back, loves her new Oldsmobile and loves weekend trips to the lake or mountains.

Sandy's conviction that politics and politicians are outside her own real world was typical, though she seemed to care more about both than many Americans we met. She didn't see anything in the political process that could satisfy her worries or hopes.

She was beguiled by the classic American delusion that everything will turn out okay—a childhood vision of happy-ever-after that captivates many Americans well into adulthood. Unlike a lot of people, Sandy caught herself and decided to become a grown-up. But she realizes that this might never have happened had her husband not died. This seemed to be what she was saying when she recalled how she had asked the child psychiatrist if her husband's death would cause "permanent-type damage" in her son. Is death permanent? She could have kicked herself for asking.

The sudden, freakish death of her husband deprived Sandy of her just deserts. This is the power of fate at its cruelest, a power enhanced by the way Americans now live, speeding from place to place, life to life, throwing themselves at the mercy of machines and forces they don't entirely understand. But that's the fun of it too—that's how you chase a dream.

5

KIDS

"Thunderstorms. Strangers. New Kids. Downtown."

Sandy Ford worries that her kids have it too soft—that they don't know the meaning of a hard day's work. She worries that they live in an insulated and comfortable world where they are cut off from reality. Her worries are as commonplace as any we found in Middle America.

Kids are everyone's reminder of how much the world has changed. Today's Middle American kids don't grow up in Cleveland or Philadelphia or Topeka or Los Angeles, but in the vast American suburb, the sea of lawns and detached houses that has washed across the countryside since World War II. Today's Tom Sawyers and Becky Thatchers have no fences to whitewash, and a ride on a raft is probably a day's drive away at an amusement park, but they have other compensations: fifty-dollar skateboards and $150 ten-speed bikes, monster movies on television, an endless variety of sports and activities. Little League used to mean baseball, but in the late 1970s it can also refer to football, soccer, motorcycle racing, tennis, golf and sailing. Children are trained as puppeteers, dancers, actors, musicians, painters, potters, karate masters.

None of this has much to do with the childhood of their parents, a fact that the parents often brood about, and that can even provoke a conversation among the kids. Upward mobility means more than improving one's life and surroundings; it also implies a steady stream of new beginnings and a loss of ties to the past.

Lowell met a fourteen-year-old named John, the son of a man who teaches in an inner-city high school in Detroit and a woman who works as a secretary. Lowell asked John what he would like to

tell the grown-ups of America on behalf of their kids, and this is
what he said:

We'd like to know what it was like when they were kids. We don't
know because they don't talk about it. We want to know what it was
like. So we can know what kind of progress has been going on. We're
going to want to compare our childhood—compare ours with theirs. Kind
of take that into consideration so we can think about how our children
are going to live when we grow up.

It seems unlikely that at fourteen, John is really worrying about
how his own children will live, but there was no doubt at all about
his craving for a sense of where he came from. John embodies just
those qualities that Sandy worries about. He is isolated in his suburban
nest, cut off from any firsthand knowledge of a world in which people
find life a struggle. His conversation is candid, but it sounds superfi-
cial—the product of a life free of dangers or threats. He is a fourteen-
year-old of our time.

While Lowell talked to John, his parents were preparing for the
next day's departure on a family excursion to California and back
in their van. John, a gangling kid with a mop-head of brown hair
and glasses, had just returned from a week at music camp, where
he had worked on his trombone and tried a hand at conducting for
the first time. He pondered Lowell's questions intently, frequently
fingering the ersatz football jersey he wore as a tee shirt:

You like school?
   Yeah.

That's a tentative yeah. What do you like and what don't you like?
   Well, some of my classes could have some changes. The time between classes could be longer, but some people object to that because
you'd be in school longer.

Any particular area of school you like better than any other?
   Math is my best. That I like. And band. Band is the greatest. I play
the trombone.

How hard do you have to work to do well in school?
   This year, lots of homework. Usually every night. You have to study

but not really that long. A few minutes, a half hour. Study every night. And do the work in school. Forty-five minutes to a class.

Is it really hard?

Some of it. There's some things you've never heard of. New concepts, ideas. But it's relatively easy.

What do you make of adults these days?

Adults? I guess they're doing a pretty good job of what they're supposed to be doing.

What are they supposed to be doing?

Watching over us. Helping younger people. Stuff like that.

Do most of the kids you talk with think their parents are doing a good job?

I don't usually talk to my friends about their parents. What they're doing.

Is there anything you think you couldn't do when you grow up?

Anything I couldn't do? Right now, I can't think of anything.

If you really wanted to be President, you could?

If I tried, maybe. If I wanted to, I could take a shot.

Could you make a lot of money?

[Casually.] Oh, I think so.

How would you do it?

I'd think about teaching, giving private lessons on the trombone. Mainly in music or some field in education. Or the law.

What would you define as a lot of money?

[Deep sigh.] Oh, well, twenty thousand dollars a year.

Have you ever wanted to do something your parents wouldn't let you do?

I can't think of anything right at the moment.

Did your parents ever tell you they couldn't afford something you wanted to do?

[Long pause.] Ummmm, no.

Do you feel at all insulated from the rest of the world?

No. I don't even think about that.

What do you like best about where you're living right now?

It's a city. You have nice neighbors and not a lot of crime. Not right here in this city. You know, murders or anything like that. There's a good police staff. Some of the bad things are we don't have our own fire department. We have to depend on another suburb. That's basically it.

When you were a little kid, what were you scared of?
Parents, crime— No, wait a minute, crime was not a problem. Usually it was thunderstorms. I dreaded those. Strangers. New kids. Downtown. Things that are strange to me.

The modern American kid does not feel "insulated," but is afraid of "downtown." That is the new reality.

Do you know any black kids?
Oh, yeah. We have an integrated school.

Do you have anything to talk about? Do you feel distant from them?
Not really. I participate in sports with them. They're in my classes.

Do you ever sit down and talk much?
With *them?* Not really. I don't really sit down and talk with them.

Why would that be true?
I don't know. Probably there's a difference in race or I'm afraid to talk to them. Something like that.

You're afraid of them and they're afraid of you?
That could be, but I've just never gotten around to talking with them. It just never happened. We do talk. We're not separate from each other. Sometimes in classes we talk about last night's basketball game or to-day's spelling test or something like that.

John's life rarely connects directly with the world described every night by Walter Cronkite, which may explain his choice of a favorite television show. He likes *60 Minutes,* the CBS documentary program, which allows him to look in on the "real" world.

I love *60 Minutes.* I think it's the greatest. They do research. And I like a couple of comedy shows. *The Love Boat.* Well, I guess just that one. *The Love Boat.*

Why "The Love Boat?"
Well, it's funny.

Why is it funny?
Well. [Long pause.] I don't know.

There's got to be something about "The Love Boat" that strikes you.
[Belligerently.] It's on a ship. I love the water.

Lowell repeatedly asked for a list of personal complaints. John—
wanting to help—could produce really only a shopping list of things
he'd read or heard about. He honestly seemed so satisfied with his
own life—whether out of inertia or enthusiasm—that he had nothing
to complain about.

Give me your list of complaints about the world.
For one thing, the energy situation. Wasting fuel. There's none to
get. And racial discrimination.

You think your parents are wasteful?
That happens, sometimes. But we've been conserving with the energy.
Most of the time. Well, I don't really think so. We don't waste paper.
We've got about twenty feet of papers in our garage. I don't think that's
being wasteful. I'm going to turn it in for a paper drive. Get money. That's
cool.

Tell me more about things that bug you personally.
Money. People are getting overpaid. Like athletes. Millions of dollars
and they're not doing anything sometimes. Take Joe Rudi. He got paid,
I don't know, two or three million dollars, and he was injured. You've
got Reggie Jackson [abrupt pause]; but he's good. So except him. The
same thing with pay for jobs. Men and women. If a man can do a certain
job and a woman can do it just as good as a man, who's going to get
paid more? The man. You know why? Because he's a man.

You said you don't understand what life was like for your parents.
No, not really.

Tell me what you think it was like.
Well, my dad was born when the war was going on and it must have
been panic. My dad lived in an apartment with his mom and dad. I remember he played sports and got a pretty good education. So did my mom.
My mom doesn't teach but she went to school with my dad.

Do you think they were able to do the same kind of things you're doing?
[Very long pause.] I think so. Except—no—my dad didn't own a bicycle.

His dad and he would rent bicycles for thirty-five cents an hour. That
was in the inner city. They had a field probably about a mile away. We
have one right here down the street. There were probably some things
they didn't have, the open space. They had a factory across the street
too. The pay is more now that it was then. At least I think so.

In other words, John's dad grew up learning to fend for himself—
to rent a bike if he couldn't afford to own one, to make his way to
a playing field a mile from home, to cope with life in an industrial
inner-city neighborhood. Resourcefulness was a crucial element in his
father's education, but it need play virtually no role at all in John's.
His trombone, his comfortable life in the suburbs, his sense of security,
all came to John by birthright—rather the way Sandy's daughter got
her fifty-dollar dresses for big nights on the town. Parents are enormously proud that they can provide all those things, and enormously
nervous about the consequences of providing them. How can a kid
who never has to struggle ever learn to struggle? Yet later life cannot
be arranged and protected the way childhood can—something parents
sense and fear.

*Tell me what you think the country's going to be like ten years from
now.*
     Ten years. Hmm. [Sigh.] Well everything is probably going to be indus-
trialized. People are going to be taken away from their jobs by machines.
You're going to have, instead of a secretary, a machine you just dictate
to. You've already got automatic typewriters.

Is that going to be good or bad for the country?
     It's probably going to be good, because these people who are going
to be fired from their jobs are going to be hired to build the machines.
They'll be getting paid. They can get oil from sand. That's good. Our
energy problem won't be that much of a burden on us. If we can put a
man on the moon, of course we can do all this other stuff.

Do you see any problems that can't be solved?
     No I don't. Maybe some diseases. Cancer. The common cold.

Do you ever envision a world in which you can't find a good job?
     [Long pause.] No, I can't.

Assuming there are kids somewhere who are better off than you are, what would they have that you haven't got?

A bigger house. Their parents are better paid.

If your parents made more money, how would that affect you?

We could probably go on longer trips. Instead of three weeks, four. Go overseas. Move to a bigger house, maybe a swimming pool in the back.

You sould like a young man who hasn't got very many complaints. Nothing makes you unhappy?

Not a lot.

6

CONTENTMENT

"It Seems Like Everybody Has Everything That They Want"

America's great mass of contented citizens disappear in the optic of our age. The oldest rule in journalism makes this happen. "Dog Bites Man" isn't news. The man has to abandon his normal position and start the biting himself to get into the newspapers or on television.

At the literal level this is fair enough. Walter Cronkite would not hold a dominant share of the television audience by opening his broadcast every night with a report that most Americans, particularly those in the vast middle class, spent another happy day today going about their business. If news truly did "mirror" the society, that sort of bulletin would indeed be a principal item on the Cronkite show nearly every night of the year. But such "news" is ordinary—it isn't really news at all—so Cronkite tells us about a lot of rabid human behavior instead. He also tells us a lot about the issues raised by the losers in American society, issues that don't play well in Middle America.

The news media are naturally drawn to "issues," "problems" and conflict of all kinds. These are the phenomena that tend to preoccupy political pundits and public opinion pollsters too. A good story for the Cronkite show or for the local newspaper is one that dramatizes something new, unexpected, contentious or sentimental. A timely poll is one that tells us how we feel about the latest speech by the President, the latest fad among the young or the fate of the dollar on the Zurich exchange.

Both the good stories and the timely polls obscure the fundamental fact about contemporary Middle America: It lives outside the issues, problems and conflicts of the day. Of course there are exceptions—

for example, when school busing comes to one's own neighborhood, or when the rate of inflation soars—but they are exceptions. The pundits regularly tell us that the country is up in arms over this or that, but in fact Middle Americans are rarely up in arms over anything at all.

If Mr. Gallup sends his representatives into the country to ask about some hot issue of the day, he will get answers. Americans don't like to look foolish when asked a serious question, and many of them welcome the opportunity to vent their spleen or wisdom. If the pollster appears at the door to ask about taxes, he is likely to hear (surprise!) that taxes are too high. When asked to rank the nation's problems in order of their gravity (usually from a list of problems handily provided), Americans respond—depending on the season, and on what issues Cronkite has recently emphasized, among other factors—that inflation or crime or whatever is the overriding problem of the day. The results of these polls are "accurate," but also profoundly misleading, because they don't reflect the fundamental contentment with the world that is typical of Middle America.

The Californians who voted for Proposition 13 in 1978 and thus created a national tax revolt—at least in the eyes of countless politicians and commentators—provide a good example of this phenomenon. In fact, the election in which Proposition 13 was on the California ballot attracted just 69 percent of the registered voters (or 45 percent of the voting-age population of California), and one-third of them voted against the proposal. So this wave of popular indignation was set off by 30 percent of the adult population of California. Moreover, Proposition 13 was the product of a very special situation: Real estate values had been rising like a hot-air balloon for many years, property taxes following them up. Many middle class citizens found themselves paying $4000 to $5000 a year in property taxes—more for taxes than for their mortgage payments. Along came a right-wing real estate man named Howard Jarvis with a proposition that offered many Californians the opportunity to reduce those taxes and put up to $1000 or more in their pockets merely by casting a yes vote—and this at a time when general inflation had given every citizen a heightened sensitivity to his personal cash flow. Yet a third of those who did vote voted against Proposition 13, and most Californians did not vote. On the basis of this result, the country was widely declared to be in the throes of a universal uprising by irate taxpayers.

The problem here is that politicians and pundits share a common stake in the game of politics as it is presently played. In fact, it is presently played by a minority of the population, and the game is dominated by issues that a majority apparently believe are irrelevant to them. Curiously, the same pollsters who do timely polls on issues like the tax revolt also do research on the mood of the citizenry that is probably much more revealing. When asked entirely personal questions about their own lives and prospects, Middle Americans are content and optimistic. We found that contentment and optimism in abundance in our conversations.

Gene and Wilma Caldwell of Springfield, Missouri, are happy Americans. He is a pharmacist, she a schoolteacher. Lowell found them tending their car and trailer in a campground on the edge of Las Vegas, where they had a conversation:

Wilma: We were at the International Holiday Rambler Rally in Colorado. There were 2200 trailers there.

What do you like about camping?
Gene: We have our own little home right with us. Our own facilities. Our own bed.
Wilma: And you can still get back in the boonies with the type of trailer we have. We love camping out in the rough, but yet we still want the niceties of a john and this type of thing, you know? Rough but not too rough.

What kind of hobbies do you have besides camping?
Gene: Gardening. Taking care of the yard. That's about it.

What kinds of things do you find boring?
Gene: We don't have time to get bored.
Wilma: Television's a bore in the summertime.
Gene: We didn't even bring our TV with us.
Wilma: We have a large home and a large yard. It takes nearly all of our time.

Why are so many Americans fat?
Gene: They don't respect their bodies, I guess. They don't stop and think. They see something they want, they have the money, they can buy it. They give in to temptation. They don't stop and think what it'll do to their body.

Wilma: And junk food is too easily obtained. At every corner there's a junk-food place. We met a fellow from Germany a couple of years ago at the Grand Canyon, and I asked him, "What are your impressions of America?" "First," he said, "I've never seen so many fat women." But he made the remark that Americans just eat all the time. Every time you turn around they have a candy bar or—

Gene: I can never get my money's worth at a smorgasbord or all-you-can-eat place.

Wilma: That's because you're not a big eater, dear.

Is your life different now than when you first got married?

Wilma: Yes. To begin with, I never thought of us as a two-car family. I started in college when my daughter was in the third grade. We got married when I was seventeen. We managed with one car all these years with the kids, you know. So here we are. We had a smaller home, we moved into a larger home. We now have three cars. Everybody has a car in the family. We're doing things we would never have thought of. Just like this trailer we're pulling. We bought a brand new Buick and paid cash for it. This type of thing. Which I never thought we'd be able to do. We pay cash for most of the things we buy rather than time payment.

Gene: That's what keeps the economy going. If everybody put it away there'd be a depression pretty quickly. I think we're like most Americans. We have the philosophy "Do it now. While you can. Tomorrow might be too late."

Willie Newbold lives in a small town about an hour's drive south from Chicago. Newbold is black, and when asked what he did for a living, replied, "I'm a railroad man." Lowell also found him in a campground, and discovered by talking to him that he and another man were driving across the country in a modest motor home with nine children. Newbold seemed remarkably at ease under the circumstances.

Did you enjoy driving out here?

Yeah. I enjoyed coming, but I don't know how I'm going to enjoy going back.

How do you like the motor home?

It's nice, but it sure was hot coming across those deserts. The air conditioning works, but when you get in that hot climate you feel like you aren't getting no air.

What do you make of the country these days?

For living expenses, I think it's getting worse. They got to cut down on the living expenses. But you know, back where we're at they aren't too high. We grow things. They don't grow nothing out here [in the Nevada desert]. That's what makes it high out here. Where I live, I grow my own stuff. Garden, hogs, chickens. I don't have problems with food.

Wesley R. Kriebek is a professor of agricultural economics at Penn State University. He is pulling his trailer across the country en route to a meeting of agricultural economists in San Diego.

We've had a travel trailer for about five years. This is the first one we've had with air conditioning.

What's your sense of where the country is going these days? Is it getting better, getting worse?

I think it's a mixed bag. We see signs of maturity in our country. The clientele at the campgrounds is just fabulous. We've found a lot of very interesting people. But as I see it, water and energy are going to be two critical factors, and I do wonder sometimes about how we're going to fare if we really get into a tight energy crunch. I think most of us are responsible people and will do our share if we see others are doing theirs. That's the way I feel.

Compared to where you thought ten years ago you were going to be today, how's your life going?

Well, you know, you set targets, set goals, achievements, where you'd like to be. Sometimes you make one step forward and one or two in reverse. But quite honestly, when I look at my life, little did I realize I would have the opportunity to travel in a nice trailer, take my family on an extended vacation. When I was a farm boy right after World War Two we didn't have the advantage of being able to see these sights. We just didn't have that opportunity, to see these national parks.

But now I see my lifestyle is so much different than that of my parents and that of my grandparents. I wonder how my children are going to be able to supersede what I've been able to provide for them. When we were at Zion National Park I saw that they are making plans to expand national parks into Alaska. I probably won't be able to afford to go into Alaska. I hope I can. So maybe there are dreams ahead for our children. I worry about our children. Just a little. You can't help but be concerned as a responsible citizen by the inflation and high unemployment we have.

The job that I have is most challenging. Coming in regular contact with youth is a challenge. We've got some very, very sharp kids in this country. It's challenging. It's exciting. I find that I frankly look forward to going to work. It may sound naïve, but it's true. There are no boring periods in my life. I enjoy every minute of it.

Margie Olafson is twenty-one, very blond, Nordic to a fault and ready to seek her fortune:

I was in Florida for a while messing around and working. I learned to handle myself around people pretty good there. But then I moved back home to St. Paul for a little bit. I thought I'd like going back. It's pretty and clean. But I didn't like it. I don't like the weather any more, and the people are all so cold. I just wasn't comfortable. So I came out here to Nevada.

What I want is to work and save some money and go to California, then work and save some money and go to Mexico. Things like that. Now is the time for me to do this kind of stuff. Even my mother said that. I can handle people. I've worked as a waitress and like that. I'll be all right.

You seem pretty confident. What about the people who can't make do very well in America these days? Do they just suffer from a lack of ambition?

That's true. It really is. I know people who are on unemployment all the time. They're lazy. They really are. I've always been able to find jobs. I don't pay a lot of attention to news reports, stuff like that, but I don't feel very sorry for those people.

But you're young, attractive and white. What if you weren't?

I don't know. Maybe it makes a difference but I don't think so. You see black models on TV commercials. Look at all the money O.J. Simpson makes. You can't be making excuses all the time. I've got friends like that. They never really try. They just complain.

Art Robertson of Toronto, Ohio, is a 320-pound bear of a man who picks up friends the way squirrels pick up acorns—instinctively. He picked up Kaiser in O'Hare airport while both were waiting in line to get on an airplane. "What are you, some kind of writer?" Robertson asked, looking at Kaiser's portable typewriter. That set

off a conversation that continued on the plane. Later, Art and his
120-pound wife, Janice, a schoolteacher, sat down for a long talk.

The Robertsons, both thirty-seven, are childless. She is a graduate
of Kent State University, he never went to college. He is a metalworker
now, working with titanium, an unusual specialty. Robertson does
most of the talking, though his wife contributes periodically, and he
is enthusiastic about every topic that arises.

What are the Robertsons dreaming about? "Oh, I don't know,"
Janice replied. "As I get older the dreams change." She sometimes
feels she would like to get away from Toronto, Ohio, and see the
world. "But at the same time I'm very security conscious. I don't
know if I could ever do it." And what about his dreams?

> Art: It's crazy, crazy. I don't have any.
> Janice: Oh, Art, yes you do. You want to own your own tavern.
> Art: That's not a dream—that's going to happen. That's a plan. I
> don't want to work for somebody, I want to work for myself.

In fact, Janice's mother owns a tavern in Toronto, and Art could
take it over someday. He already spends a lot of time there. The
regulars in the tavern contributed $3800 to help finance trips to Florida
and Buffalo by the 120-pound football team Art coaches.

"I feel I could have done more with myself than what I have,
but I don't really regret it that much." He played halfback in high
school and turned down numerous college scholarships. He actually
signed a letter of intent to attend the University of Miami. "But I
had a new car, a job paying $150 a week, so a week before I was
supposed to show up down there I called 'em and said, 'Maybe I'll
come next year.' And the next year the same, and I never went."
Instead he took up coaching young boys. "Instead of going to college,
I guess this is where I get my big thing out of life."

His boys are now a favorite topic of conversation. He recites the
names of former players who went on to big-time college football,
several of whom he expects to play professionally. "There's even one
guy who got an appointment at West Point."

"Christmastime is unreal at my house. You can't get in the door,
so many of 'em come to see me." And when a former player asks
for guidance about going to college, "I try to give them better advice

than I got. I tell 'em, just try it, go for a year. If you don't like it, O.K."

Art said he has been asked to get into politics, and that he has helped his best friend run for several elected offices, but somehow— he can't explain just why—he wasn't interested.

I think I'd rather sit back, and if somebody I know is involved in politics, I'd rather call him and say, "Hey, look, we've got a problem, it's up to you to take care of it." I think I would rather have myself tell someone, "You take care of this," instead of having someone tell that to me. Maybe that's what it is. Maybe I don't want to be a public servant, and that's what a politician is, a public servant.

And how are things going in the United States in the late 1970s?

I don't think it's getting better, but I don't think it's getting worse either. I think people are more loose right now than they have ever been. Everybody's driving new cars. Seems like even though the percentage of people that's unemployed is way up, it seems like everybody has everything that they want. I don't know very many people who want for anything, do you? Of course, in a small community like Toronto we're not seeing the country as a whole. But as far as the people in the country, I don't think they're hurting.

Don Godsey is a boyish, exuberant thirty-two-year-old father of two who sells specialty advertising gimmicks for the Kingston Corporation in Hixson, Tennessee.

Where's Hixson?

Hixson is near Chattanooga. We're thinkin' about annexin' Chattanooga shortly.

How'd you get into this business?

Well, I used to be a pilot, and this company had a plane, and all I did was fly for 'em. But you don't make any money flyin' planes. So I came into the business with the idea of learnin' it from the bottom up, which I did. I worked in the factory for a year, and became a purchasin' agent, and eventually was a plant manager, and then into sales. The money's in sales. I enjoy sales, enjoy meetin' people. I'm on the road eighty percent of the time. Cover primarily the Southeast, sometimes get up into Ohio, Illinois.

What are you selling the most of?

Right now? I believe this item right here. [He shows off the "Kwiz King," a triangular piece of plastic with fifteen holes punched in it, accompanied by fourteen little plastic pegs. It is a game based vaguely on checkers.] Now this is an item what's been around a long time. It has been made out of wood, and they used golf tees for pegs. When you go into a restaurant and order your food, when do you want your food? Right then, don't you? The reason fast-food chains are doin' so good is that they give such fast service and quality food. But people—especially families—still like to take their wife and children and sit down and order something. Takes ten or fifteen minutes to get it. You don't want to sit there and wait on it. So this game gives you somethin' to do. Your mind's occupied with playin' the game, you're not wonderin' whether the steak's gettin' cooked right, and the kids aren't squirmin' and all this. We made this board so you could imprint it [with the name of a commercial establishment], and instead of usin' golf tees, we use these pegs with the round flat tops because you can imprint on it too, and turn it into a co-op-type situation. Co-op meaning you could put Coca-Cola on the pegs and Joe's Barbecue on the board part. It's a good item goin' for us right now. The factory's runnin' six days, two shifts makin' it right now.

Another new item for us is the all-plastic yardstick [which can be imprinted with an advertiser's message and given away]. The reason we're going plastic— I'm not goin' to tell you there's a shortage of wood, but there is a shortage of wood for yardsticks. Yardstick wood cannot have knots in it, cannot have poor grain. The guy that sells us blank sticks says he can make more money makin' two-by-fours than sticks. So we went to plastic because we can give a better product for less cost.

When did you learn to fly?

I learned to fly when I was sixteen, out of a cow pasture. In fact, the first time I flew I stole the plane and flew it. Lucky I'm alive. Very lucky.

What kind of education do you have?

I have a B.S. degree in agriculture. From Middle Tennessee State University. My big goal was to fly with the airlines, and I went to college just for that. [He never did get an airline job.] I went when I was twenty-five years old, just to get the degree. I didn't care if it was music. Well, I was raised on a farm, so agriculture was an easy thing for me to go through college with.

This is because the airlines require all pilots to have a college degree?
Yeah, a degree. They didn't care if it was in music or what. It's a screening process, you know.

Is that something that's wrong with this country now, these formalistic requirements?
Sure it is. And you go take their tests, they're formalistic too. You know, they don't want a guy too smart and they don't want a guy too dumb, they want a guy that's in the medium of these tests. I took a test with Southern Airways, and the guy told me that a genius is too smart to be a pilot. They'd be unsatisfied with that kind of work. He [a genius] couldn't sit up there flyin' an airplane—he'd be wantin' to run the whole airline in three months. He'd be unhappy, and eventually this could cause problems right in the cockpit. I don't know how they figure it. It's psychologists do all that stuff.

Godsey has his own psychology of sales, at which he appears to be doing well. "Sales are made on enthusiasm. Enthusiasm is probably 75 percent of it." He has more than enough.

In your travels around your territory, how do you find the state of the nation these days?
The state of the nation as far as I'm concerned is in excellent condition. You know, you'll always have your problems of poverty and crimes— you'll always have that. Any time you got masses of people you're gonna have it. But I think it's no worse than it was in the 1930s, it's just exploited more. Don't you think so?

Exploited by whom?
Oh, the news! No, TV, I mean. [He seems to remember suddenly that he is talking to a journalist.] I don't mean they're throwin' it out of proportion, I'm just sayin' you hear more about it faster. Uh, 1930, if they had— Let's say a union had a riot at the steel mills, you probably wouldn't have heard about it for five days. And it seems like if it doesn't make big news its easier to calm it down. But once it makes big news— you know, "Look what we did!"—then that's not bad news reporting, but I think it kind of kindles— I think our nation is in much better shape than the world, in my opinion. I mean inflationwise, and the whole route. [He gets off the subject of news reporting that quickly, in mid-thought.]

Thinking ahead in your own life ten or fifteen years from now, what are you hoping for, what do you see down the road?

Me, I like to think that down the road I'll have more customers, therefore more sales and more success. And more success means your family has more success from the material standpoint. I'm a very optimistic person. I'm not pessimistic. I don't believe in a depression over the horizon, or a recession even.

What do you worry about?

The only thing that would knock me down would be an illness. Of course everybody worries about their health. I guess when you get past thirty you think, Well, if my health went down, that's it, that's my job.

But I don't worry about anything as far as a job or job security. If they decided, Look, we can't afford you any more, well, that's partly my fault if they can't afford me. It would mean I'm not keepin' my sales up. But I feel like I can go to ten other people in the industry and get a job. I'm not worried securitywise or anything like this.

The contented American is a common phenomenon. We heard scores of voices like these, recounting lives that inevitably include the predictable range of pain and frustration, but which strike the people who are living them as essentially happy, comfortable, interesting. We repeatedly heard the ring of authentic enthusiasm. "I never thought of us as a two-car family," said Mrs. Caldwell—and now they have three.

A false index of happiness? No, it isn't false. It is not complete either. The Caldwells also seemed to like their work and to like each other. But the car—or the trailer it pulled, which provided their access to all kinds of unexpected pleasures—was no small contribution to the fun they were having.

Another common sentiment was the one not quite articulated by Art Robertson: "Seems like everybody has everything that they want. I don't know very many people who want for anything, do you?" In other words, my friends, my family are doing well—in fact, the world I live in is filled with people who are doing well, and I rarely see people who aren't. Robertson himself mentioned one of the obvious challenges to that impression: "The percentage of people that's unemployed is way up." But he didn't know those people, and it was clear from his conversation that he was not convinced of their existence or their plight.

Margie Olafson had a similar thought: "Look at all the money O. J. Simpson makes." Or, things aren't really so bad for black people, are they? She didn't think so. Reports of our social ills are greatly exaggerated—or so it seems to many Middle Americans.

Art Robertson said something else that was echoed in many of our conversations. Asked how things were going in the United States, he didn't think the country was getting better, "but I don't think it's getting worse either."

Wesley Kriebek put the same uncertainty about the future in a different context (one we heard repeatedly): "I wonder how my children are going to be able to supersede what I've been able to provide for them."

7

OPTIMISM

"The Calamity-Cryers Are the Sad Part of Our Country"

The idea that an entire society could be built on optimism was invented in America. Without an extraordinary display of optimism at the very beginning there could have been no America. We have been living on it ever since. Wilma Ray is living on it:

I'm going to Los Angeles next week. I'm going to be on *Hollywood Squares.* My girlfriend won fifteen hundred dollars on the show, and she recommended me. She told them, "I have a girlfriend who's even nuttier than I am; you'd like her." So they invited me down for an audition. I'm going to win the fifty-three-day cruise. It's the secret square, the grand prize. My husband says he couldn't take that long a trip. My sister would probably like it.

Where does the cruise go?
    Well, I don't know the shape of the world very well, you know? Rio de Janeiro—can you get there on a boat?

Yes.
    Well, that's one of the stops.

Irving Shapiro, a kosher caterer from New York, is also thriving on optimism:

Is it a problem for your business that fewer and fewer Jews respect the kosher laws in their own lives?
    No, no it isn't. It's a question that's often raised with us. A customer will say, "Gee, we're not kosher, but we have to have a kosher affair." See, the groom's family will be kosher, or somebody's grandfather or

uncle or something. A rabbi once said to me, "We can satisfy everybody by having kosher food served, but when we serve non-kosher food we may be hurting somebody. So let's stay with kosher food only." No, I don't think kosher catering has dropped off because of people not being kosher.

The late 1970s have been a boom time for optimism in America. This is one subject on which Mr. Gallup's polls are probably very accurate. Every year he asks his sample cross section of Americans whether they are confident about the future—nothing specific about politics or public issues, a simple question of confidence. In 1973, barely half Gallup's sample answered affirmatively. By the time Jimmy Carter was inaugurated President, the number of optimists had jumped to two-thirds of the population, the highest figure Gallup had recorded since the early 1960s. And among the Americans who concern us here, the percentage of optimists was much higher. The gloomiest generally don't quality as Middle Americans; they have too much to be gloomy about.

We found optimism in such quantity we could have bottled it for commercial exploitation—stubborn optimism, professional optimism, ridiculous optimism, indomitable optimism.

Jess Kirk, for example, a Harvard graduate who intended to be a doctor but became a nightclub maitre d' instead:

Oh, one worries about the country now and then. So much of the world has a very dim view of our future. And I think that's sad. I don't think it's a dim view at all. Well, for instance, they say the world is so overpopulated we'll never be able to feed ourselves, and that sort of thing. But you can drive through our country and you'll see millions of acres of tillable land lying idle, doing nothing. So I'm not impressed by all the crying that you hear. I think we could have four times the population and still feed our country quite well. Japan is quite well off, a hundred million people on an area not near as big as Nevada. If we did it the way they do, we could feed a billion people very nicely in this beautiful country. So the calamity-cryers are the sad part of our country.

And then there are those who are forever dissatisfied with conditions—"He's getting better opportunities than I am," that sort of thing. And he expects somebody to hand it to him, instead of going out and struggling for it. I was a hillbilly kid and I went to Harvard myself with no money. Anybody could who really tried and wanted to. Anybody in the world can have most anything he wants if he'll give it a fair, honest try.

Or Jane Z——, a working woman of about fifty-five, mother of three grown children, who recently had a breast removed because of cancer:

I had a mastectomy eight months ago. I'm under chemotherapy now. Another three and a half months more to go. So I was infected with cancer, and it gives me a feeling that, um, "You're lucky to be alive." Really. And I've taken it in my stride. I would not let myself break down over it. I'm very fortunate that I caught it in time and that I'm as well as I am. And, uh, I just— We just take every day the way it comes. I've never cried over it.

These damn women who write books on breast cancer. I read one of them—*The Day That I Cried.* I've read the book *Breast Cancer.* I just sat there—this was about three months after my operation—and I sat there for two solid days absorbing every word in that book. And I was a nervous wreck, not because of what happened to me, but to read how this woman explained it, in a way that could frighten so many people. And 95,000 women a year are having mastectomies. I mean this is an unbelievable, terrible thing. If I were to write a book on this— and it would be a best seller—I would write just the opposite. My book would say, "Damn it, women, aren't you lucky? Aren't you damn lucky? Don't just sit there and cry over this." I was very unnerved by what I read, because I think that as much as they could see the worst part of this, there is a happy part of it too.

Or Wade Colgate, a young man, age twenty-three, who makes his living as a dancer:

I like America. I believe in America. I really believe in the concepts of this government. The concepts of freedom. Individual pursuit. The idea of free expression. I really believe in the integrity of the individual human, the value of the individual human. There are a lot of problems, but at least people are aware of them a lot more than they are in some other places.

I'm bisexual. I think homosexuality will come out of the closet and become more acceptable. People have been brought up thinking, Bad, wrong. A cattle prod goes off in their brain as soon as it's mentioned. Now people have confronted it, thought about it, which is probably more than they've ever done before. The younger people are much more tolerant. One of my theories is that younger people are so much more aware, and it has to be television. I have a younger brother and sister who are seven years younger than I am. Every step of the way, they've been five years ahead of where I was. All these television shows, television situation comedies, where you sit down and they play out human drama, and it's played for laughs, which has taken the edge off. We've been taking ourselves too seriously. Now people are much more able to look at life and shrug their shoulders.

The important thing for humanity is the relaxation of the values that say "No, you can't be this, or do that." The American concept that you can be and do anything you want is essential. People have to express who they really are.

I think America is entering a humanistic period. Whereas you could say on the surface that America has always been very humanistically oriented, I don't think it has. I think it's just beginning; we've just scratched the surface.

We met a young architect in Las Vegas who had already designed a large hotel-casino though he was not yet thirty years old. His name is Tony Marnell, and he offered a theory about American optimism:

When you find the high points of any architectural period, you'll usually find that the civilization at that time was on the breach of a new spirit or a new hope. Well, you tell me what the new spirit or the new hope is for twentieth-century man. What is he looking forward to? He is looking forward to being dictated to by the machine. The machine has him, it's inevitable. He can't exist without the machine knowing how he exists, where he exists, when he exists. And what do those people out there— What's their hope? They live under the optimism that the machine is going to solve the problem. To me there's a very big difference between hope and optimism, and you know, we are not living in an age of hope, we're living in an age of optimism.

8

AMBITION

The successful fulfillment of most Middle American dreams requires ambition, but ambition alarms many Americans. This is a dicey subject. Doing well, getting ahead, working hard and the rest are all perfectly acceptable, but being pushy is not. The distinction may be purely cosmetic—ambition is fine, provided one disguises it.

But not everyone bothers to disguise it. Many Americans sense that as long as the Horatio Alger mythology is generally accepted, even crude ambition will also be accepted. Hence the currency of "Nice guys finish last" and similar sentiments. Those whose ambitions are large and undisguised often feel they are trading the affection of their peers for respect. Why not?

We met quite a number of these ambitious people—people who have volunteered for duty on the front line of the struggle for personal betterment, even if the costs are high. Two of them deserve special notice, one whose ambitions have been largely fulfilled, another who is still hoping.

"Cattle . . . Flies . . . Rabbits, or Whatever You Want to Call 'Em"

Donald Widenhouse is a go-it-alone American, a breed celebrated in our culture. We like Lone Rangers, self-reliance, "self-made" men. Widenhouse has made himself rather wealthy with his wits and his instincts. A country boy from North Carolina originally, he now stages gimmicky promotions for businessmen who are trying to attract clients. The promotions are based on Widenhouse's instincts about what his fellow Americans will respond to. He has pursued his ambition by adhering to a personal theory of human nature:

Anything that's free [he laughs a small laugh] attracts people. I've always found really that to move people—that's what you're doing—you don't *like* to really treat 'em like cattle, but people talk about people as cattle. To move people, the one thing that makes a guy react is something that's free. I could give away ice cream free and attract a segment, and I could add candy and I'd attract a few more people, and chocolate candy and a few more. Every time I've ever made a dime it's been by giving something away free. People respond to it.

Ten years ago, you could use in mailing—direct mail, as an example—you could use the word "free" very easily. In the heading of a mailing I could say to you, "Bob Kaiser, you just won three days in fabulous Florida absolutely free!" And it would attract, say, twenty, twenty-five percent return from people sending you ten, fifteen dollars as a handling charge. Then you would in turn take that person and sell him—virtually sell that body—to, say, a land company or something of that nature. Not knowing much about land companies, I liked to do business with them in the beginning, and I made money with 'em. It was something I couldn't turn down. But they're very—I'd say a prostitute-type business, you know, very unethical type business. . . .

But as far as moving people, it's the carrot and the stick—carrot and a rabbit. He'll just follow it around. You've gotta find out what you want to cater to your rabbits, or whatever you want to call 'em. . . . Your big companies, Kellogg's, all these people do it. Coupons. There you see ten cents off or twenty cents off, and people use 'em. Really, it's simple.

How big is the— I want to say the "sucker factor," but I don't mean to be so derogatory. How smart are people? I mean, you say something is free—

People are smarter today than they were ten or fifteen years ago, from exposure, and the media—as far as understanding things. But people are basically the same evidently, because percentages don't change with your mail order things. Like, say, a "free" gimmick that you might have run different ways ten years ago would run, say, from ten to twenty-five percent return, and today it still runs about ten to twelve percent. That's an example.

Donald Widenhouse was born in the Piedmont of western North Carolina. "I was raised in a one-room schoolhouse with five grades in there." His father sent him to college, but he didn't understand the possibilities then, to his great regret now. "I didn't appreciate education, I didn't go after it like I should. I had it and pissed it

away. I went to college, but it was like a farce to me—it was a party."
All this came out in a long talk in his office in a bungalow in a
residential neighborhood. At the end of that talk Widenhouse revealed
that he sometimes dreamt about giving up the business and going to
law school. "You know how it is, how sometimes you know you
could do something really well? Well, I could be a damn good attorney."

Widenhouse has discovered that the gambling industry makes good
use of his talents. Most of his business now is with smallish Nevada
casinos. Widenhouse devises promotional campaigns based on intro-
ductory free gambling gimmicks to attract people to his clients' establishments. He claims enormous success. Doubling a casino's business
is not unusual, he says. A small man with boyish good looks, he
says all of this while looking you right in the eye, with conviction.
Widenhouse is a master of the skills taught by Dale Carnegie. You
believe him. Also, he makes it sound simple: "It's like me saying,
'Here, play this dollar in nickels for me,' or 'Here, play this five-
dollar chip,' and the first thing you know, right away you're playing
again, but it's with your own money. I got you right up to the table
and set you down is what I did, right? You know what I mean?"
Yes.

*Do you ever have the feeling that you're kind of a great puppeteer, pulling
strings, and the people are dancing down at the other end?*
    No-oh. [With feeling.] No, I don't. I enjoy doing what I do, and I like
people—much as people are hard to find that you can like. Can't like
many people. It's hard, hard to find a friend, you know what I mean? A
person who's really truthful. Because most people are after what they're
after.
    I just look at it like a fairy-tale thing, with the guy—the peed piper,
right, or the pied piper, whatever you call it. And if you've got honey, I
guess you'll attract flies. And, of course, other things attract flies too.
You can attract people with good or bad. I guess that's what I'm trying
to say, you know? People really don't know the damn difference until
they get in there and see—"Well, it's not honey." But then they don't
come back. But you can still attract 'em. I guess it's like a magnet, certain
things to certain people.

*Do you feel that this kind of work develops a kind of cynical attitude
about human nature?*

Oh, yeah, I would say so. Yeah. A guy shakes your hand and you—just watch out! Just watch out. I went home on a vacation, and I see my brothers and sisters are about the same way. It's just to me a very unhappy situation sometimes that I even try to become friends with people. Cause I end up getting fucked. When they start becoming friends with me, I start wondering, Well, what do they want? What are they after? What's the end result? And, of course, it's good to be that way, I guess. Some people say it's not, some say it's bad, some say it's good. To me it's good because I lose less, whether it be from a monetary standpoint or just a mental thing. You follow me?

We of course live better, I guess, than any place on the earth. You probably know more about that. I haven't traveled that much outside the States. But hell, just in the States you see a lot of poverty, you know? Mexico, which is not the States, but to me it is. Hell, I can go home and see poor people, see them everywhere. Sometimes I think about it and I get sad, you know, because I think, where the hell am I going? And the only reason I think— Well, it's my love for my daughter and my wife that keep me going.

Do you ever think what kind of world your daughter is going to have to deal with?

Oh, God. Yeah. Maybe it won't change a lot. [He is thinking about this with some care.] When I say people won't change, I mean our beliefs, our earthiness, or whatever the word might be. She's gonna see many changes, I guess, like I have. I can remember running a drive-in theater and seeing a picture about Las Vegas and wondering if I would ever get there. I was thirteen years old, twelve. I'm thirty-seven. A few years ago I was in the country.

It's gonna be an exciting world for her. If she makes it that way. It's going to be—a lot of open space, you know, a lot of new frontiers if a guy wants to make 'em, lot of new frontiers, lot of land.

So she's got a lot to look forward to, talking about my daughter. She's got a great personality. She's loved, and the only thing she's got to look forward to is learning that people are going to hurt her, which I try to teach her. It's hard— Sometimes it's not hard, cause it just happens every day when somebody's a snob or says dirty things to you at school. Kids grow up awful fast.

One of the realizations we've come to, talking to as many people as we have for this book, is that this country works for an awful lot of people.

Oh, yeah.

The general sense that you can get a fair shake if you work hard is very strong. It makes you nervous in a political sense—because it's working so well for so many people, those poor people in the Piedmont of North Carolina, or in the ghettos of Washington, or wherever, disappear from view very easily.

Well, we lost track of them, you follow me? I'll be honest with you. I bought a car the other day— To tell you the way I think sometimes— and I never told this to anybody—about eight months ago I bought this new Mercedes. O.K.? The car cost what—twenty-two, twenty-three thousand dollars. O.K.? And when I ride down the street, a lot of times I'll see poor people, what I consider poor, straggly-looking with two or three kids and an old beat-up car. Knowing the wage scale that man is probably capable of earning, I feel sad, you know?

Well, I like to make donations. I like to help people, so I do that to boys clubs and things of this nature, because you can't— It's hard to find an individual to help.

See again, most people when they're in that category are happy. I thought they were not, not too long ago. But they are. That poor boy and that poor man in some cases is happier than you or I with our whatever we might have. And he knows there are other things out there, and I think he knows he can get 'em if he wants 'em, but he doesn't want 'em. And they're perfectly content with their way and their life, and they make whatever they make a week, and they're happy, and they go out, and they do their poker playing on Friday night and their drinking on Saturday and their church on Sunday. That's the way it is.

The American way.
That's it, yeah.

Kaiser met Widenhouse in an auditorium in the local convention center. The room was filled with moms and dads. Kids were all over the place, most of them girls, most in party dresses, many with elaborate hairdos. A local disc jockey was trying to hold the crowd's attention with his presentations of successive diminutive contestants. This was the *Our Little Miss* pageant. The winners would go to Buffalo for the national finals, if they could pay their own way.

The girls had memorized brief walking routines—across the stage, curtsy, keep smiling!, twirl about, walk off. Of the younger girls, Gabriella Widenhouse, five, did this best, or so the judges concluded. She won the Miss LaPetite trophy, about as big as herself, and the trip to Buffalo, which her father could afford thanks to his success in business.

Gabriella gave this interview moments after her victory was announced:

How did you learn to walk across the stage? [She had an elaborate routine, punctuated with curtsies.]
I did it by learning.

Who taught you?
Nobody.

How do you feel about winning?
I like it.

Did you think you were going to be the winner?
Yes.

Why did you think that?
Cause I was doing good.

Necessity's Daughter

Unlike Donald Widenhouse, Shirley Walker has no marketable skills, at least in the conventional sense. She is a classic ambitious American nevertheless.

Americans have always loved inventions and understood that necessity is their mother. Shirley Walker is an inventor. Her self-designed project isn't quite ready for a patent yet, but when it is, it should be in the finest tradition of the better mousetrap. Having examined the likely endgame of life in a broken home on a dirt-poor farm in Missouri, Shirley Walker reinvented herself. She did this with considerable thought, some risk and a remarkable understanding of the potential benefits and probable losses:

Someday I won't be twenty-five years old. Someday I'll be fifty years old. And I don't want to worry about making a living. When I'm fifty years old I want to have it made. And I will.

Lowell first met her in a hotel bar. Shirley's presence there was unusual. At the time, she was the first woman ever to work as a bartender in a major Las Vegas hotel. She had left home in the Ozark country of Missouri only six months earlier, so getting this job was an important accomplishment.

Moves are as important to sex symbolism as they are to basketball or ballet, and Shirley behind her bar had them. The momentary glance at a staring man was masterful. So was the throaty laugh—as much a barrier as a signal of appreciation. Yet nothing in her manner or her laugh cut a man off completely; she always left a residue of hope. And she never stopped performing behind the bar. Her thrusts of bust and bottom—less than bumps and grinds, but more than accidental—provided a sort of street-theater burlesque.

The props Shirley used for her performance combined natural assets with some outside help. She is pretty in an accessible, straightforward way—smallish, with thick dark hair, open bright eyes of a brownish hue, a small nose and a charmingly askew mouth. Those were all gifts of nature. Added later—parts of her invention—were the perfectly straight capped teeth, the well-modulated voice and the large, erect breasts. When working behind the bar she wore a tight tee shirt, no bra.

Shirley's ambition is security. When we met her she was certain that her best shot at security was through the money of a man—a man she hadn't yet met, but who was due any moment. She understood that she was shooting high, especially for a woman with no education and no middle class credentials. But she was utterly certain that there was room for her at the top. Well, she said she was certain.

I just knew that there would be a certain time in my life when I would be ready to make a move and I would be knowledgeable enough to make a move successfully, without anyone being able to put one over on me. If people can put one over on you, you're dead, because there are so many people out there to do it. So you have to be worldly. You have to be aware of what's going on and what can happen to you if you're not smart.

When the time came, Shirley made her move to Las Vegas. "It's like years ago when people used to pioneer to California hoping to strike it rich," she explained. "People come to Las Vegas hoping to strike it rich, because right now it's the last boom town."

Why did you come here?
For money.

Where does money lead you?
Where does money lead me? It just pays my bills. And I want to save money. In the Midwest you can't make a living anymore. You just can't make it.

Save for what?
Save for what? To invest. Property. Probably start with a sixplex or something like that, go from there.

Have you ever been married?
No.

Do you have any interest in getting married?
No.

Why?
Right now it's not to my benefit, getting married.

That suggests that if the owner of Caesar's Palace [the poshest of Las Vegas hotels] was an attractive man you might marry him?
Possibly yes. Because love is here today and gone tomorrow, but security lasts forever. That's just the way it is. Its a hard, cruel fact of life. When the love is gone and the arguments start and all the nonsense starts, at least if you have somewhere where you can get away—like your own ranch or this and that and the other. But if you're poor and the arguments start, where are you going to go? When you're fifty years old? Where are you going to go?

How did you end up arriving at these conclusions, when a lot of people your age have ideas that are very different?
Observing—observing women who at one time were very beautiful and got anything they wanted, but when they get older, it's difficult, they can't make it, they just can't make it anymore. Intelligent people that I know—widows, this, that and the other—when they get older, what have they got?

What about your own parents?
I've never known my real father. My mother— When I was young I observed what my mother did and watched her totally ruin her life. She could have had everything. She was beautiful, a gorgeous woman, she could have married some very intelligent, worthwhile people. Instead she settled for a factory worker—who is now going with someone thirty years

his junior. You know, where is she at? She's nowhere. She can't leave, because she is so insecure about herself she thinks no one else would want her. She's only forty-four years old; she's never furthered her education beyond high school, because she's been too busy breaking her back in the factory to make it. Like she told me, "What am I gonna do now?" You know, as far as she's concerned—nothing. And that isn't going to be me when I'm forty-four, I'm not going to be dependent on some man to make me happy. No way. I want to travel and see things.

What happened to your father?
They divorced when I was three years old.

Did your mother ever tell you about him?
I have a picture of him. He was a very attractive man. I understand very intelligent—he had like a genius IQ. He was in a mental institution for a few years. He had frequent problems in that area. He had to have shock treatments all the time; he was very violent with her on a number of occasions, that's why she had to divorce him. That's all I know.

You know, it's a funny thing. I knew where he was, and I drove right through the town where he was when I drove out here, and I wondered if I should stop and see him after all these years, see what he's really like? And then I thought not, evidently that wasn't meant to be, because he could have found me and he didn't. So I'm gonna leave all that behind. You can't be emotional about it.

Shirley's own program for self-enrichment and (later) self-improvement had its origins back in the Ozark country. If one person apart from Shirley herself was instrumental in its formulation, that was the woman Shirley called her best friend.

My best friend is a lady in Illinois who is totally opposite to my background. She's sixty-five years old. She was brought up in New York and educated in Italy. She was head of the Red Cross in Burma, had her picture on the cover of *Harper's Bazaar.* Married one of the most intelligent lawyers in this country. In fact, I think he had some of the highest marks at Yale University. He's dead now. Died of acute alcoholism. She had such an interesting life. An antique dealer, she was all over the world. So I used to go up there for dinner every night and talk to her.

She'd say "Shirley, for god's sake, what is somebody, young, an attractive girl, why are you coming around here with me? Don't you want to be out with the young kids having fun?"

I'd say, "No, I don't want to be, because they can't teach me anything. They can't prepare me for anything that's going to happen to me."

My background was very—rustic, let's say. So every time I would say something wrong, I'd tell her, "correct me." Every time I would do something wrong, I would tell her to correct me. I was just so eager to learn, because my mom and her husband didn't want me to go to college. They absolutely forbid it. They wanted me to go to work in a factory, stay in the factory, marry somebody in the factory and do the whole thing.

Why was that important to them?

Because they were intimidated by the fact they can't handle somebody that is different. I'm different from all the rest of the family. They were either farmers or factory workers, that's all they've ever known, that's all they ever wanted to be. I was always different. I'd go to the library and read every day. That type of thing. My mother used to look at me, she'd say, "How can you like to read?" I used to read all the time. About the rest of the world. She couldn't understand. She hated to read. She wanted to make me like her and I just wasn't like her. So I guess I was a big disappointment to her in many ways.

I wanted to join VISTA when I was eighteen. I was made to feel like a complete idiot for even thinking about it. How could I think about that? Giving away my work free? When I could do something like putting a radio together for fifty bucks a week?

Shirley laughed at that idea, the kind of deep but edgy laugh that people who have been kicked around a little often develop. Laughing provides a certain essential distance. Other reactions are not to be trusted. They might imply vulnerability, a luxury not permitted by the Walker Plan.

My father had some Apache Indian blood in him, so I was interested in working with them. My mother thought I was completely berserk. But I've always been the mother, actually, and she's always been the child. I've always been the stronger individual. She couldn't even— She's never flown in an airplane. She's only been in three or four states. She could never think of doing something like I did. I packed my car, told the landlord I was leaving, paid all my bills and drove out here. Alone. As far as a job or anything, or where I was going to live, I didn't know anything. So many of my friends said, "How can you do it? I think you'd be afraid to

do it." Well, I said, "I'd think you'd be afraid to stay here." But they
didn't understand what I meant.

Her own ability to cast off one life and begin another came largely
from the inspiration provided by her older friend in Illinois:

I admired her so much. And, uh, unfortunately—it's bad to put it this
way but that's the way it is—money gives you the freedom and independence that everybody wants. That gave her the freedom to be educated
in Europe, it gave her the freedom to be able to live in Burma and be
head of the Red Cross there. She had the connections because of her
money.

When I met her and her [new] husband, and these people had been
in the biggest circles, all over the world, and they kept telling me that I
had something that I could use to further myself, then I realized that I
must have something that I should utilize before it's gone, before I get
old. Because, unfortunately, when people get older they're not taken
very seriously. I don't understand why. Myself, I enjoy older people, and
I think they have much more to offer than a younger person. You can
learn from these people because they've had the experience. So those
were the type of people I try to surround myself with.

Talking about her ambition, Shirley could be brutally direct:

I made a big decision when I got to be twenty-four that it was time
to get to the business of getting ahead in life. I had bills and I had this
and that. There were things I wanted to do, and I needed a wardrobe.

It was such a coincidence—it was really wild. There was this man
in Illinois who had been trying to date me for three or four years. A
very attractive man, an older man, married, who had three or four car
agencies. Very wealthy man. So there were things I wanted to do, and
to do them I had to have money. The wildest thing was I hadn't even
thought about this. He called me. I was sitting on the couch thinking
about what I was going to do with my life: "I know I can't spend it here
in this house all alone. I want to see things, do things."

So he called me. He'd asked me out a million times, but I'd never
go. He said, "Would you come down and have a drink with me." He'd
had a heart attack, and he said, "I really need someone to talk to." He
said, "This is going to sound strange, but I need to do something with

someone I really like, and I've always really liked you." I said, "I don't know what to say to you."

So the next day he came by for coffee. So I said to myself, We'll see if this guy is really the high roller he pretends to be. Or if he's just a lot of bullshit. As he was leaving, I said, "Oh, by the way, you mentioned you wanted to do something for me. Well, I need three thousand dollars." It was in a bank the next day.

He had his own jet. We'd fly all over. We used to go to dinner in Kansas. We'd fly over. I bought a lot of clothes. But always in the back of my mind I knew I'd be leaving. I just didn't know when.

So this relationship lasted about six months. It started like in June. At the end of November he got a divorce after thirty years of marriage, which was something I hadn't expected. At this time I really did think a lot of this man. He was basically a good person, a really good person. A week later he found out he had a very, very serious heart condition and he had to have surgery. Take the veins out of his legs and everything. They put him on all this medication and he became so depressed and so upset— It was just not going where it had been going before.

I had told him when we first started going together that by the end of this year, if things aren't happening one way or the other for me, I'm afraid I'll have to leave. No matter what your situation is. That's what I did.

I called him once from Las Vegas. I didn't let him know exactly what my phone number was or anything. He went through the surgery in February. He was absolutely sure he was going to die. No doubt in his mind. I told him there was no way he would, it would be all right. I really felt that way, that he would make it—I don't know why. And he did make it. So I called him in May and asked him how he felt. We talked for about an hour. I said it will take you about a year to get feeling better, but if you ever decide to see me again, as a friend or whatever, feel free to call me or come out.

How to you feel about all that now?
I don't regret doing it. For a moment.

Could you put it back together?
There are too many complications. His family. His mother and father are still alive and very, very, very religious. He had a daughter I graduated with and another who is four years older. There are too many complications. I didn't just do it for myself. I decided it would be best for everyone

concerned. It was the most practical thing to do. So by the time I'm thirty I'll have something put together. There's no doubt in my mind.

Why did she end the story with that prediction about what she would accomplish by age thirty?

Working at the bar of a Las Vegas casino, Shirley was a regular recipient of all sorts of advances. Cash offers were part of her working day. She had learned to smile and reply, "It will cost you five thousand, and that's not for all night." What would happen if someone tossed the $5000 on the bar? "I'd think about it," she said with a warm grin.

I haven't been to bed with anybody to get anything I wanted out here. People are so— It makes them mad because I'm not fitting into the general thing. If you're a woman you go to bed with someone, you're used as a utensil for whatever, you know. And the thing was, when they asked me to go to work at the hotel, I said, "Look, I know what the program is at the hotels, so I want to tell you up front, I don't go to bed with anybody to get a job. I don't go to bed with anybody to keep a job. It's up to you."

Women have done it to themselves, to themselves. If they would just make themselves a little hard to get—a prize and not just something that anybody can do, just like that, for a few bucks in the pocket—then they would be respected much more than they are today.

But you tend bar in a tee shirt without a bra, so you obviously know this part of the program as well, right?
Sure.

Your idea or the hotel's?
My idea.

One day at the bar the subject of cosmetic plastic surgery came up. Shirley mostly listened. Then she remarked that the quality of cosmetic surgery done in Las Vegas was poor—she would never have an operation done there.

"I had that operation in Illinois," she said, matter of fact. "Silicone implants—not shots, that's illegal. I stayed in the hospital five days, I took real good care of myself."

"Plastic surgery isn't a physical thing," Shirley explained. "It's a head trip. I did it for myself. Not for anybody else."

And that wasn't all. She pointed to her capped front teeth. "I paid six hundred dollars to do these," she said.

From time to time Shirley would announce that she had met someone important, or would be flying to California for the weekend to see some influential people, or something of the kind—intimations of large successes, but always delivered across her bar. Difficult to evaluate. She once said that she had been approached "indirectly" with a proposition to pose for *Penthouse* magazine. This could be worth $10,000 to her, Shirley understood (was it some guy's line?), and she wasn't rejecting it out of hand. She'd been to a Las Vegas photographer who took some discreet pictures of her in the nude, which she took out of a purse and displayed one afternoon. Would she take the $10,000 to pose for that sort of picture?

Oh, I don't know. I would have to put myself in a certain frame of mind, you know? This is not me. It's not me. The things they do now are so gross. There's nothing sensuous about it. It's whether I want to subject myself to that. Or can I look at it from this standpoint—let them get off on whatever they're doing, and take advantage of the system? Ten thousand dollars would be a nice down payment on a nice piece of property. I told them they'd have to talk to my lawyer. I know what the program is. How girls get screwed over. I'm not one of them.

What's your reaction to the fact that there is so much money around to pose for those pictures?

To me it means the world's a little bit sicker than I thought it was. I can't imagine why people want to sit around and look at nude bodies in a magazine. Don't they have anything better to do?

What about the guys at the bar who are sneaking a peak at your braless tee shirt?

Oh, yeah. I think it's so funny. In my own mind I'm just laughing. There's a million bodies running around. You see 'em all over. They can pick up a magazine and see a nude girl, but wow, let 'em come in here and they think they're almost seeing something. That's the secret. *Almost* seeing something but not quite seeing it. Almost getting something but not quite getting it.

When you are thinking about ten thousand dollars to pose that way, how does your own sense of self-esteem and dignity fit into what you're thinking about?

When I was eighteen I couldn't do that type of thing. Since I'm older—
If you want to get ahead, you have to take advantage of the system.
The way things are. And not be sad or embarrassed.

*Now wait a second. You just told us the benefits of pre-empting "the
system" by saying, "I know what the rules are and I'm not going to
play."*

When you go to the point where you'll go to bed with some guy to
get a job, right away you've lost his respect. That's just the way it is,
even though there are girls who do it. When it comes to a magazine,
that's a different type of situation. I don't know why it is, but it is. They
might have conquered you pictorially, but they still haven't conquered
you physically. That's still left to be done. As long as you can leave
something left undone, then you're still interesting. Then you're still in
demand.

Do you think of yourself as being happy?
No. Just existing right now. But not happy.

Does that make you sad?
Well, if you let yourself think about it, dwell on it, you know, you're
gonna be sad. But I can't do that either. Because mental attitude has
a lot to do with how you're going to make a success or not make a
success of yourself. You have to be careful not to let yourself get into
that slump. Well, I'm just going to save money so I can do things. Travel,
being able to travel, not being confined. Yeah, but essentially money.
Because it isn't the money itself, but the freedom the money gives you.
If you talk like that, if you have the guts to talk like that, people think
you're a gold digger, but I'm not a gold digger. It's just that money gives
you the freedom to get away from the nine-to-five bullshit and get back
to the business of living. Living is more to me than going to work and
shoving out a bunch of drinks.

Do you ever feel lonely?
Yeah. I can't find too many people to relate to, you know?

9

TECHNOLOGY'S TOYS

Conquering the American Imagination

The great American buffet is piled high with all sorts of dishes, from Drambuie to divorce, but there would be no buffet at all without the contributions of modern American technology. Technology was the crucial tangible element in the great postwar boom, and it is now the central tangible element in the daily lives of Middle Americans. Indeed, the fruits of technology are the principal defining elements of modern American culture. Which only means that without the automobile and television, there would be no modern American culture remotely like the one we know.

Automobiles and television offer irrefutable evidence of the power of the middle classes in American life. It has long been fashionable to decry both the cars produced in Detroit and the television programs produced mostly in Hollywood, but the criticism rarely has the slightest effect. This is because both the cars and the programs remain enormously popular in Middle America. General Motors and ABC both understand that they are not making products to please social critics but to please people—ordinary Middle American people. Sure they manipulate the market, but they cannot defy the market, nor would they dare to try.

Middle America is the rich part of the national marketplace—the target audience, the key segment. Middle Americans buy most of the new cars (the lower classes buy them used). Middle American families are the mass consumers at whom the bulk of television advertising is aimed. Middle America is the heart of the matter.

The automobile has allowed middle class Americans to reshape the country, turning countryside into suburbia and moving downtown shopping districts lock, stock and drugstore to shopping centers and now to downtownlike shopping malls. American kids grew up dreaming not of sunken treasure but of cars—just as Sandy Ford dreamt of her first station wagon. The car won over the American imagination, a less formidable accomplishment than it might seem, since there was no serious opposition.

Until television. Now American kids can also dream of winning the jackpot on *Hollywood Squares,* or of poking Howard Cosell in the nose. Middle Americans virtually created an entire popular culture by their choice of television entertainment, ratifying the "sexual revolution" by accepting *Soap,* or redistributing the nation's wealth by buying enough razor blades and beer to finance the assent of star athletes into the economic stratosphere.

"There's an Ass for Every Seat"

One day in Las Vegas, Lowell happened upon a convention of Cadillac dealers gathered for a preview of next year's models. Here is a sample of what Cadillac dealers talk about. First a man who now sells Cadillacs in Indianapolis reflecting on the symbolism of success:

I bought my first Cadillac in 1963. It was a Sedan DeVille, a silver car with red leather interior. I hadn't had the car too long and I went to sell an incentive program to an insurance company in Dallas. I had a one-thirty appointment with the guy who was vice president of sales. I came in and waited for him in his little reception area and pretty soon he barged in. I heard him say to his secretary, "Well, whoever owns that Cadillac out there certainly doesn't need our business."

I kind of turned green, yellow, blue and every other color. So happened I was the next guy in his office. He asked me to sit down. I said, "Before I sit down maybe I better tell you I couldn't help overhearing you. I'm the guy who owns that Cadillac out there."

The guy was very nice, but he said "Is that so?" I said, "Yes. And could I say just one more thing. I just want to explain I earned that Cadillac. Nobody gave it to me. I earned that Cadillac by doing what you called me over here to do and by being the best in my company at doing it."

Naturally, he made the sale.

A Cadillac dealer from Louisville: "I think one of the great Cadillac ads—I think it ranks with the greatest they've ever run—is the 'Someday' ad. [Someday, You Too Can Own a Cadillac.] That's the American free enterprise system: Someday we'll do better than we did today."

As a matter of fact, today a lot of us are doing better than we did yesterday. Another Cadillac dealer: "You got to remember one thing. There is no more carriage trade. The carriage trade is gone. Cadillac is a volume car; its going to be a more volume car in the future."

And another: "Don't identify Cadillac with rich people. That would be a great mistake."

Al Rosen, the American League's Most Valuable Player in 1953, then the third baseman for the Cleveland Indians and now the president of the New York Yankees, has a simple explanation of American society: "We're a nation of sports addicts and automobile addicts, and I think if you took away those two things this country would dry up and wither away."

We also have blue jeans, hamburgers, one or two others. But surely automobiles come at the beginning of any list. There would be no mass American culture without automobiles, no familiar status ladder, nothing for kids to aspire to—no McDonald's! Of course, Rosen is wrong about the country withering away. Girdled and bandaged as it is by the Interstate Highway System, it could never do that.

There are more licensed cars in America than color television sets. Americans spend three times more on cars each year than on education. We have 1.5 miles of paved road in this country for every citizen— adult and child. Each day Americans consume more gasoline than milk. Two of every ten working Americans work at producing cars or satisfying their needs.

Whatever they may do to the air or the balance of payments, cars are fun. Our Middle Americans like them as much as anything in their lives. They provide status, mobility, a basis for daily life. Millions of Americans, it appears, think of the car they drive as the best concrete symbol of *who they are.* Someday, you too . . .

Gary Press, proprietor of Prestige Motors, purveyor of Rolls-Royce, Jaguar, BMW and Volkswagen:

The BMW owners know that there's only a select 28,000 people in the United States that get a BMW every year, and that's the way they feel about it—that "I have something not everyone can have." Certainly a Rolls-Royce owner feels that way. A Jaguar owner is a guy all by himself, you know. That's a guy who knows the Jaguar image is that it is somewhat of a troublesome car; it takes a lot of hose tightening and things. So they know that people who see them in their prestigious Jaguar know that they're a special kind of guy that wants to go for that type car. We change the look of a lot of our Volkswagens by adding pinstripes and deluxe this and that—try to make our cars look a little different than other Volkswagen cars. So our whole image is prestige. We put a lot of luxury items in our cars. We have a lot of Volkswagens with "cruise control" that the other dealer [in town] doesn't have.

Do you think there's something crazy about us, that we spend all this time and energy on cars, worry so much about cars?
Uh, I think it's— I think it's an independence thing. I really think it's something for a guy to go out and spend ten thousand or fifteen thousand dollars of his income—especially to a guy that's making twenty thousand dollars a year—to spend fifty percent of his income on a car is probably more of a major purchase than a home. The home used to be the major purchase, but now a guy might have five or six ten-thousand-dollar cars in a span of ten years, so he's spending more on his cars than he is on his home. You know, it's— It is kind of a crazy thing. I don't know what makes people do that.
We have a term here, "There's an ass for every seat." Once in a while you get a car that's ugly. It's turquoise with yellow seats or something, you know. It's a car that you think, Oh my gosh, nobody's ever going to buy *that* car. And sure enough, somebody'll come in and say, "Just what I've always wanted." It doesn't seem that the cars can become too expensive.

Tom Barrett is blond, good-looking, overweight and rich. He is a real estate developer from Scottsdale, Arizona, a collector of "antique" automobiles and an organizer of automobile auctions for collectors. At the time we talked he owned one of the world's 240 Duesenberg's, among several dozen other cars.

Why have the old cars become so popular?
Well, finally the cars have been discovered by the public, especially the cars of years ago, the 'twenties and 'thirties, as works of art. And there's such a limited amount of them in the world, and there's so many

people that love the old automobiles—it's just caught on in every state in the union.

They're excellent investments. They're better than the stock market. I'd much rather have my money in metal and rubber and something I could enjoy, see and drive than in some stock that fluctuates every day on the Big Board. And they've been climbing in price anywhere from fifteen to thirty percent a year; they've really been skyrocketing in price.

What does this say to you about what kind of people we are, that we have this romantic attachment?

Well, the man has always had a romantic attachment. And of course you've got a great thing in America. It's a melting pot of a lot of different nationalities that have come here over the last two-hundred years and ninety-nine percent of them came here without a quarter. Some of them came as late as just thirty years ago. They made a lot of money, and they've always dreamed of owning cars like this. They're stepping up and buying them. But besides owning 'em and buying 'em, they're buying 'em as an investment. They're a great investment.

Where do you see this in fifteen or twenty years?

Well take the Duesenberg market right now, which is your highest market, it ranges in price—Duesenberg automobiles will bring usually two to three hundred thousand. Now they will probably go—in the next ten years—to five and six hundred thousand. After all there's only 240 of them in existence. They only built 580 of them in their heyday. With the population explosion and the amount of money that's around and all the different people that are getting into it—it's the one hobby in the world that the whole family can participate in. A fella can have a bunch of stamps at home, but he enjoys 'em, the kids hate 'em and the wife hates 'em. But the cars—everybody and their brother can get in the enjoy. It's a family outing, it's the great American circus, which makes America great, you know. Every little boy from the time he's old enough to walk and ride with his father in the car begins dreaming about automobiles.

One of those little boys grew up in Minnesota and spent the first dollar he ever earned on a car. "I was twelve. I bought a car and sold it. I love cars." His name is Will, and he grew up to be a wealthy real estate operator, but he never lost that affection for automobiles. He was at the auction that Tom Barrett had organized, and he was buying cars.

"It's nostalgia, mostly," Will says of the booming interest in old cars, "wanting to go back to the old days when things were good. That's my attitude." He quenches the nostalgia with a collection of several dozen cars, which he recently moved from Minnesota to a new home in Southern California. He moved for "the weather." Before the move Will decided to sell off about twenty cars—"the ones I figured were worth less than ten thousand. I sold them at an auction up north. Actually I got more than ten for some, thirteen for one, but less on others. It averages out."

How does one keep so many cars? "I just bought a building, eight thousand square feet, air conditioned. I'll just leave 'em there. I had my own mechanic in Wisconsin. I haven't hired one yet down here, but I will."

This conversation took place just after Will had acquired a 1960 Lincoln Continental with an unusual customized body for $6500. He is very pleased with the price. While he talks, a green 1955 Ford Thunderbird comes up for sale, and Will's wife is interested. "Watch this. She likes to buy too," he says.

She gets up from her seat, walks over to look at the car, then has a word with one of the men dressed in white tuxedos trimmed with black piping who are helping run the auction for an Indiana firm of auctioneers. She returns to her seat and sits down, but gives no signals to the auctioneer.

"Are you in it?" Will asks her. She nods almost imperceptibly. The price is bid up to $6000. "If you want it you better bid," Will advises.

"I've got the high bid," she mumbles. "It's mine." So it was.

Their seventeen-year-old son has been looking over the newly acquired Continental and returns to say it looks fine. "Your mother bought a car while you were away," Will tells him with a grin.

"She did? What kind?" The boy looks bemused.

"T-Bird. Little green-turquoise one."

"With portals?" he asks.

"No, it's a 'fifty-five," says Will.

This is a family hobby. "We all drive 'em. The boys love to work on the cars." They have dogs too. "They're part of the family. Because of the dogs, we only drive cars with leather seats."

"I keep a car in every city where I have an office," Will says, and recites the list: an old Chrysler New Yorker in Miami, a Cadillac in St. Paul, a Lincoln in Minneapolis. "Sometimes I drive an old Ford pickup truck. And I got a new Cadillac that we drive on trips."

Ever buy a foreign car? "No. I don't want to spend any American currency on any foreign product. It's a principle with me. I know the profit's already been made [on an old foreign car], but still I don't want to do it. This is a good country, we ought to spend our money here. Anyhow, there's enough foreign parts in them [American cars] already."

Will strikes a new acquaintance as a happy man.

"I am happy. I really am."

But Is It Paid For?

Margaret Donaldson is a professional auto repossessor in a Midwestern city whose name—like hers—had best be disguised here. Auto repossession is a huge American industry. People like Margaret work for banks and finance companies whose customers fail to make the monthly payments on their cars. Then she retrieves the cars.

The cars themselves, I think, are a status symbol to everyone. And it just depends on how important it is to you—I mean the status. We don't particularly take more Cadillacs than any other kind of car. But one of the interesting phases of the business is that there are fewer four-door than two-door cars ever repossessed. The reason being the people who buy four-door cars are more substantial people. They aren't gonna lose 'em. As a matter of fact, that car over there [a four-door Chrysler] is one of the few I have ever been able to get as a repossession.

Now the business itself is a little different from what everybody presumes—that you're the meanest person in the world. Because to a banker you're a hero. The banker that holds the note on one of these cars and wants it back thinks I'm the greatest thing that ever happened if I can get it. If I can't, at least I've tried for him. Now he doesn't have the guts to come out here and do what I'm doing.

The other night Marty [her young assistant] and I stole six cars in one night. Brought 'em in. This Mercury was one of them. Just before we took this, in sight of this, we took a Chrysler New Yorker and a travel trailer. We stole the Chrysler New Yorker, went around the block with it, and hooked on the guy's special equalizer bumper, then came back and stole his travel trailer with his own equalizer hookup. Now that guy, for instance, had disappeared on 'em—had never made any payments on that Chrysler or the travel trailer at all, and he was something like a year and a half disappearing. The way they found out he was here was, the other night he called his ex-wife, and evidently got melancholy or something, and gave her his address. She called the bank the next day and give them the address. They'd been hunting all over the country, had no idea where he was.

Now there's all sorts of gimmicks we use to try to find out information, and it's getting much harder all the time. More and more people have unlisted telephone numbers, so that becomes a very difficult thing. I can't tell you how, but I finally established someone who would look up unlisted phone numbers for me. And I pay pretty dearly for it. It's well worth it. And it used to be that the police department came to us, through another source that I had, to get them.

They used to publish every electric power cut-on, but they are no longer allowed to. I now have someone at the power company who can look up current customers. Up until the last three weeks I've had a way to break post office boxes. A lot of people live just using a post office box. I've just this morning reestablished a way to do it. These are the little tricky things. If you've got the right contacts you can do anything.

A lot of it is just really using common sense. I've established a policy that at no point is any vehicle worth anyone getting physically hurt over. I try to be as nice to people when they do come into the office as I know how to, as long as they're nice to me. If they get raunchy with me I'll ask 'em to leave, but I've only had the police out here twice in all the time I've owned the business.

Margaret took the business over from her brother, who had a heart attack and decided he had to give it up. Women are not commonplace in auto repossessing, she says, but neither are they unheard of. Margaret is well into middle age now, no longer as handsome as she was, nor as trim, but still effervescent, full of laughs.

There's a story that goes around in our ranks, that in order to get a good repossessor you've got to get somebody who loves to steal. Now Marty is a kid, learned to be a locksmith when he was fifteen, and he used to pick locks and drive cars out and around for an evening and then park them someplace else, then walk away from 'em, wipe his fingerprints off. The other night he stole the wrong jeep and did the same thing. It's part of the fun of it.

We work late at night, when most people are asleep. The law says "peaceful repossession." Well, it's peaceful if you don't hear me take it. We go out about midnight to two o'clock, depending on how many we have to do. And I always memorize the name of the person as I get out of the car, so that if they do catch us and do come out—"Hi, Mr. Waltham, I'm Mrs. Donaldson from Ajax Auto Recovery"—right away! Now, the fact that you speak to him by name means you're not a car thief, you know. And I've never had anyone actually shoot at me.

Now one night a guy put a gun right here [Margaret sticks a finger under her chin]. And I had a sheriff's deputy standing right behind me, six foot four with the big hat and the big badge and the whole nine yards, and this clown, halfway drunk, says to me, "You're not takin' my car." And I say, "Now wait a minute, they just want to store it"—gave him my usual pitch. He said, "I don't know who you are and you're not takin' my car." And I said, "Well, let me show you my identification." And he said, "I don't even know who he is." And when he pulled that gun the deputy said to me, "Very slowly, just step back a step at a time." And I did that, and the guy didn't shoot. That's about as close as I've ever come.

I'll tell you that the ones I hate the worst are repossessing motorcycles. That kid with that motorcycle, as far as status, he is more concerned about that motorcycle than anybody is with their brand-new Cadillac. That means more to him. But the other part of it is, to me, I have no place to hide. When I walk away with that guy's motorcycle I'm a sitting duck. I've done it a couple of times in the moonlight, walking across a back yard, and I'll tell you, these Westerns that you see with all the elements, I've gone through 'em.

The people generally? As my brother always said, you should let 'em wind down like a three-dollar watch. In other words, they're mad at themselves, they're down on their luck. And you take their wheels away from them, they're pretty lost, you know. Our society has become very transportation-conscious.

"He Just Fades Right into the Picture"

Cars were a crucial ingredient in the recipe that made the new America. They gave us all mobility—indeed, they gave us access to one another. But it was left to television to actually bring us together by providing the common experiences that Americans now share.

Television is the one acquaintance that virtually every American has in common. It is now probably the most important element in the chemical mixture that makes America a nation. It gives us shared experience, shared heroes, something to talk about and a sense of who we are. We couldn't live without it. Paul Delguidice couldn't live without it.

He can barely find room to live with it, either. Sitting in his fiancée's small suburban apartment, surrounded by electronic equipment worth about $10,000, Delguidice extols the virtues of television—not the message, the medium. To his left are stacks of stereo equipment and an enormous six-foot television screen. On his right are video tape decks, controllers for video games, stacks of video cassettes and the keyboard and screen for a home computer. In the center of the tiny living room is a color television projector the size of a small refrigerator.

Delguidice is twenty years old, pale, well-groomed—a pleasant young man who works in his father's family restaurant. Before he is thirty, Delguidice (pronounced Del-Jew-Dus) says with the confidence of an expert enthusiast, Americans will be watching three-dimensional television in their homes. Not some schlocky trick involving movie screens and special cardboard sunglasses, but holographic television using laser-based technology.

We've got projection of still holograms now, but in Russia, supposedly, they've perfected motion picture holograms. They've got a thing set up for audiences of two hundred. You'd have *Star Wars,* and instead of pictures on a screen, you'd have battles and stuff right in the room in front of you. That's definitely going to happen in the next ten years. You'll probably have holographic television. Football games right in your living room.

Delguidice is one of television's children, and he loves it. Not in the form the networks pump out—the *Gong Show* and *Masterpiece Theater* are for spectators. He is a participant in the wonders of electronic circuitry, the transmutation of invisible impulses into sights, sounds—an electronic life apart.

Isn't it expensive? Cheaper than sports cars, boats or light planes, he points out. And for him, more fun:

A lot of people are starting to get into this type of electronics. Let's turn this off [he switches off a nearly life-size projection of Linda Ronstadt singing on the *Midnight Special*]. This is basically electronic baseball. You push this down like that and it sets up a field for you. [The field is projected on the six-foot screen.] This guy bats and that guy will pitch. You can move your fielders back and forth. The games are on these carts [cassettes], and they're fifteen to thirty dollars apiece, depending on how complicated the games are. They're just really versatile. You can curve the ball and stuff like that. They're really starting to get into complicated games. Like these players here look more real than the people who are on the Ping-Pong and tennis games. There are games coming out where it looks like actual little people playing and stuff like that. The thing that's interesting is the number of people you get in here, older people, who say they aren't really interested and then they just can't leave it alone. Like this one here. [He switches to a game involving moving ships, minefields and electronically controlled submarine torpedo launchers. His fiancée, Molly, says quietly, "That's my favorite."]

It all looks simple, but the electronics behind something like that are just unbelievable. [Pointing to his collection]: This is the product of years of collecting. This is all top line. This is *the* thing with electronics now. A lot of people were into stereos and things like that, but this is the new type of electronics. It's something to get into.

You've got a home computer too?

Yeah, I'll show you that right now. This one here is a Radio Shack one. As far as quality, it's a decent quality computer and everything. Let me show you. [He turns on the computer, fiddles with some tape cassettes.] I had programs on this tape but I erased them by accident. Let's use this one. All this one is, basically, is a blackjack game. But the thing that's nice about a computer is it's almost like another person after you get used to playing with it, you enter it in, and it asks you *What* and things like that because it can't figure out what you want to do.

Delguidice at the keyboard of his computer takes on a look of self-absorbed concentration reminiscent of a church organist. When he is explaining how it works, he seems to be talking to himself as much as anyone else in the room.

Right now, each time it flashes, it's recording a line right off the tape. There are games in computer magazines that involve eight or ten thousand steps. They simulate a trip out West or going through different countries with different political schemes and stuff like that. It's just all basic math. The computer has a form of logic. Basically, that is just entertainment. Like I've got the video games and if I wanted to play blackjack, I've got that with one of the games. It's nice to play, but that's all you do. You plug it in and it works. You don't know how it works. With this thing, you play it for a while, and the more you play with it, the more you see how to make it do stuff.

The computer begins asking questions such as the names of the players, whether we want to play with one deck or two and how much money each of us is using as a stake. Delguidice's eyes never leave the screen of the computer as he stops the program, taps several keys and instantly the equations involved in the blackjack program appear on the screen.

Now it stops the program and you can see like the basic math involved. See, I had the computer print this and here's the logic for the computer. It *knows* by this equation. It's a long program. These are all the steps just to play this simple game. But when it's all done with, electronics is pretty simple. With those video games, all it is is little circuit boards. It does all this automatically. But the math behind it is pretty complicated. That's why I like this. When you're playing, you're still learning something.

Paul's fiancée, Molly, is a pretty, slender young woman who speaks in a soft voice that sounds like it's modulated to avoid interrupting something somebody might be watching. They share a passion for their electronic equipment, although for different reasons.

Paul: Ever since I was nine or ten years old, I've always been playing with stereos. It's not so much listening to the music or watching the movies, it's the electronic-type draw.

Some people suggest this kind of equipment tempts people to withdraw from the world—create their own world and live in it.
Paul: I know. It gets like that, especially when you first get the equipment. When I first got the giant television, I stayed here and watched television for a long time. And when we first got the deck, we recorded everything.
Molly: Sometimes, I'll sit here until six in the morning watching television.
Paul: It's definitely something you can do at home and it keeps you occupied. I've played with it all day quite a few times.

With their marriage fast approaching, Paul and Molly are busily planning their first home. At the top of their list of priorities is creation of a special environment for their electronic offspring.

Paul: Right now, we have plans to just design the basement totally around this equipment.

Molly: You know the sound rooms in the good hi-fi stores? That's what we're going to do. Kind of seal off the basement with a bar. We've got it all on paper right now. Designed. We've been to several furniture stores already looking for things. You know those sectional couches, they call the playpens, we've already got that. We've got racks for the equipment. It'll look like a showroom.

What about the suggestion that Americans spend too much time watching television?

Paul: As far as watching television, what's on the network, I couldn't do it. Not after having the recording equipment. You get too selective. You turn on Channel Four or Channel Seven, and there are commercials every four minutes.

Molly: That's what drives me crazy. What I enjoy watching are *Three's Company,* silly programs, things like that. But there are the commercials. But we've got two decks so I can record from one to the other and dub out the commercials. That's a lot of hassle but it saves the program. I couldn't sit here Tuesday, Wednesday, Thursday and Friday and just go through the *TV Guide.* That would drive me crazy. I'd go to the movies or something.

What if somebody told you that you ought to be out playing tennis or jogging or something.

Molly [laughing]: I do that in the morning. I watch in the afternoon.

Paul: It probably affects your activism a little bit. Maybe a little.

What about the idea that when people used to have parties, they talked. Now they sit around and stare at things like this.

Molly: Yeah. That's true. That's a big disadvantage.

Paul: Especially with the big-screen television. Lot's of times we'll have parties at my parents' house and I'll bring the big television or the deck. If I hook the deck up to a regular television, people will still talk. You can ignore that little screen. But with this six-foot screen it's hard. A friend has his set up in the family room so you can see it from the kitchen and stuff. You'll be sitting at the kitchen table talking and the screen is just so big and lifelike that every time there's some little motion your eyes are just attracted. Because of the size of it. That's definitely a problem with that size television. If you're in the room, you're going to be watching television. It's very hard to watch regular television after watching this.

Molly: Yeah it is. To go back to that little screen is really hard.

Paul and Molly see nothing Orwellian or unhealthy about the role electronics play in their lives. By any conventional yardstick they would be a completely normal middle class couple, different only in the fact that as far as home electronics goes, they are the people the Joneses will be keeping up with. Paul talks with great enthusiasm about the special wall switches he is having installed in their new home:

It looks like a stainless steel switch plate, but its got a little digital readout which is the time. And it's got two "on" and "off" buttons. You can program them so they turn your lights on and off automatically. When you're not home, instead of being like a timer on a lamp, say at 9:30 your living-room lights went off. Then at 9:32 your hallway lights would go on. At 9:37 your bedroom light would go on and your hallway light would go off. Minor security things. I'm looking at electronic burglar alarms and there's just so much stuff.

Do you think these are things that everybody will have before long?

Paul: The giant televisions, yes. I've shown this television to friends of my mother and father. These people find it unbelievably impressive. It becomes something they're seriously talking about getting. They just never saw it before. And video tape too. If a person's got the money, I can't see saying, I'll wait five years and the stuff will be better, or cheaper." It's like saying, "I won't buy a car this year because five years from now the cars will be better."

Molly: It's just like we're moving into a house and we're talking furniture, carpets, drapes, things like that, and that's big bucks. Something like this, if you look at it as furniture, another part of your house, it's in the same league.

Paul: People just don't realize how affordable things are.

Paul and Molly have found a way to resolve the deep ambivalence Americans feel about television. They have bought Marshal McLuhan's whole hog: the medium really is the message in their lives. They spend hours gaping at technological phenomena, not at *The Love Boat* or *The Newlyweds' Game.* Television has become a friend to invite over for the evening. Every evening. This is the case in tens of millions of American households.

In fact, television has become a member of the family, and is loved and resented, respected and ignored accordingly. In many American homes the thing is turned on all the time, whether or not anyone is paying attention. This is something the Nielsen ratings can't take into account, but the networks' own surveys have discovered the truth—the fact that the set is turned on doesn't mean it's being watched. Walter Cronkite's voice at the end of the day can be soothing, reassuring; it doesn't matter what he is saying.

Americans are often of two minds about what they see on television, just as they are often ambivalent about their personal friends or jobs. A sixteen-year-old named David from Santa Clara, California, made a representative comment:

> Soap operas—certain people just really lose reality, it becomes part of their life, you know? That's dumb to me. Like *Edge of Night.* People became like part of the families that are on TV. You know—"Oh, my sister died!" Like my friend Bill Vincent, he gets into the soap operas, he becomes a part of those things. Like the TV absorbs him, he just fades right into the picture.
>
> *How much do you watch TV?*
> I've timed myself—I usually spend seven hours a day in front of the TV. I almost had to wear glasses.
>
> *Does that seem sort of silly to you now?*
> Yeah, yeah.

Does it really seem silly? Probably not. Like most Americans, David knew what he was supposed to say, and he said it. But nobody makes him sit there for seven hours a day.

Advertisers are now spending about $8.8 billion a year on television. The average American family allegedly spends twenty-nine hours a week in front of his tube. Viewing has dropped off a little, according to the Nielsen figures, but this could be due to the fact that increasing numbers of women are going to work (the most noticeable loss of viewers has been for daytime programs). On some evenings 100 million

Americans are simultaneously sitting at home watching their television sets. Sometimes the future Molly Delguidice sits in her apartment until six A.M. watching TV.

This is more than an important element in the national fabric. Without television the national fabric would be unrecognizable.

10

SHAPING UP

"Silicone Still Has a Place in Medicine. No Question About It."

The great American buffet offers technological solutions to what were once considered non-technical problems—for instance, an inadequate body. Traditionally the shape of one's body had to be taken pretty much as it came. No longer.

"The Masters and Johnson of Cosmetic Breast Surgery"

Dr. George Tippit certainly realizes that big breasts—"I'd prefer to say well-proportioned breasts"—are an object of dreams for many, many Americans, both men and women. But he doesn't know why, though he has tried to figure it out. "One of my friends asked me once when I first got so interested in breast surgery," Dr. Tippit recalled. "I thought for a while and finally came up with a very honest answer: I think I was about eleven years of age when I got interested in breasts. Maybe twelve." Is this something Freudian, something to do with Mother? No, Dr. Tippit doesn't think so. Too many of the world's cultures don't share the American mania for breasts. Baffling.

There are very few surgeons who will say this, but this operation someday will probably be an operation of historical interest only, because—whether it's fortunate or unfortunate—this generation, the last generation, and for a number of years, we've been livin' in a more and more youth-oriented society. Clothes—just about everything is sort of oriented toward the breast, in regards to women. And let's face it, three or four generations ago it was ankles and knees, and a hundred years from now it might be ears. We don't know. Seriously, someday what

we consider a very gratifyin', happy operation might be considered something rather ridiculous.

Two or three hundred times a year, by his own count, Nathaniel
George Tippit, M.D., trained in surgery at the renowned Mayo Clinic
in Rochester, Minnesota, who voluntarily gave up "a quarter of a
million dollar, gross, general surgical practice" in San Antonio, Texas,
slips a new pair of breasts into another patient. "I would guess as
many cosmetic breast operations as any single surgeon in the United
States," said Dr. Tippit.

Dr. Tippit has an office and his own little operating room in the
shopping arcade of the MGM Grand Hotel in Las Vegas, just next
to the barber shop. He had to sign "a ten-year ironclad" lease with
the hotel, and when his "cosmetic breast surgery clinic" got off to a
slow start, that lease made him nervous. This is understandable; one
cannot easily imagine a strong market for miniature operating rooms
located in resort hotel shopping arcades. But everything worked out
for the best—or even better than that, judging by the happy, prosperous
visages of Dr. and Mrs. Tippit. At about $2000 per operation, the
clinic is now grossing half a million dollars a year.

Dr. Tippit grew up in Louisiana, and his smooth, musical voice
echoes those origins. About fifty, he is a big handsome man who
dresses with care: shiny white loafers, white slacks, a purple blazer
and a sports shirt whose giant collar points dropped over the blazer's
lapels. Mrs. Tippit—the second Mrs. Tippit, whose name is Ingrid—
was born in Germany, and talks like Marlene Dietrich. She has a
pretty, sexy face, with high cheekbones and a full mouth. She wore
a pale blue gown with a gathered skirt and high neckline which did
nothing to conceal a large bust.

They were interviewed in Dr. Tippit's office, a carefully decorated
room done in white and tweeds, whose walls were covered with paint-
ings. The pictures were done in the romantic-realistic style favored
by hotel lobby art shops—like the one a hundred yards from their
office in the MGM Grand. Virtually every one of the pictures depicted
a nude woman with large breasts.

Both of the Tippits were extraordinarily friendly and talkative.
Dr. Tippit began by describing his own history in the medical profession, taking the story to San Antonio, where he was exhausting himself

with a surgical practice that covered the gamut, but seemed to include a steadily increasing number of radical surgeries for cancer.

Originally I thought that as you got older, then this would bother you less, it would be less depressing. But in my case—possibly I'm just a sentimentalist—it seemed that as I got older the only thing happened was I had more of 'em sent to me. And it became more and more difficult to go in and see these patients.

You put them in the hospital with the little lump in the breast, and you've told 'em that they were going to have a little shot in the arm the next morning, and they'd go to sleep, and they'd have to sign an operative permit, which would allow you to take out that lump. If there was nothing to it, you'd tell 'em they could go home the next day. Or, if it was reported by the pathologist as being malignant, then you'd have to do a very radical excision of the breast, all the muscles and lymph nodes, and then you would go by and see 'em that evening. They wouldn't ask you what was the outcome, because they had a huge bandage on and they couldn't tell by feeling whether they had their breast or not. Surprisingly, it was usually about the second or third day before they would have enough nerve to come right out—you'd be seein' 'em twice a day, once in the morning, once in the evening—and on one of these trips, usually on the third day, she would finally get the nerve up to say, "Doctor, was it cancer?"

I mean, the word "cancer" is something patients don't like to use, especially if it's referrin' to themselves or their family. So then you have to pull up a chair, sit down, say, "Well yes, it was," and try to be very optimistic and, uh, cheerful, but at the same time be honest, you know, as far as the statistical evidence and what their chances were, which they would usually ask you.

How many doctors admit that their work depresses them? Dr. Tippit and his wife (who worked with him as an assistant) began to consider their options. He wanted less exhausting and happier work.

I'd reached the stage, and the age, the state of maturity, I'd rather put it, to where I realized there was much more to life than bein' dedicated to that extent.

Also, he thought the government and the private insurance companies were meddling too much in his general surgical practice. And he wanted to move somewhere that his grown children would find attractive, so they would visit. "Frankly, none of them liked San Antonio." He had done some cosmetic breast surgery in Texas, liked it and felt he was getting good at it. He and Ingrid both liked Las Vegas—they had gone there often on vacations—so they decided to move there. They opened the clinic in the shopping arcade. After a slow beginning, business is booming.

Not only that, it's fun: "Really, we have frequently discussed keepin' a diary of some of the cute things that some of the patients say." Mrs. Tippit likes to tell about the wonderful looks on patients' faces when they look at their new shapes for the first time. She thinks it takes a special kind of spunk to undertake this operation, and the women who have it "are really fun people." Mrs. Tippit:

This is an operation that takes a little guts. You know, people have to think about it. They say, "Gee, I don't know anybody who has had this done, maybe it's a good idea, maybe it's not a good idea." But they say, "Well, the heck with it, I'm going to try it." And later on we get the letters, with the results, the comments of the neighbors. We just sit here sometimes and laugh! We just got this letter from this girl in Chicago. She said she invested six grand on having her teeth capped, and now, she says, "I could be gumming—nobody looks at my teeth!"

Dr. Tippit: Nobody looks at her teeth! She literally wasted six thousand dollars on having porcelain caps, and she spent about one-third of that amount having a mammaplasty and she said, literally she used the term, she could be gummin' and nobody would pay any attention.

Enough chitchat. Dr. Tippit wanted to explain what he does. He got up from his desk and walked around it to a bookcase, where he reached up and pushed a button. A movie screen descended. Across the room Dr. Tippit had a slide projector, which he now turned on. The lights dimmed.

Let me show you something very briefly, it might be of interest to you. This is something we looked for for three and a half years, what we would consider the perfect model patient—a girl who couldn't possibly afford to have this done, but we wanted a girl who had a very fresh Coca-Cola girl–type of appearance. So I sort of spread the word throughout this area and also in the Texas area. We had maybe twenty-eight or thirty girls who came to us, who wanted to have an operation done free in return for their written legal permission to show these pictures for educational and consultation purposes only. The first twenty-nine or thirty or possibly forty of them that were referred to us literally looked like old retired madams. Finally, two months ago, there was a very cute girl, just a precious girl, who was from Hastings, Minnesota, who was out here visiting a friend of hers, and she heard about this, so she came by. She turned out to be the ideal model, and two months ago we did her.

Then the slide show began. The pictures had been taken by a professional photographer, whose wife, "by coincidence," had received new breasts from Dr. Tippit two years earlier.*

This one [slide] shows me showin' the implant to the patient. Have you ever felt one of these? It has a very strange feel, because it's at room temperature. This material was pioneered and perfected by Dow Chemical. [It is a plastic bag filled with an inert, clear gel.]

They can modify the consistency of it. This happens to be almost exactly the consistency of normal breast tissue, for obvious reasons. I meet a lot of men who say, "Well, have you got one of these I could just carry around in my pocket and take a feel of it every once in a while?" [He laughs.]

This [the next slide] is one of the preliminary examinations. The main thing it shows is this little, saggy breast outline here—in a very lovely girl otherwise. She's twenty-two.

This picture shows us taking some measurements, which are quite important in determining the exact size and shape implant to use for the particular individual girl. However, the most important thing involved is your experience and the expertise you've developed over a period of years. And frankly—not many surgeons like to say this—ten percent of this operation is surgical technique, and ninety percent of it is an artistic sense of proportion. That's one of the things that makes it so much fun.

The slide show continued for nearly an hour, with Dr. Tippit explaining each stage of the surgery. First, he cuts a tiny slit in the

* When Dr. Tippit hired an interior decorator to design his clinic, they exchanged services: "I operated on his wife, and he decorated our offices."

fold of skin behind and beneath the breast. The natural breast tissue lies on the chest and can be quite easily detached—a job Dr. Tippit performs mostly with his finger. The implant, a plastic bag filled with the soft silicone material that hangs naturally in the shape of the breast, is inserted behind the breast tissue and fixed in place.

This way you don't cut any breast tissue, and you don't cut any nerves to the breast, and you don't cut any of the major blood vessels to the breast. This girl, if she has four children, she'll be able to nurse all four of them. Not just as well, but even better, because the implant pushes the nipple out, and the baby will be able to grab it.

Now when we've got the implant in perfect position we've got a very tight, specially designed bra. She has to wear this for three weeks, day and night. Incidentally, sexual relations, they can resume that night, or the next night.

Mrs. Tippit: Marilyn [the nurse who works in the clinic] has a nice answer for that question. She says, "The doctor would like you to use a certain amount of discretion about it; he would prefer that you wait until you get out of the office."

Dr. Tippit [switching to the next slide]: She has just walked into this office [which has an enormous mirror on one wall, and the young girl is pictured gaping into it]. Look at this look of disbelief the photographer captured. First of all they have this look of disbelief—"Could this be me?"

Mrs. Tippit: They often say, "You mean I get to keep these now?"

Dr. Tippit [showing the next slide]: And this is the next reaction—a big, big grin. Now look at her beautiful profile. Now this little girl, I told her, "For goodness' sakes, don't go back and marry a farmer in Minnesota." She is a natural born model. This isn't posed. She's really a very lovely girl, and she was really admiring herself.

Now she was supposed to come back this week, it's been eight weeks now, and we're paying for her transportation back, just to get post-op pictures, without the bra, and get a series of 'em with her sitting, standing and lyin' down. Lyin' down mostly to show how flat they are, and soft, because they have a very fluid, natural feel afterwards. And that's forever. But her mother's dyin' of cancer, unfortunately, and it may be weeks before she gets back here.

Besides the slide show, Dr. Tippit has photo albums of "before" and "after" pictures to show prospective patients. He takes pictures of every patient with a Polaroid camera, in part for "medical-legal reasons," as protection against malpractice suits. One of his albums shows only "re-do's," or "ones that were done before by someone else," as Mrs. Tippit put it.

There are other types of implants. This [holding up another plastic device] is a waterbag implant. We took this— We've taken a lot of these out of girls. They are put in through an incision which is made underneath the nipple. Sometimes they have to cut through the breast tissue, which cuts through milk ducts and major nerves and arteries, and frankly it's one I personally disapprove of very much. It's an easier operation, because these are put in totally collapsed. But on the other hand they're all perfectly round, and the earliest I remember bein' interested in breasts, I was about eleven, and since then I don't recall havin' seen a girl with round breasts. They simply don't make 'em. Whereas if you've noticed, this [the implant he uses] is what they call the contoured, or some of 'em call it the teardrop-shaped implant. Now, they also make this waterbag or saline-filled implant in the teardrop or contoured shape, but they're easy to put in, because they're put in collapsed, then after they're put in, they open this valve up here and take a syringe full of sterile, normal saline and pump this up. I want you to feel that [the hard plastic valve], that's underneath their nipple for the rest of their life, and some of 'em become very self-conscious about it.

One of the girls that we took one of these out of, when she filled out her form [he asks all patients to fill in a questionnaire] she put down, where it said allergies, "Grapefruit." Her name was Penelope, and later I asked her, I said, "Penelope, what happens when you eat grapefruit, do you break out in hives or a rash or what?" She said, "I don't mean that kind of grapefruit, I mean this kind," pointing to her breasts. 'Cause that's what it felt like to her, and particularly durin' her sexual relations.

Dr. Tippit talked about who wants new breasts, and how he decides whether a particular woman is a suitable patient:

After goin' through the early amenities, one of the first things I will ask the patient is, "Why do you want to have this operation done?" I tell 'em it may sound like a silly question but it's a very important one. And I'll get a lot of different answers, and usually most of 'em are sort of ambiguous. They beat around the bush; they don't come out with it directly. But what it really boils down to, the majority of them, and the reason that we want to hear, most importantly, is that in effect what they're sayin' is that it's for their egocentric, selfish reasons. "To improve my self-image of myself," and not because "My boyfriend wants it done," "My husband wants me to have it done," or "My husband's runnin' around with his nineteen-year-old secretary." If we get a girl like that, we refuse to do her, because you can't cure a broken marriage with an operation. And, if she has it done, and then she continues to have very serious psychosexual problems, then who's she goin' to blame it on? Me. We turn down approximately twenty-five percent of the girls that want to be done.

The Tippits are convinced that the operation does bring a new self-image, and with it new well-being.

Let me show you one of the most classical examples. This girl is only four feet nine inches tall, she was thirty-four at the time, she's married to a local physician. You can see she had already started developin' quite a little tummy. She said every time she had a baby—she had three of 'em—her breasts had shrunk up and atrophied more.

Now she was supposed to come back six weeks after her operation. She didn't. So in three months we called her and insisted that she come in, and these pictures were taken. [He pointed to the "after" photos.]

Now tryin' to ignore the beautiful bust line, which is not too easy, look at the tremendous difference in the way this girl holds herself and the change in her psychological self-image of herself. First of all she started dietin', exercisin', she started playin' tennis and water skiin' with her husband. In twenty-seven years this is the first girl—at least to my face—has ever called me a liar. She absolutely denied that these were her ["before"] pictures. Psychologically, in three months' time she could not believe that she had ever looked like this. I think this illustrates that the primary advantage of this operation is primarily psychological.

I always like to have Ingrid sit in with our consultations, and particularly if girls fly out here by themselves, because my feeling about it is this: If they fly out here by themselves, and especially the younger they are the more important it is, instead of sitting across the table from a male doctor, a dirty old man, if you want to use that term, they're sitting across a desk talking to a husband-wife team.

Not long ago we did a girl from St. Louis—we do a surprising number from St. Louis—and after she had come in here and admired herself [in the mirror], and Ingrid and the girls had helped her get dressed, she said as she was goin' out—you know this Middle Western accent—she said, "You know, you guys remind me of the Masters and Johnson of breast surgery."

Mrs. Tippit: One of the cutest compliments.

Dr. Tippit: Really, I told her, that's one of the nicest compliments we've ever had.

Mrs. Tippit: Really, the other interesting thing is—excuse me for interrupting you—patients develop such a— Well, when I'm around they're more apt to ask questions that they wouldn't ask George alone. For example, they would say, "Well, when can I resume my marital relations?" They probably wouldn't ask him this. Or, sexually oriented questions, mostly.

Dr. Tippit: Or, "How will this affect the way I feel afterwards?" "Does it affect the feeling of my nipples?"

Mrs. Tippit: See, my husband did my operation—what, seven years ago, eight years ago?

Dr. Tippit: Eight years ago.

Mrs. Tippit: Ya.

You had this operation?

Mrs. Tippit: Um-hum.

Dr. Tippit: Yes. In fact, I did Ingrid—

Mrs. Tippit: He did mine, he did my stepdaughter [his daughter]. For her twentieth birthday he gave it to her. He did—

Dr. Tippit: Daughter-in-law.

Mrs. Tippit: One of our daughter-in-laws. And my sister is coming out in September from Germany. In fact, both of my sisters are coming out, and the other one, the more she thinks about it, the more she wants to have it done too.

Dr. Tippit: Next month we're doin' her sister from Germany.

There's More Than One Way to . . .

Dr. Edward B. Frankel is also in cosmetic surgery, but on a different scale. "I enjoy being a businessman, personally," he says. Dr. Frankel is a practicing dermatologist, and a specialist in transplanting hair into the scalps of bald men and women. He invented the "Frankel Power Punch" to help perform this operation. But it has grown beyond mere dermatology now—Dr. Frankel is an entrepreneur with a large clinic on Wilshire Boulevard in Los Angeles, a modern medical facility that Dr. Frankel designed himself. He has other clinics in San Diego and Orange County, and he talks about finding a way to franchise his system across the country. "I just really enjoy expanding a business enterprise."

Dr. Frankel advertises his services on radio and television and in newspapers. This makes him controversial in the medical profession. He also promotes himself assiduously.

Our first direct contact with Dr. Frankel was a telephone conversation between him and Lowell. During that talk, he said he would be glad to talk to one of us, provided there was something in it for him. Specifically, he told Kaiser in a second telephone conversation, he would like an assurance that we would mention him in this book. So Kaiser wrote him a letter: "I am writing to assure you that Jon Lowell and I intend to quote your comments in our forthcoming book . . . and to use your name and to describe your work and the services you offer."

This letter was on his desk when Kaiser sat down in Dr. Frankel's office. Kaiser glanced at it and noticed that something had been added to it at the bottom of the page. He soon handed it over, and Kaiser read: "In consideration of an interview with Edward B. Frankel, M.D., I agree that the value of this interview is $10,000. In turn, Dr. Frankel agrees that this sum will be waived if the . . . description and location of the office is noted in the forthcoming book."

Below this addendum he had left a blank for his signature, and for Kaiser's. So the interview began with a brief signing ceremony.*

Then Dr. Frankel proposed a tour of his clinic, a large, bustling establishment with more than a dozen employees, including three who were apparently surgeons. Dr. Frankel declined to say just how big the staff was. He declined to answer any questions that might have given aid or comfort to a competitor in his line of business.

Dr. Frankel was proud of his design for the clinic, and proud of the facilities, including three operating rooms for cosmetic surgery, four for transplants, numerous consultation rooms, and lots of medical equipment. He showed off almost every room, even inviting Kaiser into the operating room to watch a face-lift, an offer he declined.

---

* For the record: Frankel's main office is at 4322 Wilshire Boulevard, Los Angeles. He offers all types of cosmetic surgery, hair transplants and various skin treatments. He accepts "most major credit cards."

As he walked around, he busily turned off the lights in unoccupied rooms. "You can see nobody around here pays the electric bill except me," he said. He greeted a surgeon coming out of the operating area and asked him to "turn off some lights." Then he shouted at a nurse to turn off the air conditioning in the waiting room—"It's freezing."

Dr. Frankel is a smallish man whose physiognomy might be called nondescript, were it not for his profession. This specialist in hair transplants is largely bald. He wears a beard that is speckled with gray.

I advertise the practice of medicine. I started advertising years ago as probably the first advertising doctor in the country. Because I advertise, there have been little hassles along the way—but, interestingly enough, not from patients. Not from people who come in and get services. Some of the criticisms have been, well, "What kind of a doctor has to advertise? Gee, he must be about as good as a used car salesman." Or, "If you advertise, then you're going to have a self-interest to do things you ought not do." My answer to that is, the self-interest is there whether the patient comes in from advertising or is recommended by the guy next door.

Dr. Frankel started advertising in the 1960s, not long after he completed his medical training at the University of Southern California and Los Angeles County General Hospital. He was asked to leave the Orange County Medical Association, the local branch of the AMA, because of his advertising, but later was invited to rejoin. At the time of this interview the Association was again asking him to leave its ranks—"a legal problem," as he put it.

Whatever its effect on his colleagues, advertising has obviously been good for business. But success in this field, according to Dr. Frankel, is as much a result of society's values and pressures as his skills as a surgeon or promoter. Frankel expressed this opinion in a discussion about whether his patients "really need" the cosmetic surgery he provides:

Does a patient whose chin recedes dramatically or whose nose is just really quite large and misshapen, or the ears are flopping in the breeze—does this patient really need surgery? The answer is Hell yes. The person who has some obvious deformity like I mentioned is going to be discriminated against, that's just the nature of our society. Now there are plenty of studies that have been out—the fact that executives tend to be not only healthier, but taller, not fat. There are lots of things you could point out about a person's physical appearance and physiognomy that do cause discrimination in this society. Some people come in and really can't look at you because of their baldness. You'd be amazed. If you don't experience this kind of feeling yourself, it's hard to appreciate it, but after you see these people you gain some appreciation. It doesn't do you any good to say, "Well, gee, why do they feel that way?" It sure as hell doesn't do you any good to say, "Well, you need a psychiatrist, not a hair transplant." They could waste a hell of a lot of money and still say, "Gee, I spent ten thousand dollars on a psychiatrist, I'm still bald, and I still don't like it," when all they needed was something on their head. It just happens that way.

O.K., so you get down to these procedures where the patient is really quite insecure, or has a feature that will cause discrimination, will cause others to mock them. Take a kid that comes in with a birthmark on their face or real floppy ears. Mother will bring them in at age five. As soon as they get into school, other kids are making fun of them, right away.

Then the things like face-lift, where a person wants to be younger. Now, whether it's because they're, uh, getting to an age where the husband is looking at younger women, whether the guy wants to attract a younger woman and he feels he can't do it when he's bald, if the reason isn't too outlandish, and it's consistent with what we know we can end up with as improvement, we'll do the procedure.

We're not looking to sit down and offer them psychotherapy and tell them, "Look, you don't have to worry about your husband, you've been married now twenty years and you're going to have a good life together." That's not part of what we're doing. We'll correct it if we can do what they're looking for. Now, whether they are actually able to keep their husband, or whether the guy is really going to be able to attract a younger female—that's now his thing. But we'll get him the hair and we'll do the face-lift, and we'll do it well.

That gets you into another issue: How much does the fact that it can be done build up a desire? The fact that there's a newer, faster car, how much does that increase the desire for someone to have it? Well, granted, the person that wants a faster car will buy it. I think we see that all over the place. I think that's just part of technology, it's part of what we create, it's part of—I think—coming out of caves. I've kind of wondered about the question in general, actually, in a philosophical sense. I think the fact that we can build tall buildings and all—we build 'em.

Dr. Frankel was not shy about quoting his prices:

For example, eyelids, upper and lower eyelids, both together you're talking about somewhere between twelve to fourteen hundred dollars. For either upper or lower you're in the range of about seven hundred dollars. If you're doing both there's a reduction, some price savings. Face-lift, you're in the area of two thousand dollars. Face and eyes, again you can save some money by getting them done together, you're around twenty-seven hundred or so. Protruding ears, depending on the person, seven hundred to one thousand dollars. Dermabrasion, which I personally do, depends on the amount of, uh, face. If you're doing, for example, the full cheeks and temple you can get into the area of five to six, seven hundred dollars. It's for facial scars, acne pits and this type of thing. Now that's a procedure that I do in this office, as well as the transplants. I also personally do some of the scar revisions. A person's in an auto accident, has scars that they need repairs, and that's another procedure that I do. A full face dermabrasion could be as much as two thousand dollars. Tattoos [i.e., their removal] can vary from one hundred dollars to five or six hundred dollars, depending on the size. It's strictly a square area–type thing. Breast implant, you're talking about twelve to fifteen hundred dollars, including the price of the implant.* Hair transplant, you're talking about ten to fifteen dollars—we're in the area of ten to twelve-fifty a plug, depending on how many you're getting. If you're getting more plugs, I can give a better price.

There are also some newer things that we're getting into, some of which have been done in, uh, particularly in Argentina. Doctors are doing what is called "pedical flap," which is basically taking an area of skin from above the ear and behind the scalp and moving it across to cover the top. Scalp reduction, which is like a face-lift—basically you're taking excessive bald skin off the scalp, closing it up, so that you're reducing the area of the baldness. . . . I think we're going to be able to transplant much larger areas of free grafts. By free I don't mean in cost, I mean not a pedical.

Those "plugs" actually grow? The new hair actually grows?
The hair grows as if it stayed in its original site, and will grow the

---

* Dr. Frankel and Dr. Tippit are of one mind on the preferred method for augmenting breasts. Dr. Frankel's surgeons also use the inert Dow Chemical insert. Dr. Frankel also agrees that the use of silicone injections was a grave error, but he adds, "Silicone still has a place in medicine. No question about it. And in cosmetic medicine. For example, there are certain depressed areas, certain problems involving both injury and congenital defects where injections of silicone are still the choice."

length of time, which is basically lifelong. I've transplanted eyebrows also. But remember on eyebrows, you're usually taking a finer hair from the side of the neck, but the hair in the back of the neck continues to grow, it doesn't stop growing like a natural eyebrow, so the patient has to understand that they're going to have to clip their brows.

Dr. Frankel is a bald man selling hair. How does that fact affect business?

Well, occasionally a person'll say, um, "Can I ask you a personal question?" That's exactly the way they frame it, and I know the question, I know the answer as soon as they say it. The answer is obvious. In my case, I'm growing a beard, I don't have the same interest in hair on my scalp.

But I can tell you this, that when I see some patients coming back and they've got nice hair growth, I get a little wistful. But I don't quite have the personal desire at this time. Maybe my beard is a substitute. I started growing it, as I look back on it, interestingly enough, at about the time when my hair was kind of ebbing away.

When I'm on TV, and I have been on a few TV things, and talked about it, I've got what I call my TV hat that I wear [he laughs], which is a hairpiece. We also happen to have hairpieces that we sell, the reason being some people simply say, "I don't want surgery."

Besides accepting credit cards, Dr. Frankel offers his own credit plan:

There's another kind of a first that I think I can say I'm responsible for [besides advertising], and that is, advertising and selling cosmetic surgery and hair transplantation on a payment plan, financing. Prior to my advertising and offering it, the reason that plastic surgeons always said, "Well, gee, we got to get money in advance, money up front"— well, why? They said the patient won't pay you, they'll figure up a little reason why they're not satisfied—their nose didn't quite go this way, there was a little wrinkle in the cheek—some reason that they won't pay you.

I can tell you [whenever Dr. Frankel says "you" it comes out more like the "ya" of his native New York City] that I successfully advertise a payment plan over a year or two, and we do not find that people are picking out little points not to pay their bill. The advertising does bring in a wide range of people, honest people who pay for what they're getting. It's the whole thing that our country is built on. To the extent that you might say our whole economy is built on credit, we can give credit also, without any problem.

Dr. Frankel takes repeat customers:

Is there any limit to the number of face-lifts one face can endure?
Well, gee, two or three is certainly not that much difficulty. And generally that takes a person through their lifetime. The elastic fibers in the skin lose their ability to tighten up as time goes on. A good analogy is to an elastic waistband. As the elastic waistband loses its elasticity, suddenly it's twice the waist size. So you could keep cutting it out, and it would still have a little pull left, and you could cut it down to the original size a number of times, but suddenly you'll reach the time when all of its elasticity is gone. Now that's like skin. So you ask how many times can you face a face-lift? Well, two or three anyway—it depends on how much stretch there is.

Dr. Frankel is proud of his efficiency and appalled at his profession's lack of it. "Part of the complaints and part of the whole federal and state uproar about medicine and the cost of medicine is really related to inefficiencies." Once he worried about the whole system: "The question was, Should I be worried about how medicine is practiced, or should I be concerned about my own practice and making a living? I can tell you, my concern about how medicine was practiced generally was the first to go." Though worried about society in general, particularly its profligacy, Dr. Frankel is bullish on his own prospects:

Looking ahead five years, ten years, what do you see for yourself and this practice?
Well, there'll be a hell of a lot more advertising than there is now. But advertising, our competition, doesn't bother me at all, because knowing my own abilities in this area, we'll go into any area no matter who's there. I *know* that we can go into any spot and succeed in both a business and a medical way.

Is it your assumption that there's a great unexploited market of potential clients out there?

Oh, no question about it, yes. You're going to find it in every metropolitan area. There's just no question about it. Sure. And then you'll see the usual ways of business competition. I personally feel that it's very hard to set up a situation where up-front looks good, and is good, let's say, and suddenly it bogs down in the back. General Motors not only carries on a good advertising campaign, they back it up with a decent car. I think it's all gotta be there.

If you've got good surgeons, you could open up an office, backing it up with the kind of backup facilities that we know is right, and with the kind of advertising that we know works—and you can waste a lot of advertising dollars finding out what works—and really that's it. You give him the backup work so that his time is spent doing as much cutting as he wants, cause really, the surgeon is the cutter. And that's really what's necessary.

"If You're Not Happy with You, You Get Depressed"

A glimpse of a face-lift operation in mid-lift was not Dr. Frankel's only offer of help. He also proposed that Kaiser talk to some of his patients before, during or after their treatment. Some women who had breast enlargements were due in that afternoon for checkups, he said. Kaiser said he'd love to meet them.

Which is how Kaiser met Mrs. X (no names, please), a sandy-haired woman with a pleasant face whose age appeared to be in that uncertain zone that begins for some unlucky women in the late twenties, for others not until thirty-five or forty—just the other side of youth. She talked in a small consulting room, sitting on an examining table wrapped in a loose gown.

It all started five years ago. After my little boy was born [her second child] I lost a lot of weight. I've never been a heavy person. And my breasts got the droopies—that's the first place you lose weight—and I just, uh, I'm very self-conscious. I think every woman is, about her shape, O.K.? I still consider myself young, I'll be thirty-one in December, but, um, I always wanted my figure to remain attractive, as much as possible, and it really bothered me.

So the first year I did nothing about it. I thought about surgery and the possibilities, and I began to get some information on it. But I wasn't sure yet if I was going to have it done. Then two years went by and I was going to doctors. O.K., free consultations. Every one in the area that had free consultations, I went to. And, uh, some of them have charges—twenty-five, thirty-five, forty-five dollars for a consultation. One doctor out in Covina, I won't mention his name, he takes his patients and transports 'em down to Mexico. His fees are naturally lower. But if you know anything about the sanitary standards down there— My answer was a definite no, thank you, I'm not interested.

So I was shopping around. Some of 'em, where they charge for a consultation, said, "Well, every woman after she has children gets the droopies. You have a fine figure, nothing to worry about." But I wasn't happy with it.

I'm also, at home, the type of person that runs around in the nude, you know? I can't stand clothes. I'm a very free person, O.K.? So I wasn't happy with me. And if you're not happy with you, you get depressed. And I was getting depressed. So I took out the phone book and started going through it, and called every single one of 'em. But when I saw the ad [Dr. Frankel's ad in the Yellow Pages] it amazed me, because his name was large print, the hours, everything. It looked like they were hiding nothing, saying, "Come, my arms are open," you know, "Come see me." So it struck me, and I called, and I came in. After all of 'em that I had looked at, I knew, after my consultation here, that this was it. I had found what I was looking for. There wasn't anybody telling me, "You don't need this surgery." There wasn't anybody telling me, "Oh, whatever questions you have, ask the nurse, I have to see my patients." They weren't in a rush to get rid of you. And they were very friendly, you know? Some of the girls have become my friends. I don't know 'em, you know, but they're my friends. They cared about me and my feelings.

What did you worry about during those years before you had the operation?

Well, if you've ever lost weight suddenly, you have these awful stretch marks. And I didn't look good in a bikini. You know, they drooped so low I could tie 'em in a bow [she's laughing], I used to tell my husband that all the time. I didn't feel comfortable in any of the V-tops or low-cut tops or anything. You know, gee, I could have 'em open to my waist and there was just nothing there, I had lost so much weight. You know, Twiggy the second.

What's changed since you had the operation?

Oh, my husband cannot believe me. He simply cannot believe me. He says I wake up in the morning, I'm happy, I get up and I make his breakfast, you know, I cook his meals for him, I run around the house naked, and I'm happy. He said I used to just sit in a corner and mope: "God, here I am a woman, and I, I look like death." And it had gotten to the point where I'd say to him, "Why don't you go out and find yourself some young stuff. It's all over for me." You know, I was really in a bad state of depression over my body. And now—forget it! I've got the most beautiful body in the world [a giggly laugh]. I've got my shape back again and I love it.

11

NATIONAL PASTIMES

"What Life Is Really About"

The American cult of youth is so pervasive that we sometimes fail to realize when it is at work. For example, our most popular national spectacles—though no one talks much about this—are kids' games. In a general climate of fear about getting old, we make national heroes out of athletes whose careers are virtually guaranteed to end by age thirty-five. Is there life after football?

Amos Fowler, twenty-two, would like to know the answer to that question, and he worries about it. Amos Fowler is a former hero who hopes to be heroic again, a great offensive lineman at the University of Southern Mississippi and now an ordinary, unnoticed guard for the Detroit Lions of the National Football League. A second-string guard, that is—a hero on the bench.

Sometimes you say to yourself, Why do I play the game? You go out there and you hate practice and everything like that, but when it comes down to the end and the game itself it's just all worth it. Just one win. It's worth everything you put behind it. Once you're not out there playin' football, that's when you really get upset.

My last game my senior year at Southern [Mississippi] I got hurt about the third play of the game. It was just like takin' my life away from me. I said to myself, This might be the last game I'll ever even participate in, and here I am hurt. So I told the doc, "Well, I got to go back out and play. Whether it's hurt or not, I got a long time to let it get healed. So I'm goin' back out."

And he did.

Amos Fowler is a product of the poor white South. He grew up in Pensacola, Florida, with three brothers and sisters and no father in a two-bedroom house. He started playing football when he was eight or nine for a midget team sponsored by the Pensacola Salvation Army. "Then I started playin' city league ball, then junior high on through high school and college." The big-time college scouts passed over Amos, but his uncle had a friend who got him a tryout at Southern Miss, and within a week he had made the team. It just got better after that, culminating in his selection in the professional football draft, the ultimate dream.

But that dream comes true without any guarantees. As a Detroit Lion, Amos has had to start over again. To keep his spirits up he writes notes to himself in the loose-leaf book of plays he is meant to study and master, notes reminding himself that when the going gets tough, the tough get going, etc. At least he knows that if things don't work out, he's got his degree from Southern Miss in building construction.

A young American who grows up the way Amos Fowler has gets an interesting view of the adult world. It is full of football fans.

We had a couple of guys at my school, their names was Two Bits and a Quarter. They were two guys and they were probably in their forties, and these two guys just tried to hang around with the college kids. They'd come around the football team and everything else and they really got into it. A lot of the ballplayers hung around with them. I didn't too much. But I liked them and all that. They invited players over to their houses, they threw parties for the team, they would help the team get up for games. Matter of fact, one of the guys donated his home one night with refreshments and everything to have a team meeting there and get everything together. They got into football like it was part of their job, part of their life. Just like that. I guess they had played football back when they were young.

Amos considered why people got so excited about football. "I guess it's just always been a thing," he said. "I know when I growed up I always looked up to an athlete. It's just like lookin' up to a big brother or something. All the girls want to go out with a football player."

Amos is a soft-spoken, almost gentle giant whose accent and courtly manners convey the sonorous warmth of the old white South, but he understands that the coarser aspects of the game he plays explain much of its appeal:

Seems like what America wants and loves is to see violence. That's why they go see fights and football games and everything else. They love the violence. I don't think the football team looks at it as violence at all. I never think of it as violence. Very seldom do I ever really get mad enough out there to want to hurt somebody. And I never do that unless a guy hurts me. Or tries to hurt one of my teammates, something on purpose.

When you're part of it, according to Amos, the violence looks different than it does on the instant replays:

Most of the players are out there because they enjoy the game. They're competin'. Tryin' to win. I think if there was another way to get around from bustin' a guy's knee on a cut block or something like that, then you would do it. Any time you cut a guy I don't think you mean to bust his knee. You feel bad about it.

I remember back one time when I was playin' in the city league. I was about twelve or thirteen. I was playin' defensive end. This guy came out, a runnin' back, and I closed down and hit on him and broke his ribs. They brought an ambulance onto the field and toted the guy off. I wanted to quit right then. It really scared me. Intimidated me. I felt like I had really hurt the guy seriously. I thought the guy was dead or something the way they was runnin' around and bringin' the ambulance out there and everything.

After all these years, Amos said, it seems like he has spent "all my life" playing football. But there is a ghost in Amos's life now, the ghost of afterwards. What will happen when football is over with?

Over with. [A pause.] I think it will be very tough. When you're playin' pro ball, there's no job security. The Detroit Lions could come to me tomorrow and say, "Amos, we don't need you any more." Boom, I'd be gone. It's a big part of my life or I wouldn't have stuck with it the whole time. It would be very hard to cope without it. To just get away from it. I know my family and my girlfriend, after the end of football season my senior year, there for a while I had nothin' to do, and they said they could tell it affected me. Wantin' to be out there playin'. When you're playin' you always complain about not havin' any time. But when it's over with you have the time and you sit there and say, "What should I do with it?" I've got this degree in buildin' construction. But I think if I got out of football I'd like to coach. But I don't have a degree in coachin'. I know I'll probably be involved in it.

I hope I'll have a son one day who can play it. I always say to my girlfriend, "If I have a son he's never playin' football." But I know deep down I'll want him to. For sure I guess it would bother me if my son didn't at least try. I wouldn't force it on him. I hope I wouldn't. But I really would like for him to play.

The more he thought about that unborn son, the more Amos knew he wanted him to be a football player. There may be life after football, but life *without* football? Unlikely.

How much did it bother Amos to have become just another player, no longer a special star?

It really bothers me that I'm not a first-teamer, because I know I can play in the professional league. I've still got things I've got to work on and come on with. You can't play this game and go through what you have to go through and not want to be on the startin' unit. Sometimes you get down and depressed and you just have to say, "I'm going to go out there and work as hard as I can." You tend to say, "I'm not gettin' anywhere, so why kill myself?" I don't want to ever get to that point. I'm out there to be on the first team. I've worked hard and I've gotten somewhere.

I'll tell you, I don't like it, not playin'. But you just have to keep tryin' and hope that someday your day's gonna come. It seems like I'm inconsistent. I'm a rookie and I'm just not mature enough, it seems like that's my biggest problem. One day I'll be out there and I'll do great, and the next day I might screw up or something.

The more he talked about this the more Amos revealed his frustration:

I don't know what it is—I can't really say. I've talked to the Lions' coaches and everything else, you know, and they just say, "Well, we're gonna get you in there, we're gonna play you." And I have played a lot, you know. I'm talkin' to some of the veteran guys, you know, and they said "Hey, I think you guys have played a lot. In my rookie year I played one play the whole year." And the games I've been in I've been pretty good, you know, and everything. I was pleased with myself.

It was no fun talking about this failure—about the fact that three other rookie linemen are starting on the team, but Amos is on the bench. After all, football has been everything to Amos Fowler, and he has always been great at it.

Did Amos feel he had missed anything in life by devoting so much of his twenty-two years to football? Yes, he thought he had:

Like in college, a lot of my buddies who didn't play football, they had plenty of time. While I was out there on the football field, they could be in there hittin' their books in the afternoon, gettin' their homework out of the way, then go out at night. You know, I still wanted my night life, to go out, and so I just couldn't get on the books as good as they could and everything, as far as that way goes. Then the social life—as far as bein' in a fraternity and all that, gettin' to mingle and everything, at my school you couldn't do it. And I couldn't play baseball or anything else. You could only play football if you were on scholarship.

Now that he is playing for money, playing as a *professional* football player, Amos senses that something important has changed. He can't describe this too specifically, but it sounds a lot like growing up:

Pro ball is more businesslike, but it's really not that much different from college. Except for now it's your job, it's a job and you've got to do it. I know in college, if you played at my school, at Southern, you didn't like the Ole Miss ballplayers or the Mississippi State ballplayers. But here now I couldn't say I dislike the Minnesota Vikings or the Chicago Bears or anyone else. I don't even know the guys. They're out there doin' a job, just like me.

There's one thing between pros and college. You used to get fired up for a ballgame, and if you won you just went crazy and everything. Here the same thing happens, but I don't think it hits you as hard, to win. In college if you won the big one it stuck with you for a long time.

Whatever happens now, Amos's future in sports is assured—as a fan. Not just football, either:

You know, I'm just crazy about sports myself. I really get into them. Just like the World Series. All of us guys on the team, we were really battlin' it down. And watchin' basketball, and everything else. No matter what sport activity I go to, I still really get fired up and excited just being in the stands and watchin' it. Just the competition, seein' people competin', one team trying to win. The atmosphere. Knowin' how I'd be feeling if I was out there competin' against 'em.

Violence, excitement and competition, a test—perhaps Americans like sports for the same reasons so many of us apparently like wars. We heard those same explanations for America's sports mania from numerous people.

But this is a complicated mania. Americans love their football, a crude and crushing game, albeit artful at times. But they equally love baseball, as subtle and intellectual a physical sport as any in the world, a game whose only regular violence involves bat and ball.

Kaiser discussed this with Art Robertson, the 320-pound giant from Toronto, Ohio, who coaches midget football there. Robertson and his wife, Janice, appeared in Chapter 6.

It was Robertson's opinion that Americans' love for football was entirely logical:

Football is a lot like what life is really about. Probably the reason people get so wrapped up in it is its being so competitive. That's a big part of anyone's life—competition, going out and proving that you're as good as the next person or possibly a little better. If you strive hard, work hard, you succeed. If you don't, you get knocked around. If you just go out there and roll over, that other team's going to roll right over you. And if you go out in the world and feel the same way, the world's going to roll right over top of you.

It's the American way.

12

RELIGION

God Isn't Dead. He Has a Marketing Problem.

If the body is a dish offered in the great American buffet, so too is the spirit. For a fee, anyone can learn to meditate with his own mantra. For a larger fee, anyone can join the sect of his choice, from the Hari Krishnas to the Scientologists to who-knows-what-next-week. Even old-fashioned American Protestantism is offering itself up in new wrappings and flavors to attract the customers.

The Reverend Bill Sharp, for example, is a gifted marketer of the old-time religion:

We're trying to put together a spiritual shopping center in a city. Already it has reached proportions beyond our imagination.

In the case of the Reverend Sharp, that is some imagination. Though forty-six, Sharp looks about thirty, with carefully styled black hair cut modishly long. On the day he was interviewed he wore a three-piece denim suit. The blue frames of his eyeglasses matched the denim. He had a gold chain around his neck that held a large silver cross with a turquoise at its center. He sat in the boiler room of an imposing geodesic dome that was once a Cinerama movie theater. Cinerama never really caught on, but God has a future, particularly with helpers like the Reverend Sharp.

I never met my real parents. I had a wonderful foster mother who adopted me when I was about six weeks old. My name was originally Rex Moore and then it was Bill Alexander and then it wound up William Martin Sharp. Dallas is my home. I went into the ministry after coming out of the Marine Corps. I had opportunities to go into professional boxing, football, maybe be an artist. I chose the ministry. I'm a lieutenant colonel in the Civil Air Patrol. I have served as the wing chaplain for Nevada. I'm taking that LaSalle law course, and I'm a pilot.

Why the correspondence law course?

I think it's helped me navigate as a minister. One of the failings of the average academic college today as far as a minister is concerned is that they really don't teach ministers how to be a minister. How do you buy land, who do you go see, how do you conduct a wedding, a funeral? These things are never talked about. You study the Bible and you get a thorough knowledge of the Bible, but there's more than preaching on Sunday, especially in today's churches.

I believe today people are gravitating to the larger, more magnetic centers, just like a supermarket. You see the big shopping center. I think the "jot-em-down" store is passé.

There is a place for the small rural church, there will always be, yet I contend the true New Testament church can't remain really small, because the Bible says "they added daily to the church." So it has to grow. Of course, the city and the surroundings have a determining influence on the growth.

In putting this together, I handled all the real estate. We paid no commissions. We saved probably $160,000 or $170,000. But there are times when I know I have reached my limitations and I have a very fine, competent attorney here in the city. He takes care of the biggies.

After I was discharged from the Marines I went to Bible college in Missouri. That's where I met my wife, Nancy. We've been happily married for twenty-five years next August twenty-second. Nancy is a vocalist; she's recorded several albums and is doing two new albums presently. She's sung with me in my ministry all over the world. I was ordained in 1955. I traveled as an evangelist for a number of years. We pioneered a church in Dallas. I was there five years and three months. Then we accepted a church in Independence, Missouri. During those years we had a very fruitful, prosperous ministry. We had a television ministry, radio ministry. Then we came here, pastored for three years, five months, then we split with our denomination, Assembly of God, over politics. I don't want to get into the grievous things. I don't want things to sound like sour grapes. It's a good denomination, but we disagreed over the handling of funds for my television ministry. I'm not opposed to denominations, other than the restrictions they sometimes impart.

During that time we began to really have to decide whether we wanted to burn our bridges and in effect start all over. Because we had—and this is not vanity, just because we had been at it long enough—achieved a certain prominence and prestige in our denomination. When we began this less than three years ago, about thirty-three months ago, it was really kind of like a leper colony. We had little hope. We couldn't find any buildings. In this city we could find nothing.

So we began at Circus, Circus.* There were times when I really wondered what was going to happen. The first Sunday, for example, I had no place to study, prepare, meditate for my first sermon. I had to go in the men's room. I had to sit in the john. Not to use the facility. Just to sit down and study. When I'm in there I hear groaning in the next stall. It's one of the men praying for the service. So while I'm in there, I hear a little voice saying, "Are you sure you're doing the right thing? You don't have to do this. You can still pastor a good church in the denomination."

A couple of weeks after we started we were having communion and we went to move a table that was covered with a drape. A guy was underneath. He'd slept under the table all night. This was at Circus, Circus. We had to use the wine cellar cage for a nursery to begin with. The kids would crawl all over the wire. We'd bring in our songbooks. It was kind of like a Billy Sunday tabernacle kind of thing. Every Sunday we'd back our truck with the baby beds up to the casino.

The new church quickly grew. For a time the Sunday services were held in another casino, then in the convention center, then in a showroom whose normal spectacle was called *The Wild World of Burlesque.* The Reverend Sharp remembered that one fondly: "The beautiful part was a guy would come forward, make a decision, and you'd hear the jackpot go off. I'd say, 'Well, folks, another one just hit the jackpot here at Christian Center.' " The congregation began with twenty-five people, "and in thirty-three months we have twenty-five hundred here." And they have bought the former Cinerama movie theater as their church.

We had a real time getting this theater. We had less than a hundred members. I walked into the Pacific Theaters offices and said, "I want to buy your theater." The good attorney inquired as to my source of

* Circus, Circus is a gaudy, family-oriented hotel-casino in Las Vegas that features live circus acts in the rafters above the casino, and a big arcade of games and gimmicks for kids. It has been extraordinarily successful.

finance. He was Jewish. I said, "The God of Abraham, Isaac and Jacob." We negotiated with them. They were very kind. We were able to purchase these ten acres for a million and a half. Right today, its worth as it sits right at three million.

We're planning to build a Christian nightclub which will be in a space needle. We've been approved by the Federal Aviation Administration to go 230 feet in the air. We're going to put in a hotel, because every year we have what we call an "International Charismatic Convention." We have outstanding people come in. Pat Boone has shared in this ministry. Elvis Presley responded financially by watching our telecasts. There are many [famous] people who come here. We don't exploit them. We don't do the "We have Clark Gable here today" thing.

We have a twenty-four-hour lifeline number—386-LIFE. Recently Clint Eastwood came. He shot a movie in Las Vegas. He wanted to use our property to blow up a car, rent our land. I didn't want to rent the land. I said, "If you'll shoot my sign with my crisis center phone number and mention the church in the movie, you don't have to pay me anything." So they agreed to that.

Merv Griffin has contacted me. I just did my third wedding on the Merv Griffin show and they just told me the ratings for that one wedding went up twenty-five percent. We reached something like fifty million people. I've had thousands of letters pour in from all over the country.

But back to the question at hand. I preach the basic fundamental doctrine—Jesus Christ crucified, resurrected, life eternal, abundant life message. I don't get on a hobby horse and preach against gambling, smoking, drinking, cussing. I don't pound the pulpit and preach against all of these things. I preach a positive gospel. I believe there's a heaven to gain and a hell to shun. I believe the Holy Spirit has to change our lives. We turn over daily the proverbial new leaf. I believe that if we could get everyone to share the basic doctrine, loving thy neighbor as thyself, we would have no wars, suicides, conflicts, whatever.

I maintain this: that if Jesus of Nazareth was in the physical form today, walking around, as he walked on the shores of Galilee, he would not, contrary to what some of my peers say, take a whip and go in and whip all of the people at the crap table. I think he might go into some of the churches and run out some of the Jezebels in the choir, the hypocrites, the double-standard women, and some of the deacons—people who don't manifest the spirit of love in Christ.

This is the thing that's driven people away from church today. They can get more sympathy in a local bar or casino than they can in church.

Don't get me wrong. I'm not saying that if Jesus was walking around the [Las Vegas] Strip that he'd be in at the dice tables or playing baccarat. But I believe he'd be in there manifesting the spirit of love. He went to the sinner. He was out and about.

The Bible says go into all the world. This is my world. Las Vegas. I believe that all that I've ever learned, all that I've ever been, all that I've ever trained for, is culminating in the destiny of this work. I've got a life sentence here as far as I'm concerned.

We want to build a Bible college here, and the Christian nightclub. The youth are not being reached in the city. And the crisis center. These are three of the facets, the multifaceted ministry that we have. We also have a coffee house ministry. In other words, we're trying to reach all kinds of people through various multiple ministries. The movies. God gave us a movie theater. So rather than dump all the equipment, why not use it? So we show family and gospel films together each week.* We always show the secular film first. If they want to leave, they can.

This is the city of weddings. That's why we're building the wedding chapel at the top of the Christian nightclub. You'll be able to walk up a ramp from the restaurant— Of course, you could have a reception there. There'll be smorgasbord in the daytime. It'll be a revolving restaurant like the space needle. It'll seat five hundred people. At the top we'll have our wedding chapel. It'll be an all-faith chapel. We'll have the Jewish Star of David, we'll have the cross representing the Catholics, and we'll have the doves representing the Protestant faiths.

We're going to give books on marriage. Our theme will be "Come, but be prepared to stay forever." Not just a fast-buck operation. We want to enhance the wedding image in this city. Do what we can in a few minutes to upgrade their marriage. We're going to provide marriage counseling if they want it. Most of them won't want it. But at least we'll place a free book in their hands when they leave about what marriage really means. I've married some celebrities and I've married some plain vanilla people, but I'm not too quick to marry any and everybody. This is going to be the world's most unique wedding chapel when we finish. We're going to advertise in all the national magazines. I'm omnidirectional. Reaching in many directions.

Our vision now is to have a national television ministry from this city. To be able to show to the world people who are, who are— What's the word I'm thinking right now? They are celebrities, yes, but they are

---

* On movie nights there's a soda fountain and candy stand in the lobby. During the week it's filled with religious pamphlets and Mrs. Sharp's records.

what we call in Texas the "bell cows." They are people that the whole world is focusing on right now. World leaders are here in various forms. Not so much in legislature as in the entertainment world. The word I was thinking of was "world communicators." We have world communicators coming to this city in every form. If we can just show how God has arc-welded their lives into something meaningful.

What we envision in ten years, if this world stays glued together, is a hotel, a facility for our conventions. See, there are a lot of Christian people who would like to come to Las Vegas, but they don't have a reason. We're going to give them a reason. Our Christian nightclub. Having a Christian breakfast on radio every Monday morning from that nightclub in the sky. The hotel, the Bible college, the network, the television, the crisis center. What I'm trying to say, in essence, is we're trying to put together a spiritual shopping center in a city. Already it has reached proportions beyond our imagination.

You've got $300,000 right now and you need ten million to do all of this?
That's true. We've raised $300,000. I don't know where the money's coming from. I don't know how I got this far. But I know we're going to make it. I've read the last chapter.

Born Again

It is a short film with a thick, sensual feel, the kind of commercial advertisement that admen boast about. An elegant young woman, bathed in a soft, lush illumination, gazes at herself in a mirror as she puts on a string of pearls for an evening out in the big city. Suddenly the picture dissolves. The same girl, now freshly scrubbed and simply dressed, is boarding a bus, apparently headed for a new life. The modulated voice of an announcer explains that she has found Jesus. No longer will she work as a prostitute.

Christian commercials on "Christian networks," Christian talk shows, born-again rock groups—all manner of electronic Christianity bounces around the land on our airwaves, another indication of the big business religion is doing in the late 1970s in America.

Is there a market? Here the available statistics are remarkable. In a recent extensive national survey on religion, the Gallup organization found that one-third of the country's adults—that would be 50 million people—profess to have been "born again" or to have experienced "a turning point in your life when you committed yourself to Christ." Even allowing for the inclination of some people to appear a little holier to a visiting poll taker than the facts might justify, this seems an astounding number.

But the sense that one has been born again is no guarantee of formal religious practice. The same Gallup study found that 87 percent of the populace considered personal religious beliefs important in their own lives, but less than 40 percent expressed high confidence in a church or organized religion. We too found countless examples of people who felt religious but did not act out those feelings in a formal religious institution.

Jack Cullinane, for one, a real estate developer from Davenport, Iowa, goes four or five times a week to a favorite spot beside a river and sits quietly watching the water. "When the pressure builds up, or there's something undecided, I go to the river. This is my religion. I belong to a church. I'm not an atheist. But I'm not religious, no way."

Cullinane's use of terminology is revealing. To be "religious" implies something formal to him, something to do with churchgoing, and he isn't interested. God isn't dead. He has a marketing problem. The Reverend Sharp's spiritual shopping center is meant to be one solution. It seems to please a large number of customers.

The reasons for the persistent strength of religious belief in modern America are a subject for another inquiry, but one important one seems obvious. The conventional feast on the buffet table—the combination of tangible goods and excitement that preoccupies so many Americans so much of the time—is spiritually neutral, empty. This does not make the conventional dishes unappealing, obviously, but it may make them unsatisfying once tried or acquired. A great many people clearly feel a need for more than things and excitement. Material security is not the same as a sense of security.

This message reached us with unexpected force. Months after our original stay in Las Vegas Kaiser returned there and found some of the people we had interviewed. First he sought out Shirley Walker, the fortune-hunting bartender from Missouri. She was still tending bar, but something important had changed. She was no longer using her moves, no longer tantalizing the male customers. She had cooled down. What happened?

After you guys left town I had a bad experience. I was very ill for about four months ["female problems," she said later], and I got down to the point of no return where I really thought I was going to die. I was very sick. And you can reach a point where things are so bad that the only thing you have to do is pray about it. And I did, and I had a real born-again experience. And from then on I started to think about things differently. Because after you guys left, my plan of getting ahold of somebody with some money and the whole bit—socking some money away—was going just fine. I was gambling with this wealthy man and I was going home with four thousand one night, six thousand the next night, and I really thought, Boy, this is it. You know: I've got it made in the shade; I'll never have another worry by the time I'm thirty.

Well, I found out that's really not where it's at. By the time I was able to go out and buy anything I wanted to and do anything I wanted to, it just wasn't fulfilling. And the only thing I had found that was fulfilling was that born-again experience. It's hard to explain that experience to anybody. You can't explain it, it's got to happen to you.

What do you realize now about the old Shirley we first met that you hadn't realized then?

Well, I realize that I was— Really, in a lot of ways, it's how a lot of people are out there. They've had a rough way to come up and the only way they can make it is by learning how to survive any way they can survive. And if this hadn't happened to me I'm sure I'd still be in it, because it was working for me just like it's worked for a lot of other women who are very financially secure today because they were very determined to make it with whatever they had to do, and they did it. But also they're miserable today, too, even with all the things they have. So now I just have a new outlook on life—this life and the next life.

What happened to your dream of financial security?

Well there's nothing wrong with financial security. I think it's great. I think that if you can obtain it there's no reason you shouldn't, if you can do it in an honest way. But if you have to do it in a dishonest way— if you have to get up every morning, look at yourself in the mirror and realize what you've done to get to that goal—it's not going to be the fulfilling thing you were looking for. You know, love of money is really a sick thing.

Now I have a lot of new ideas about what I'd like to do with my life, and things I'm looking forward to—working with children, with kids that are going through the kind of life that I went through as a child, and realizing that if somebody would have been there to help me when I needed help, I wouldn't have had to struggle and go all the wrong ways to try to obtain happiness. What I would like to do eventually is get involved in some kind of nationwide thing to help abused and unwanted children, neglected children. There are even unwanted, neglected children in upper-class homes that need someone who can identify with them. [She said this as though it were a discovery.]

And what about that problem of not being able to find people you can identify with?

Oh, now I've found some I can identify with, people that have had the same experience that I've had. Nothing's accidental. I met one woman in the restroom at the hotel, and through her I met another woman who is a fundamental Bible teacher. None of us go to church. We find the church is very hypocritical, and they don't teach anybody anything. They just sing and have rituals and do whatever they do. But we're just getting into the true word of God, which is the true Bible, and living by the guidelines of that. It's a great way to live, a very fulfilling way to live, a happy way to live.

I have a class on Mondays and Friday nights. She has other classes also, but then I work during those times.

Have you been able to make any personal relationships that carry over outside the class too?

Oh, yeah, especially with my Bible teacher. She's a really fun and interesting person. Very experienced. She's seventy-three years old, so has a lot to talk about. She's lived like a lot of us lived. She's had a pretty wild life, like I had.

And that was that—stunning news, but easy enough to believe after a moment's reflection. Shirley did seem headed for trouble—though also conceivably success—on her old route. Apparently she caught on too.

It was curious that she had once again found an elderly woman who was her friend and guide, but there seemed no reason to belabor the coincidence. She truly had changed; she radiated entirely different signals.

But the lesson did not end there. Soon after he found Shirley, Kaiser found Neil Slocum, the divorce lawyer whose prediction that virtually all marriages may someday end in divorce appears in Chapter 2. Slocum had a new office, bigger and several stories higher than his old one, in downtown Las Vegas's highest office tower. He also had a new drawing of Christ decorating the office wall. It took him about forty-five seconds to get around to the fact that his life had been transformed. He had been born again.

I was very, very depressed in many, many ways, and particularly about the status of my [second] marriage and personal life and the pressures of my practice. I think I was probably about as badly depressed as you can be and not commit suicide. [Slocum was speaking of a time about six months after his first meeting with Kaiser, and this admission came as a surprise. He had seemed fine the last time they met. Slocum said things had gotten worse in a hurry.] This was shortly after my divorce with my second wife [at the first meeting he said the marriage was in trouble]. I was just very depressed about the whole thing and I called Nancy, my present wife, and asked her for a date, and told her I was divorced. I'd known her—she'd been one of my clients earlier [for a divorce]. She'd called me up and taken me to lunch about a year earlier and told me how she'd become a Christian. And I cut it short—literally just sort of said, "Well, here's a crazy one, leave me alone," and I raced off. But after my own divorce, for some reason I called her and asked for a date.

She said yes and we went out to dinner. She asked me if I would like to go to a church picnic with her. I said yes I'd do that, so I went on this little picnic. They had a service, and pretty soon the minister began to talk to me. At least I thought he did, and at the time I thought it really was *it*. And he said, "Well, would you like to accept Jesus Christ as your savior?" And I said, "Well, I'm not ready yet." And he said, "Oh, yeah, you are." I said, "No, I'm not." He said, "Yes, you are. Come on." So I did.

He just said, "Come and kneel down," which I did; and there's something called the sinner's prayer, which is essentially—you ask Jesus to come into your heart, and then you say, "Lord, I am a sinner, forgive me for my sins, and please come into my heart." And for me it really was a physical feeling. It was like something being poured into my body. Now that's peculiar, very peculiar, because I was totally non-religious, anti-religious in many things. But I still am anti-religious in that I am still strongly opposed to most organized religion, because they're really bureaucracies, they're not doing anything.

What I'm involved in now is a small group of Christians who study the Bible and act in the word of the Bible. I haven't lost a bit of my skepticism or a bit of my analytical ability, whatever I had, and I have yet to hear anything or read anything in the Bible that is contrary to what I can believe. I used to think that people who believed in the Bible were really fundamentalist types who were going to argue with the theory of evolution at the drop of a hat and all that sort of thing, and that really is irrelevant. I mean you could argue it still, I guess, but it's irrelevant. What is relevant is the real, living power that Jesus Christ has in the world. He does have a power to change lives. He changed mine. My problems didn't go away at all. They're even worse than they ever were [a laugh]. But I can handle them. And my relationship with Nancy improved dramatically. We did get married. I adopted her two children, giving me a total of eight that I'm responsible for. My business has picked up. I seem to be getting more and more complex problems in the family law area. I seem to be able to handle them a lot better than I could.

Had Slocum's views about divorce changed at all after this experience? Not really, he said—not at all.

Until this remarkable coincidence occurred, neither of us really believed the Gallup contention that 50 million Americans had been "born again." Now we believe it.

13

INGENUITY

"I Did a Computer Machine That Ate People"

Cars and television are products of the functional era of technological progress—both of them are useful. But the American romance with technology has gone far beyond that stage. In the era of the great buffet, we have redirected traditional American ingenuity. We have passed from inventing television to inventing that realistic game of electronic baseball that can be played—after wiring up the right connections—on one's own six-foot home television screen. Progress.

Americans still believe in their own ingenuity. We encountered dozens of ingenious new schemes, theories, would-be inventions and concoctions in our conversations. We also found stubborn confidence that inventions would continue to appear that could help solve humanity's problems. Everything can be worked out.

Jack Gordon has a lot of that confidence, though he has pretty much stayed away from humanity's problems. He concentrates on amusements. Lowell first discovered him in the columns of a provincial newspaper that described his creative exploits. So without the intense inventor saying so, Lowell knew he had invented a machine that caused people to pay money to play tick-tack-toe against a live chicken.

Lowell arrived at Gordon's nondescript office on a Saturday morning as the inventor was ushering out an Irish doctor who handles Gordon's machines in Ireland. The doctor paused long enough to make small talk, noting with approval that he was seeing a growing number of American patients and they invariably paid cash. Gordon welcomed Lowell in.

Late thirties, carefully styled hair, a nest of gold chains around his neck—first impression. Then he started gobbling the Rolaids by the fistful and chain-smoking Pall Malls and generally handling himself like a hyperactive child, and you saw the real inventor. His office is dominated by a painting of Samson destroying the temple. Instead of a frame, the picture is surrounded by real, cracked marble pillars.

I make a button machine which takes a picture with a Polaroid camera. It puts your picture on a button in one minute. I make a poster machine. You insert a picture in the machine. You push a button and obtain a twenty- by twenty-four-inch poster in one minute. I manufacture a penny machine. You put a penny in, an actual penny, turn a handle and it'll say the Lord's Prayer, "Welcome to Las Vegas," "I had a dream with Martin Luther King." Whatever you want it to say. Boom. There's no inventory involved. You use the customer's penny. You sell him back his own penny for fifty cents.

And I manufacture a chicken machine, which is a machine that plays tick-tack-toe. The chicken plays tick-tack-toe with a human being. You will never beat the chicken, because the chicken goes first. Which is the advantage in tick-tack-toe. Okay, you can tie. But you can never beat him.

Where do you get the ideas for these things?

My entire family created things. My uncle invented the miner's lamp. My grandfather invented the skill saw. Hereditary or whatever, I create these other things.

Explain the genesis of the chicken machine.

I just had an idea one night. I keep a notebook beside me. If an idea pops into my head, I'll jot it down. Then I'll throw it to a machinist and say, "Here's what I want." Then it will go onto a drawing board. Can it be done? And our whole basis is, if you can put a man onto the moon you can do anything. Our belief is that anything can be done. I firmly believe that.

So the chicken machine just popped into your head?

Yeah. I play tick-tack-toe with my children. So I said, "Could a live animal play tick-tack-toe with a human being?" What was the dumbest animal that could play tick-tack-toe? Well a chicken has no brain. Could they play it? The answer was yes. Now they play it. They play it well [tight laugh]. The machines generate thousands of dollars.

Are there problems with the chickens?

No, not really. The machine comes with two chickens. [They're fed grain as a reward for making a correct "move" and tend to get sated.] You use one chicken for like three hours and then you let it out and put another chicken in. I have an animal trainer in Hollywood who trains animals for motion pictures. And I pay $150 per chicken, which cost them like twenty cents each. They train 'em for a couple of weeks and send 'em to me, and I put 'em into the game. The machine costs five thousand dollars.

Will any kind of barnyard chicken do?

Yeah. Any kind. I also have rabbits that take pictures. I have a reindeer that runs a printing press. He's in St. Louis. At the zoo.

This seems to be the amusement machine age.

Of course. What happened is this. During the Depression, okay, there were two businesses that existed and lived. The carnival industry and the movies. Because when people are depressed and have no money they want to be entertained. That's why amusement parks are doing so well. Games are inside those amusement parks. Take more money off them. This is the game age. Bigger and better than ever. And growing.

What does a machine have to have to make people play it?

Glamour. Noise. People are attracted by noise. Take slot machines for example. Why do bells ring on a slot machine? There's no reason for bells to ring—okay?—but people like to hear noise. Noise creates excitement and excitement draws money. They should look unusual, intriguing, so curiosity seekers want to know exactly what it does.

Describe a machine you invented that never got into production.

I did a computer machine that had a thing that ate people.

Ate people?

A computerized thing. While you were swimming, like barracudas would attack. You'd get eaten if you went off the line. Okay. And it was too ghastly. I had red blood dropping out. That type of thing. The children really were afraid of it. I developed that [computerized] killer car game. I developed that, but I didn't like it. Because hitting pedestrians, I thought, was a bad thing. So I backed away. I just gave the drawings away.

You must have some kind of idea for an ultimate game machine.

Yeah, I do. It's kind of a trade secret. I'll sell this company and then I'll go into a new field of machines. I'll produce it, develop it and retire totally. I retired once for two years. I traveled around the world. Now I'll develop the one machine which I can't divulge now. Then I'll probably retire for two or three years. And then do it again. I enjoy working hard for two or three years and then I get very tired, bored with it. Even if business is fantastic, I just reach a point of boredom.

Some people must think you're a little goofy.

Yeah. You can never explain a chicken machine. Those who know me, know that I'm very serious. Those who don't know me, I show them brochures. I never tell them I've got a chicken that plays tick-tack-toe. Because the reaction is, "The kid's crazy." So what I do is I have a brochure. I don't try and project it without having the figures in front of me and a descriptive brochure that says this is what happens.

At this point, Lowell was offered the chance to contest a bored-looking white chicken. While Lowell lost several games to the chicken, Gordon offered a running commentary:

You've got to remember, the chicken always wins. Watch how the chicken watches you. We train him to watch you. They're the healthiest chickens in the world. But you have to really take care of them. The manual tells how to take care of them. This one's being shipped out Thursday, so we have to get another chicken.

This is incredible.

Oh, yeah.

In fact, the chicken is triggering a computer?

Oh, yeah, but he goes first. We have three signs: "Bird Wins," "Time's Up"—because you only have so many seconds to make your move—or "It's a Tie." It never says "You Win," because you can't win.

You're a peculiar kind of American genius.

Yes, yes . . . oh yes.

14

ROLLING THE DICE

"Maybe One Day You Might Strike It"

For many years "tax reform" has been a political issue in Washington. Liberal politicians, and in recent years Jimmy Carter, have argued that the tax code should be revised, eliminating tax loopholes and special provisions that really benefit only the wealthy, so that ordinary people carry less of the tax burden. Year after year tax reform proposals are offered in Congress, and year after year they are defeated, usually by large majorities.

Theoretically, taxing a few rich people at higher rates in order to help tens of millions of ordinary citizens ought to appeal to sensible politicians, but it doesn't. Partly this is a function of the clever lobbying that rich people finance in Washington, but lobbying is a minor factor. The real reason Congress votes against tax reform is that Americans aren't really interested in punishing rich people. Americans are interested in *becoming* rich people. And who knows? Maybe next week "My train will come in," or "Things will go my way," or "I'll get lucky." And if that happens, any sensible citizen would want to know that those tax loopholes will be there for him to exploit.

Lady Luck is an All-American girl. The American language is full of special phrases to describe past or anticipated encounters with fate. We are constantly "taking a plunge," or talking about one; "shooting the moon," or regretting having tried; or simply "taking our chances." Americans both get rich quick and go bankrupt in staggering numbers, no doubt a reflection of the national willingness to go for broke.

At the most obvious level, Americans love to gamble. According to a national gambling commission that reported to the government in 1976, about two-thirds of the adult population wagers money on some sporting event or game of chance each year. The amount of money involved is not known, since so much of it is gambled illegally, but just legal games and racetracks take in nearly $20 billion a year.

Making a killing at the track, the big win at the crap table—these are great American dreams too. Some pursue the big win as a contest with the gods; others calculate that they can outsmart fate or outsmart the system.

A Man Who Beat the System. Briefly.

Mark Estes is twenty-nine but looks nineteen. He is thin, blond, smooth-cheeked, friendly and open—a nice American kid. He is also a hard worker, who masters whatever subject he takes on. He mastered mechanical engineering at Case Western Reserve University in Cleveland. Then he mastered blackjack, and won tens of thousands of dollars.

More than that, actually. There was a time, as you will soon see, when Estes and a friend were $180,000 ahead of the Las Vegas casinos, flying high. At that level Estes became one of those rare people whose daydreams actually happen.

But that moment didn't last. The system fought back, and before long Estes found himself getting beaten up by security guards in a back room of a big Las Vegas casino (or so he says.) An American Melodrama that actually happened:

My father was senior vice president and general counsel of the General Electric Company. He's retired now. I grew up in a real middle class—upper middle class—type of environment. We moved around a lot. I was born in Syracuse, New York, and moved to Owensboro, Kentucky, then Hinsdale, Illinois, which is just outside of Chicago, then Louisville, Kentucky, then Rye, New York, and I went to school in Cleveland, Ohio, for six years.

I started—let's see how I can tell this best—I started playing blackjack about four years ago. My fiancée and I drove out to Las Vegas, and I had just read a couple of articles on blackjack, and it totally absorbed me. We stayed about a week. I went back home and got all the information I could and started practicing. And I would practice blackjack, probably on the average for the next two years, about three hours a day. I played four different blackjack systems.* I really never thought that I would do it for a living until my fiancée left me.

I lived with my fiancée for four and a half years. She decided that she didn't want, you know, that she didn't want me to live with her any more. So I had to get away from there, and Las Vegas was really the only place that I considered ever going, because, well, I was really fascinated by card games, and I got fascinated when I realized it was possible to beat blackjack. Casinos were just totally fascinating, totally absorbing. You know, I was totally absorbed in it, that I could beat a game that was taking hundreds of millions of dollars from the American public, from the normal people. That really fascinated me—that they offered a game where that was possible to do, given enough skill. So I moved out to Las Vegas. It was interesting, because the first twenty-one days—I've got records of every day I've ever played blackjack—the first twenty-one days I made over four thousand dollars playing blackjack.

I decided that I wasn't playing big enough money. I figured, Well, if I could make four thousand dollars playing with five-dollar chips in twenty-one days, then if I play with twenty-five-dollar chips then I can make twenty thousand dollars in the same period of time. So I started playing with twenty-five dollar chips, and in four days I lost three thousand dollars. And it turned out that in the first ninety days that I was losing an average of twenty-five dollars a day. In other words, with all the time and energy that I put into playing blackjack, I had lost a pretty significant amount of money—about two thousand dollars. I was pretty discouraged at that point.

I would be in casinos, running around town, about ten hours a day. Actual playing, maybe only six hours. It was amazing, you know, I never lost my interest, excitement for playing blackjack. And I moved in with a friend when I first came to Las Vegas, and his family. He kind of had the same drives that I had, but his drives were to become the richest man in the world. At the time he had a wife, three kids and about five thousand dollars to his name. And I had seven thousand dollars. But my interest was just in supporting myself. I wasn't interested in becoming the richest man in the world. The first three months that I lived here, we were trying to formulate a game plan for how we were going to make

* Estes' blackjack systems are all based on remembering the cards that are played as a game progresses. Different systems attach different values to various cards, and the player keeps a running count of those values in his head as he plays. When the remaining deck or decks in the dealer's hand contain a disproportionate number of face cards and other high-value cards, the odds become much more favorable to the player. A "counter," as a blackjack player who uses these systems is called, will bet much more money when the dealer's deck is "rich."

money in Las Vegas. And starting in January of 1976 we put our game plan into action. And in the first five months of 1976, between us we won $180,000 playing blackjack.

Our game plan was to check into a hotel for a weekend—we'd go to different hotels—and play blackjack just for those four days. We ended up playing for twenty-one weekends together. We had an arrangement worked out where we split up our money. The amazing part of it was, as I look back on it now, is that in the twenty-one weekends that we played, we only lost twice. We had one weekend where we lost like three thousand dollars and we had another weekend where we lost a thousand dollars. [The rest of the time they won.] Which is— You know, the chances of that happening are phenomenally against winning that much, even with the system.

As a team it worked out great for the first six months that my friend and I played blackjack. I had enough money at that point— I mean I was happy. And I didn't have the overwhelming desire to play blackjack any more. But the more money that my friend made, the more he wanted to play. And I wanted to go out and play golf and play tennis and do things like that. And so it came to the point where we just couldn't work it out any more, so we decided that we'd split up the arrangement. And it did turn out that he made a lot more money—you know, he contributed a lot more than I did to the winnings. Because he had the ability to win a tremendous amount of money. I mean he could go into a casino— Well, he won fifty thousand dollars in one twenty-hour period at Caesar's Palace. I just couldn't do that.

Did he have a better memory than you?

No, in fact his system stunk. He's a very poor player as far as counting cards or something. His system isn't very good and he doesn't like to study it, he doesn't like to practice, and he doesn't know that much about blackjack theory.

Nevertheless, he won, usually more than Estes. Did that mean there was such a thing as luck? Estes would not admit it, nor would he deny that his partner had a special quality that enabled him to blend into a casino crowd, look like every average Joe in the place, but leave with a lot of money.

Estes always liked games, he said. He played basketball in high school and college, and for two years he toured the country as a professional bowler. Since he became a blackjack addict he has also taken up bridge, and begun to study its laws of averages.

The collapse of his successful blackjack partnership did not end his career in "21," however. He went from his lucky friend to a team of professional card counters organized by Ken Huston, an MIT mathematician whose blackjack exploits have put him on the cover of *The New York Times Magazine:*

That was fascinating to me, you know, to meet Ken Huston and a team of expert blackjack players. Actually it was probably mainly because of social thing. I had a couple of friends, but this was like a whole group of people that were expert blackjack players.

The first thing we did was go to the Bahamas and play blackjack at the El Casino. We played for two weeks and ended up losing $150. Then we came back to Las Vegas and I became a big player.

The way the team concept works is that you take four or five people into a casino, and they sit down at different tables and count the shoe, the four-deck shoe [a box containing four decks of cards from which the dealer deals]. When the shoe gets rich—which means when it's favorable for the player—then they give a signal and the big player comes in and bets amounts ranging from a hundred dollars to a thousand dollars.* That was the level that I was betting at.

The counters sit at the table and they're betting the table minimum, and whenever their decks get hot they have a signal to call the player— it's the placement of the hand on the face. Then they give two more signals. One of 'em is to tell the big player what the count is, and one of 'em is to tell him how many aces are left in the deck. And these signals are really blatantly obvious. I can't understand how the team concept worked for so long. The picture is, you know, a casino, and five people playing at blackjack tables, and one player just jumping around from table to table with piles of hundred-dollar chips, and then after the shoe is over picking up his chips, going over to another table, and then somebody at that table will give those signals—sounds amazing.

But we had, you know, the swings. The swings that blackjack players have are just totally incredible. In playing that concept, I lost $9900 one time at the Desert Inn, and won over ten thousand dollars a couple of times at Caesar's Palace. But the interesting thing about counters is

---

* In other words, the counters who sit down at the blackjack table first keep track of the cards in their own minds as they are dealt. If a disproportionate number of low cards appear in the first part of the game, then the deck will be "rich" toward the end. When this situation arose, a counter would signal the big player to sit down and begin betting.

that they have to have a tremendous amount of money to make any money. Something that nobody really knows is that a blackjack player's maximum edge is about half a percent. At least this has been Ken Huston's team's winning percentage—one half of one percent of the money they put into action. In other words, for every hundred dollars that they bet they win less than fifty cents. So an hourly win for a blackjack player whose average bet (per hand) is three hundred dollars will be $150.

We're not using the team concept any more, because the casinos have finally caught on to that.

For Estes this was a simple matter of fact; the casinos had caught on, so the team system could no longer be used.

This was not his first encounter with the power of casino managements in Nevada. Not long after his arrival in Las Vegas he discovered that card counters like himself—blackjack players who apparently cannot disguise the concentration and deliberateness with which they play from well-trained casino employees—are not welcome in the casinos. This was the story:

Very early when I started playing I was playing at this casino, and I was playing really small stakes, and I'd just been playing for a very short period of time, about twenty minutes. I made a ten-dollar bet on one hand, then I made a fifty-dollar bet on the next hand, and after I did that I looked up and there was a casino man to my right and a floor man to my left and a floor man behind me and a security guard behind me. This was the Riviera Hotel, which has a tremendous amount of money played on it. There were people at my table playing a lot more money than I was, and it was very crowded. I was really surprised when it happened.

The security guard tapped me on the shoulder and said, "Come with me." So he took me over to the security guard's stand and he asked for my ID and he wanted to know where I was staying and why I was in Las Vegas. So I told him all that. Then a floor man came over and read me the trespassing act, which says if you're ever seen in these premises again you can be thrown in jail. Which I thought was kind of harsh treatment. I ended up winning forty dollars, totally, for that session.

I came back in the [Riviera] hotel about six weeks later, and I actually only came to the coffee shop to eat breakfast. But after I ate I decided that, well, I'll go play a couple of hands. And the reason I thought I could do it was because it was on a totally different shift. It was five

o'clock in the afternoon when I got asked to leave, and this was five
o'clock in the morning. And I played for about fifteen minutes, I lost
$220, and I started walking out the door. The security man stopped me
and said, "Could I see your ID please?" I said, "Sure, here's my ID,"
and he said, "O.K., come with me."

He took me into the back room and asked me a whole lot of questions.
And he had me sit and wait. We waited for about forty-five minutes,
and then two men from SWAT came. They had a badge that said
S-W-A-T.* And they put handcuffs on me and put me against the back
wall and frisked me down and took me to the police station, and took
all my clothes off, put on a prison uniform, and took my picture, and
fingerprinted me. And then they let me go. I was arrested for trespassing.
In six months that was the only casino I had been barred from or had
any problems with.

On one other occasion Estes had been spotted as a counter and
asked not to play blackjack any more. That happened at the Las
Vegas Hilton, a 2000-room hotel with a huge casino that generates
more than a third the profits of the entire worldwide chain of Hilton
Hotels:

I was playing for about three hours, and I ended up losing a little
bit of money. And there was one floor man that was particularly interested
in my game. So I went over and asked him if he could buy me dinner,
which is common for a person that's playing a lot of money, to ask the
casino to do things for 'em. I just wanted to have dinner in the coffee
shop. And he said sure, O.K., and he went and got a slip of paper and
gave it to me. And then he said, "And when you come back, you can
play any other games, but we'd rather not have you play Twenty-one."
And I said, well, you know, "Why?" And he said, well, "I think you know
why." He said, "I don't blame you, cause I'm a counter too. But we've
watched you play, and you're just too good. So we don't want you to
play." So that was really nice.

That happened in February. In November Estes went back to the
Hilton with a friend of his whom he backed to play blackjack. The
friend was playing, Estes was watching.

* Special Weapons and Tactics, an acronym made notorious by a television series called
S.W.A.T.

I watched him play for about fifteen minutes, and then he left. We were about to leave the hotel, and three plainclothes security guards came over, and one of them asked for our ID's, and we showed him our ID's. The security guard told my friend to cash his chips and leave the hotel, and that if he ever came back he'd be thrown in jail. He had won a couple of hundred dollars. Very rare for him to do!

And they told me that if I ever came back in the hotel, I'd be thrown in jail. And I said, "Why? I don't understand. All I was doing was watching my friend play blackjack."

And they said, "If you don't leave this hotel immediately, we are going to arrest you and take you to jail." And I said, "Do you have the authority to do that?" And one of the guards, his face got very red, he got into a rage, picked me up, threw me against a row of phone booths, and told the other two security guards to take me into the security room.* And he told somebody else to call the police and have me taken to jail.

So the two security guards lifted me up so that my feet were just, you know, dangling, and not quite touching the ground, and they carried me into the security room. Now one of these guys was six-four and 230, and the other guy was really solid; they were both really gorillas. And that is the total thing that I said. I didn't want to get these guys aggravated.

But I liked going into the Hilton. The shows are good there, and they've got a discotheque there. I wanted to know what I had done to get the treatment.

One of them said, "Would you take your ID out so it will be ready when the police come?" And I said, well, I'd rather wait for the police. Because I wasn't really happy with the way I'd been handled so far. And I knew you are not required to hand over your ID to security guards.

When I said that, the same guy got—the same thing happened to him. He got really upset, picked me up, threw me on the ground, held me by the head and pounded my head into the ground. And this six-foot-four, two-hundred-and-whatever-pound security guard started kicking me in the ribs. The guy slid me across the floor, and all the time he was sliding me he was beating, pounding my head, the other guy was kicking me, he yanked me up, threw me up against the back wall, then they jarred my hands up behind my back, then they forced handcuffs on me so that I had really deep bruises on my hands, then they threw

---

* This accusation and the rest of Estes's story here are, of course, his side of a disputed incident that has ended up in court. Hilton denies the accuracy of Estes's account.

me back down on the chair. And at different times, each of them said that if we ever see you again we're going to take you out in the desert, shoot you.

Then the police came. I said, well, "Finally the police are coming, so I'm going to be able to get out." You know, there's going to be some justice finally. But it seemed like the police and these security guards were really good friends.

Then they took me down to put me in jail, and they took all my clothes off, then they sprayed me, they have some kind of bug spray that they spray you with [a little laugh], then they put me into a cell. I was in a cell with about thirteen other people, fourteen other people, a really small cell, with cigarette butts that were all over the floor, and it stank of urine, and it was really not a real comfortable place to be. Finally they called me, and my friend had come with bail, so I left.

I went to the hospital to have my bruises diagnosed, you know, so that I would have a hospital record, and then I went to a professional photographer and had pictures taken of the bruises.

That incident has led to two lawsuits, one in which the American Civil Liberties Union is helping Estes challenge the constitutionality of the Nevada trespass law, another in which his father is helping him sue the Hilton Corporation for damages.

It also helped persuade Estes to try to give up blackjack. When we talked, he was living on the proceeds of his earlier wins, then much depleted.

I really didn't come to Las Vegas to make a lot of money. Actually, I came— I also am going to school now. I'm getting a master's in business administration, did I mention that? That's just what I told my parents my original—my reason for coming out here was. I guess I told myself that was my reason for coming out here too.

In his heart, though, Estes knew better. He went to Las Vegas out of a compulsion to play blackjack.

It seemed logical that Estes should have been bitter about his blackjack career, particularly about the way it was ended. Did he feel cheated?

Oh, no, not all all. I really don't think I do. I feel like it was, you know, a bonus to have that opportunity to make money. They're not obligated to let you beat 'em, you know? It's their game, and they should be able to offer the type of game they want to offer. I don't feel like I was cheated at all. A lot of blackjack players do, a lot of players feel like the casinos owed them a living. These are the people that get into playing with the dealers, and the other methods of illegally playing blackjack.

What are the other methods?

[A heavy sigh.] Marking cards. Putting waves in cards. Having— Well, there are several ways of doing it with dealers. There's methods of standing behind the dealers, and when they look at the hole card [the card they put face up on the bottom of the deck], have the hole card signaled to one of your friends, who signals it to you. If you're looking directly at the person who's looking at the hole card, then the casino can catch on to that, but not if you're looking at someone else.

Cheating upsets Estes. "I think a lot of money that the casinos think is taken out by [blackjack] counters is really taken out by people who are cheating." At first he didn't believe cheating was widespread, but he became convinced. He described one cheater he knew:

He's been working with dealers for about three months now, and he's got about thirty dealers in Las Vegas who will play with him. And he's got about five or six floor men that will also play with him. And he knows several dealers who are good enough dealing cards that they can peek and deal seconds; and they can tell you they're peeking and dealing seconds, and you can't see it. Which is really scary.* What they do to make up for the money that they pass off is, they take it from people who are playing on the square, to balance the table out.

For the first year that I lived in Las Vegas I didn't think that that happened. I mean I really didn't think that dealers would do that. I thought they'd lose their jobs if they were caught doing that. But they're good enough that they don't get caught at all. And if they lose their job they'll just get another one. It's amazing. Amazing. But they do it.

It was clear from Estes's conversation that he was totally absorbed by cards, mathematical probabilities, gambling stories and the like.

---

* As he said this, Estes demonstrated how a dealer can sneak a peek at the top card in the deck in his hand, then deal out the card underneath it if he wants to, doing both so quickly that an unwitting observer notices nothing unusual.

The coffee table in his bland, undecorated one-bedroom apartment was covered with books about cards. On a card table nearby was a calculator and a pad of paper with figures written on the top sheet. There was no hint either in his manner or in his surroundings that he had any other interests in the world.

So Kaiser tried to ask Estes some philosophical questions, questions that ought to make him at least reflect a little on his place in the world. But Estes couldn't cope with such questions.

Have you reached any private philosophical conclusions from all this? What have you learned about the world and your place in it?

[A pause.] Hmm. [Another pause.] Gosh. [Another pause, and a small laugh.] That's funny. I imagine I should have some—should have reached some conclusions. Uh, I know that I will always be happy doing whatever I'm doing. I also know that I— Like for the last ten years, I've always really been worried about what I'm going to be doing next year, and what the future's going to hold. And it doesn't bother me any more. Like, uh, I don't have the slightest idea what I'm going to be doing a year from now. There's some possibilities. One of them is I may start going around the country playing bridge. Or I may get a straight job as a mechanical engineer. I really enjoy working on computers. I may, independently, with some of my friends, buy some computers and do consulting work.

On cards?

Ah, yeah. Maybe. Card games. I've got a good friend that— We're thinking about making strategy for Pan, which is another game, Pangini, that's played in Las Vegas, where no theoretical work has been done at all. I may write papers on the technical aspects of playing blackjack.

Has your attitude about how the system works in America changed from all this?

Yeah. [Pause.] I haven't really formulated it all out, but, um, [pause]— I don't think people are honest anymore. I don't. I think everybody just tries to get what they can get.

Why do you say that?

[Long pause.] Because, uh, well, you know. The strongest thing is the dishonesty of the dealers and the number of cheating players there are. Another thing is the different attitudes that floor men'll have toward a person who's a good player and a person who's a bad player. I mean, if they see the potential of a person losing a lot of money, then they'll be real friendly. But if they see that a person may be a threat, then the same floor man'll just be completely different to him. I mean, like his personality doesn't matter. It's how much money you can get out.

Is that really a surprise, though, given that this is a gambling industry we're talking about?

No, I guess it's totally consistent. But, you know, that was something I really hadn't realized before. You know, I think I was just naïve when I came out. You know, I thought, I really thought that a person who has any dishonesty in him is an exception, you know, was a real exception.

And now you'd say what?

Um, I—I—I wouldn't be surprised if anybody that I did business with tried to cheat me. I guess that means I don't trust anybody. I couldn't totally trust anybody. But I—I guess I don't think that. Well, I don't know, you know. I knew that there are some people that I could trust before. And I'm not really sure now. I'm not really sure now. [Pause. Sigh.]

Estes was having a genuinely hard time answering these questions. He was struggling to find the right words. He wanted to find the right words.

After this experience do you have a more cynical or a more hopeful view of the country and its prospects?

Hm. I don't know. I guess all I can say about that question is, I'm confused, you know. Well, actually, to tell you the truth, maybe that's something that I block out. That's not something I think about. I—like really, my whole life is involved. I guess I live kind of, uh [pause], unaware-of-what's-going-on-around-me type of existence.

This whole line of questioning was bothering Estes. Finally Kaiser gave it up and asked one he liked:

What are the things that you do think about now?

O.K., good. That's good. I think about what the probability is of getting what your expected value is in certain blackjack situations and bridge situations. My cards right now occupy my life. And I guess I kind of block out— I surround myself with people who do the same type of thing. I guess I kind of live isolated from the things that concern most of the people in the country, you know?

Do you get worried—having learned that this first obsession of playing blackjack wasn't a permanent one—do you ever worry that you're going to wake up at age forty-five and say, "Holy shit, I've wasted half my life on these silly cards?"

I used to worry about that, but it doesn't bother me anymore. Because I've found out that it's very satisfying to me to work with cards and to work with figures. My fascination has not gotten less. In fact, I've gotten more fascinated. And I've thought to myself at various times, Well, this is stupid, this is ridiculous, nobody does this. People— You're not supposed to be fascinated with cards; you're supposed to find something so that you can contribute to society, and you're supposed to find a job that you can be happy with, that you can make money with. But I'm just more— You know, it's more fulfilling to me to—play.

Do you still miss that fiancée?

Uh, yeah. Yeah I do. I do.

Later Kaiser talked to Estes about the appeal of gambling. The national gambling commission sponsored an elaborate public opinion survey which concluded that people liked to gamble because they found it exciting and challenging. About half the gamblers surveyed regarded gambling as a good way to "make money." Was it as simple as that?

Yeah, I think people do have fun gambling. I know that while people are doing it— I guess it's kind of like getting drunk; you have a lot of fun while you're doing it because you're kind of losing yourself in something, but then after it's over, especially if you lose as much as you're supposed to lose [by the law of averages], you feel kind of bad about it, like you do when you have a hangover. Gamblers definitely lose the other problems that they have while they're gambling. It's a great release.

Estes was struck by the illogic of most gamblers' play:

People don't seem to want to apply the logic they use in their normal activities when they come to a gaming table. It's incredible. In a game of chance, people feel like the fact that they won the last few bets has something to do with them winning the next bets. There's no reason at all that they should feel that way.

Which is just another way of saying that Estes refuses to believe in magic, a refusal that probably sets him apart from most Americans, particularly the gamblers.

But if Estes can't share the illogic of the average deep plunger, he certainly does know about the sensations that come with the big win.

I saw somebody last night at the Dunes [casino] who was playing roulette and he cashed out for $44,000. It was incredible. And he looked like—the look in his eye was just not to be believed; he just looked so powerful. I guess it's true—if you do win, it just gives you a great sense of power.

Some months later Estes said he was getting out of Las Vegas. He planned to begin a new career on the floor of the Pacific Stock Exchange in San Francisco, where his original blackjack partner had discovered that he could earn a six-figure income by using the mathematical skills they developed for cards. Estes said he would be a "market maker," the person who decides what price stocks should open at each day, and by how much they should be allowed to move up or down.

Mark Estes broke through the romantic illusions that surround casino gambling—illusions that suggest big winners aren't really so rare, or that casino managements encourage big winners as good for business, or that the whole thing is run in a spirit of sportsmanship and good fun. Most American gamblers seem to like those illusions. They are comforting.

But they are illusions. The truth erupted one night from a senior executive of one of Las Vegas's biggest hotels, a man who seemed to surprise even himself when these words came out of his mouth:

This town was invented by people who knew how to exploit the frailties of their fellow citizens. I don't like it. I'm here because I can do extremely well here. And I guess—at my age—I don't think I could do as well if I tried anything else.

The surveys we take now, the polls of tourists, they all come back saying that now the biggest attraction in Las Vegas is the entertainment. That's crap. The attraction is the gambling, period. You can get entertainment in a lot of other places. Why, Sinatra is playing cities now that he never even heard of. They open a new theater, and Sinatra plays it. You can get better horseback riding in Utah, better golf anyplace, better tennis a lot of places, better water skiing in Hawaii. No, the reason they come here is to gamble.

And we love it. If we had our way, we wouldn't let anybody get out of town with *carfare*. You'll hear people say that there's no better advertisement for a casino than a big winner every once in a while. Crap. We *hate* winners. Of course there are very few winners.

The River of Gold

Mark Estes had the brains, self-confidence and opportunity to take a plunge as a big-time gambler. Few Middle Americans could do the same, but many share the same urge—for example, Mr. and Mrs. Ray Lee and Mr. and Mrs. Jim Kendrick.

"You don't care if we curse?" Jim Kendrick asked as the tape recorder was turned on. "We're bad talkers once in a while."

It had taken some time to find Kendrick's house trailer on the outskirts of town, and finding it was not enough. Like most of the trailers in the neighborhood, Kendrick's was surrounded by a fence and patrolled by a ferocious-looking dog. Everyone was inside the air-conditioned trailer when Kaiser arrived, and there seemed no way to get their attention, except by challenging the dog. Finally he went to the next-door trailer and called them up on the telephone.

Kendrick is a fireman. His good friend Ray Lee used to be a fireman. They both have the same hobby. They are investing their spare time and some of their spare money out in the mountains west of town looking for the River of Gold.

This all started on the CB radio. A few years ago, when CB was more popular than it has become, Kendrick used to spend a lot of time talking to truckers and other people on the CB. One day he met a man on the radio who was involved in the search for the River of Gold. They all went up and took a look, and that hooked them. Since then they've been introduced to a whole new world.

Kendrick: The cave people, if you talk to 'em, why they know they're a little different breed. They go into caves head first. *Head first.* Just start crawlin' down between cracks of rocks and stuff. I like to have a place where I can back out and turn around, but it don't make no difference to them. Now we went down in this one day—what, about fifteen hundred feet or so—and we got down there and the lights went out. Generator went out. And I'm talkin' about a hole that's just big enough that you can just crawl through and you're fifteen hundred feet down there. But like they say, if you're tired, just lay down and go to sleep. Nothin' will bother you down there. There's no bugs, no snakes, won't nothin' bother you.

Mrs. Lee: Old bones.

Kendrick: Old bones—the place is full of old bones.

Lee: But it's supposed to be enough there where, if they strike it, it's supposed to be enough to flood the market for gold. They call it the "River of Gold."

Kendrick: And it's in black sand. It's just a matter of pumping it up. There's no work to it. That's what makes it so valuable. And if we don't strike the River of Gold, we're supposed to be able to turn this over and—there are huge caverns down there, you can't image how big they are—they're gonna put restaurants, barrooms, dance halls and make a tourist stop, and take you on a train through the whole mountain. So how can you go wrong?

I usually get a report every couple of months on the progress. They called us one night here at eleven, told us they've made it—"We're in." And we went over there. They broke into a cavern. It was—what, about a half mile underground. Nobody's ever been there before. A big cavern, sealed cavern. I guess it's eight hundred feet to the top of it. We went over there at night, the air is forty-two degrees, and everything in there is wet and slimy. And they're still getting forty-two degree air out of it. Well where is it coming from? It ain't comin' from this desert out there, I'll tell you that.

Have they been in there now?

Kendrick: Oh, they went. They dead-ended everywhere, that's all. That's what's happening. They cut through the mountain and open up these caverns. They go in, they climb up, they climb down and they just dead-end.

Lee: It's just a void in there.

Kendrick: Void. It's real interesting. That's how we spend a lot of time anyway, crawling across the mountains and into the old caves and stuff. You can go up there right now. You can go to work and they'll log your time. If they ever find the river, then your time is just as good as gold. And that's the way this thing has been done.

How much have you put into this operation?

Kendrick: Oh, I don't know. I think everybody's got a thousand or better in it.

Lee: It's just like a long shot. You bet on somethin'. You just don't worry about it. Once you've put it in, you just kind of write it off. Then, if anything happens, great. If it don't, why you don't worry about it. It's nothin' that you're lookin' for.

What is it about Americans we like to take that kind of plunge?

Kendrick: Get rich quick, I guess. Ain't that the way you feel? You know, you always sat here and said, "What if I'd bought that down there? I had a chance to buy it and I didn't buy it."

Mrs. Lee: We lost all the roughness when we become Americans and had everything so good. This is kinda like going back or somethin'. It's fun, it's real fun. It isn't put a pretty dress on and put your makeup on. It's real fun. Somethin' to talk about, somethin' to relive, and it's just healthy good fun, that's all.

Lee: Well, I think another thing what it is, it's the class you're in. In other words, if you had a million dollars to go hit the stock market up there, you'd probably play that. But if you don't have that kind of money, why this is some type of thing that you can take a long shot on. Maybe one day you might strike it.

Kendrick: We all went into this knowin' there's more money put in a mine than is ever taken out. This is a known fact. This isn't really minin'. This is treasure huntin'.

At that point, everybody in the mobile home laughed out loud.

The Bowling Ball Story

A magazine writer once confronted a Southern stock car driver with the rumor that his racing team made a practice of bending the rules of the sport into a pretzel. "Don't you get caught a lot?" the writer demanded to know.

"Yep," came the deadpan reply, "but we don't get caught a lot, too."

Or, life is just a roll of the dice anyway, isn't it? Lots of Americans think so. Gambling is by no means the only gamble one expects to encounter. On the contrary, the whole experience of living often seems like one gamble right after another.

The thought that life itself is a lottery is—philosophically—a banality, but it has a profound effect on middle class Americans. The potential trauma in the lottery can be captured in a single word: "cancer." This must be a curse fully equal to anything that terrified primitive cultures or feudal man.

Here is a central dilemma of life in Middle America: The miracles of science and technology have eliminated so many of the traditional dangers in human existence that one could easily assume (as people often do until their thirtieth or thirty-fifth birthday) that life is downright *safe*. But the way we have organized human existence in this new epoch has created a full range of new dangers that more than compensates for the removal of the old.

Besides the obvious menaces posed by cancer and interstate highways, we have new social structures that are inherently risky. Americans have willingly cast off most of the traditional sources of stability and predictability in life. We have shrunk and fractionalized the family, abandoned traditional communities and communal behavior, encouraged self-reliance and ambition. And the culture endures a level of violence and mayhem that guarantees unexpected tragedies and disasters.

Nothing affects people more deeply than the unexpected force of fate, perhaps because nothing else so challenges the basic human drive for a sense of security. Security is valued in American culture, but the same culture puts security constantly at risk.

Eddy Elias's story about the bowling ball is a quintessential tale of the power of fate, and it illustrates the point we are trying to make here. Elias is in his mid-thirties now, though he is not yet acknowledging the end of his youth. He is a talkative man of swiftly changing moods, and his life has been rich and complicated—and only occasionally successful. When he told this story he was suffering through a rough patch, selling aluminum siding and hoping something better would come up.

Talk is Elias's most marketable skill. He can exude what amounts to a fog of self-confidence, demonstrating considerable wit and charm in the process. He has a ready explanation for virtually everything that has ever happened to him, except the bowling ball story:

I had a traumatic experience when I was seventeen. Myself and two buddies, we were out—we were not really the hell-raising variety, but we were bored, and I was a big clown; I was always doing things to shock people. So we walked through the bowling alley, and as they were walking ahead of me, as we walked out I picked up a bowling ball off the rack, I just stuck it under my arm. We walked out nonchalantly and as they were getting into the car I said, "Hey, take this, will you?" It was supposed to be a big ha-ha, and we were supposed to take the ball back, but one thing led to another and we decided to find some sport. We went over to my house in West Cleveland. It wasn't late at night or anything. I think it was about nine o'clock. So we stationed one guy at each corner. There were no cars on this one street, and we wanted to see how far the thing would roll, how far we could make it roll. Each guy would take a corner and watch for cars. It wasn't malicious activity. It was theft—we stole a bowling ball. But what started out to be a really fun, ha-ha evening turned into a very traumatic affair.

It rolled under this guy's car. I think it was my roll. I rolled it two and a half blocks, a pretty good roll, and the conversation went back and forth. "Let's just leave it there"—you know—"The game's over. Let's not screw around and get caught with a stolen bowling ball."

We weren't even drinking that night, although most nights there was beer in the car. One kid who was with me was Barry Carter, an all-A student, starting center on the basketball team. The other kid, Jim Farmer, was an Eagle Scout, church choir, all-A student right down the line. The good All-American-kid type.

So Jim went after the ball, and I said, "We'll drive down a block past and we'll meet you down there after you get it." And so we drove down a block. We were just laughing like hell; we thought how funny it would be if this guy came out and how was Jim going to explain a bowling ball under his car? So we were down a block, and the guy *did* come out. We were just hysterical laughing, but then I noticed Jim was backing up funny.

And I remember I said, "I wonder if that guy has a gun or something," because it looked so peculiar. It wasn't just a conversation back and forth between Jim and the guy. So I started the car and went back up the street. He did in fact have a gun.

Now this is on a well-lit residential street; this isn't down in the slums at three A.M. And this wasn't a kid who was obviously rifling the car. The ball was there for the guy to see. Well, so he had Jim up against the house with a gun, a twelve-gauge shotgun.

And we said, "Sir, please don't point the gun." We were talking to him. He said the police were coming. I said great. We were out of the car at that point; we were standing by the car, Barry and I.

Jim was up against the house, and this guy was between us with the gun. The conversation kept running back and forth, and I kept asking, "Please don't point that gun, it really makes me nervous." "We're not armed," I said. "We're not going anywhere; we'll wait for the police to get here." We were trying to explain to the guy what we were doing, and the fact that we weren't doing anything to his car. This went on and on. Nobody got there for the longest time. And I'm not really clear now— I can only recall what I think happened. Of course with this particular thing I had a nightmare every night for three years. So I asked him again about not pointing the gun and he turned the gun over toward us and told us to shut up.

It came out later that he was a drunk, beat his wife, beat his kids, had chased kids down the street with the gun before. Then Jim said something to him and he turned back. It wasn't a fast thing—it wasn't like he turned back and fired—he turned back and put the gun to his shoulder and pulled the trigger.

Of course his claim was that Jim was running toward him, but in fact they took pictures of where Jim fell flat against the house. He hadn't moved.

I was trying to talk to Jim, to see if he was all right, and where he was hit. I could hear him breathing, he was breathing forced and loud, and then we were just hoping. We asked the guy what kind of shell he used. We asked him if we could go to him and help him. He said, "No, don't move. I've got four more in here for you." And he had the gun on us. And we were pleading with him to let us go help Jim and he wouldn't let us.

He didn't say much, he really didn't say much. I said, "Are you sure your wife called the police? Would you please tell her to call the police." It had been twenty or twenty-five minutes, no police. She called again, put in a call for a man shot, and about ten minutes more went by, then police cars came in from all directions.

Of course they came on the scene and they found two kids and a good citizen in a residential area, one kid shot, and they were pretty rough with us—damn rough. I broke away from one cop—he was trying to take me to the car—and I broke away to go to Jim to see if he was all right. Of course he was dead. I saw all the blood and everything. The guy shot him right in the throat. It was at about twelve feet with a buckshot load. It didn't have any chance to dissipate. So it just plowed him right through the chest and throat and killed him.

They charged him with manslaughter. I think his wife had a heart attack and died during the trial. They let him off in three months, let him out of jail. He plea-bargained. Everything we said was corroborated.

The neighbors heard us pleading with the guy, calling him sir. The bowling ball was there. Jim had told him the bowling ball was under the car, we were just retrieving it. Everything was corroborated. This guy just wanted to kill somebody. Really. This guy just wanted to kill somebody.

15

I WANT TO BE SOMEBODY

The Middle America we are dealing with here consists of more than 100 million people. Members of this tribe know that whatever one's comforts or accomplishments, the chances are overwhelming that one is *sharing* them all the time. The Americans who escaped the old cities since the war, beginning new lives in new suburban communities, inevitably found themselves surrounded by people like themselves. An auto worker in Detroit may buy himself a cabin by a lake in northern Michigan, but it will not be a private lake—it will be surrounded with cabins like his. You don't get a quiet table by yourself at McDonald's. Life in this Middle America is crowded.

There is a source of deep frustration here. On one hand, the accomplishment of achieving the comforts and security of the middle class is a basis for great pride. On the other hand, middle class society doesn't seem to recognize the enormousness of this accomplishment. Indeed, it routinely goes unrecognized, except perhaps by one's immediate family. The culmination of a lifetime of hard work can easily be an existence that one has to share with a throng of neighbors. Individual versions of the good life may differ no more than a Malibu differs from a Cougar.

The culture abounds with reminders of our sameness and does little to reinforce old-fashioned American individualism. It is not easy to support a claim to a unique "I." But we found many Americans who were making the effort.

This chapter is devoted to the urge to be somebody. There is no American dream more widely shared than this one.

"Everyone Wants to Be a Star"

Donn Arden gets his name on billboards by inventing spectacular entertainments. He explained what is involved:

I know the audience likes to be entertained and amused in every area. I don't care whether it's jugglers or iron jaw acts or— You know, I believe that every revue has to have *everything;* it has to have good singing, good dancing, good music, beautiful people, talented people. And then, you know, I am noted as the guy who is constantly incorporating disasters. I'm the one who sunk the *Titanic* on stage—and I did it better than it has been done, if I say so myself. I have exploded the *Hindenburg* in the air, men falling on stage aflame. I've done all of this. I've done all the Phantom-of-the-Operas and Notre-Dame catastrophes. It's something that my audiences expect from me. Right now I'm going to do the damnedest San Francisco number—turn of the century—and boy, I'm really going to earthquake that whole theater. It's all Sensaround, that whole stage setting is going to be aflame and collapsing and falling. I really go in for the fire brigades and the screaming people. It's excitement to the audience. It overwhelms them. And we have a first-class challenge, because we have to do these things not like in the movies—you film it and it's in the can. Ours is twice a night and three times on Saturday. We do it live. So we do a hell of a lot of magic, but we do it real.

So who is Donn Arden? A Ziegfeld of our time, but this is not exactly the time of Ziegfeld. The most popular stage show in America is an Arden spectacular; it has never played New York, and it never will. The show is called *Hallelujah Hollywood!* and it cost $3 million to stage. Nearly 4 million people have paid more than $60 million to see *Hallelujah Hollywood!* during a run that began in the spring of 1974. Twice every night, three times on Saturday, 900 people troop into a blue-and-silver show room in Las Vegas to see *Hallelujah Hollywood!* and with rare exceptions they love it.

No wonder. "I guess the idea is to overwhelm them," Arden admitted—"you know, bedazzle 'em, give them too much, so they can't absorb it all in one seating." So *Hallelujah Hollywood!* includes the best magic act ever (two magicians make a live Bengal tiger disappear on stage), the best juggling act ever, the best elephant act ever, the largest number of bare breasts ever, the most expensive and extraordinary feathers and rhinestones and ermine—all run together with style, color, grand old show tunes, endless waves of dancers, pacing and pizazz. For several years there was a virtually nude girl who swam underwater in a huge glass tank with a dolphin, each of them behaving suggestively; but the Society for Prevention of Cruelty to Animals put an end to that. (Now the girl swims alone.) But the life-sized pirate galleon still sinks before your eyes at every performance. It is the Ed Sullivan show gone berserk—not crushed into the little electronic box, but bigger than life, spread across a 150-foot stage, with walkways up in the sky and off to the sides and through the middle of the audience, wraparound music, wraparound feathers, wraparound tits and ass. The great American entertainment. Phew.

Show Business—even the phrase is thoroughly American, more vivid because it is ungrammatical. Popular American culture is built upon fantasy, and show business is the great American fantasy. We talk about every American kid having a chance to grow up to be President, but the fantasy that really engages American parents is a different one: My child could be a *star!* Why not?

Donn Arden had those fantasies himself. As a young dancer in the 1930s he dreamed of becoming the new Fred Astaire. "But now, when I look back at myself, I didn't have an ounce of sex appeal, you know?" Arden gave up dreams of Astaire-dom for a career as a producer. He gave up fantasies for the manufacture of fantasy. "We do a hell of a lot of magic, but we do it real."

Arden's formula is as old as show business: Give 'em the old razzle-dazzle. "I believe everyone likes American shows best," Arden said when we met much later. "I mean, we have more spirit, more speed, more pace, more punch." Razzle-dazzle. And no fear of being old-fashioned: "I love animal acts. If I had the budget, I'd incorporate a dog act into every show I do.

"But, you know, I'm always very aware," Arden said. "If it's soft rock, I try to incorporate it. If it goes to hard rock, I try to incorporate it. I try to be aware of what is current, be it acid rock or country music or what have you. I don't just do nostalgia."

Soft rock, hard rock, acid rock, country music—those are America's inventions. Sure we have the totems of European culture—the orchestras and ballets and museums—but most of that is not for most Americans. What Americans respond to, dream about, rely on, is the popular culture, show business culture. That is where the styles are set, the idols manufactured. In a nation of immigrants, few of them here very long, show business becomes part of the shared tradition—a national adhesive. (Sports have this same quality.)

Donn Arden's secret is the secret of Mom's apple pie—careful preparation and just the right amount of pizazz. So for example: "Any idiot knows the difference between white rabbit and white mink. If you pay for Woolworth's, you get Woolworth's. If you pay for Tiffany, you get Tiffany." In the land of conspicuous consumption, "you spend money to make money." You buy mink.

And you work hard. More revealing than talking to Donn Arden is watching him work—for example, in the show room of the Stardust Hotel, the venue for Arden's other big show in Las Vegas, *The Lido*. From the late 1940s to the '60s, and now again in the '70s, Arden has staged the *Lido* show in Paris. In 1954 he opened a *Lido* show at the Stardust, revamping it every two or three years since. When Kaiser watched him he was holding auditions for a new version of the show.

Arden is in his sixties now, but he is still vigorous, and still handsome in a delicate, rather effeminate way. Gray hair waves back from a pleasant face which can be very expressive. He dresses Hollywood casual: open shirts, white jackets, patent-leather loafers. When he opens his mouth to speak, his tongue often precedes the first noise for a quick lick of the lips. He smokes almost constantly.

An audition to which the public has literally been invited (in newspaper advertisements) to take a stab at show business became a confrontation between dreams and reality. There was a small roundish Italian man who drove a taxi and sang arias; a six-foot woman with large girth and small bust who expected to be selected as a nude showgirl; a tap dancer whom all the kids in school thought was just great. Besides dreamers there were strivers—dancers in an Arden show who wanted to become singers, students of dance or singing who wondered if they were ready for the big time somewhat earlier than they *were* ready.

Arden sat in a booth that at night is the best seat in the house for the show, surrounded by empty tables and a somewhat dilapidated room of red carpet and red velvet that accommodates 1500 people twice every night, thrice on Saturdays.

There were perhaps 200 people around the room, girls and boys in leotards, beautiful women, homely women, men sitting nervously in a corner, men laughing loudly in groups. Some were old hands in the Las Vegas show rooms; some had driven all night from Oklahoma City or Spokane to be there. Arden looked around the banked auditorium at all the people: "This is going to be a long haul," he predicted with a sigh.

The first to audition were boy singers. There were more than two dozen of them. Mr. Arden had an announcement. (He had a microphone tapped into the theater's sound system, so his voice boomed around the room.)

"Boy and girl singers—please. I don't have time for ten-minute auditions. Please give me your best sixteen bars." Then the parade of hopefuls began.

The first impression, once the singing began, was that Arden was a son of a bitch. Mike tried to sing a few bars, and Arden cut him off: "Mike, sorry, you're not the type for this show." Mike had to take that like a man, nod, and put the microphone back on top of its stand in the middle of the empty stage.

A tall, dark and handsome gent who had obviously been through this many times before sang briefly but well. "See me down here," Arden said into the microphone. The singer came down to his booth and Arden asked if he was only looking for "principal work." Yes, that's what the fellow wanted. "For the chorus it will be $450 a week for a six-day week," Arden told him. No, the singer wanted to be a principal. "I just want to know if you're interested. It's a question of job or no job—$450 a week," Arden said. The singer looked about forty-five, and like a man who is constantly looking over a precipice that he'd rather not admit was close by. He never quite rejected the implict offer of a place in the chorus. Arden turned to Kaiser as the singer walked away. "Everyone wants to be a star," he confided.

As the morning progressed, there was a series of brusque public commentaries: "You'd better try for the dancing audition too" (to a dancer who is trying to be a singer). "Thank you, Janice. I'm sorry you're too short." "Sorry, not right for this show."

But eventually it became clear that Arden was only cruel to those who he felt had no business being there. When he saw someone with talent, he tried to be encouraging, not always successfully. A girl named Micheline sang with a warbly but strong and appealing voice, and Arden called her down for a private chat. "Can you get rid of the vibrato? I hate vibrato. Let me see you. Pull your hair back. What shows have you done? Can I see your teeth?"

And when he really liked someone he would put himself out. One boyish blond with a fine singing voice could not return at the appointed hour for a second audition, so Arden arranged a special time and came in early the next morning just to hear him.

At the end of one day's auditions the stage was cleared for a couple who tap-danced together. They were both small and danced with ferocious energy and good coordination, but it all looked like hard work, not dance. "Look at it," Arden said, exasperated. "These people called me from Vancouver to come down for an audition. Look at the money they spent. And there's no chance that they could play anywhere in this town—not in a toilet!"

Arden is preoccupied with the size and attractiveness of bodies. His advertisement said any male in the show would have to be at least five feet ten and any female at least five eight. Many who showed up hoped he didn't really *mean* that, but he did.

"You might as well have a good-looking cast. If I can get the best-looking eighteen boys that ever appeared on a stage, why shouldn't I?" But he quickly added that auditions like these don't usually turn up such talent. "It's all right to do this if you find a Nureyev—but only if you find a Nureyev.

"It comes down to face, teeth—and I undress them too, in these days of, of, of—pornography." He demonstrated that a short time later, after the girls auditioning as "dancing nudes" had pranced around the stage for a bit. "Tops off, please," came the command, and all of them quickly complied. About half of the dozen girls on stage did not measure up to Arden's expectations. The rest, Arden said, would have to be studied carefully: "The appendix scars, the silicone, the stretch marks—a lot can go wrong with a girl."

Donn Arden started out in show business in the 1920s, which meant vaudeville. Sophie Tucker picked him up as a boy dancer and wrote him into her act with Ted Shapiro. "They carried me around with them, in the days when Sophie was the big red hot mamma with the chiffon kerchief, and the big orchid display, naturally." They played "the better places."

From his earliest days Arden was drawn to dancing girls. He said he had his "first line of dancing girls" at sixteen, and soon theater managements all over the country were seeking him out. "Oh, I'm telling you, if I could write my memoirs. I don't care if it's Peoria or Paducah, Kentucky, or Sioux City, Ioway, I have played them all!"

Vaudeville died, and Arden's specialty became shows for supper clubs, big nightclubs and gambling casinos, always built around dancing girls:

I've never approved of too much energy from girls. I've rather almost preferred for my girls to look beautiful—not sweat, not huff and puff. I would generally accept an assignment for less money if I knew that my budget was big enough to make my girls truly look beautiful. So I sort of got to be known for having my fingertips on the prettiest girls in the country, and also the girls that were the best dressed, and the most glamorous come-ons, which is what girls are. My shows had a richness about them, and they still do today.

In the 1940s Arden did shows for Lou Walters—Barbara's father—at the old Latin Quarter in Boston, and for the Riviera, a casino and club in Union City, New Jersey. In 1948 he did his first *Lido* show, and in 1950 his first Las Vegas extravaganza, *American Pizazz*, at the old Desert Inn.

So Arden went from being a dreamer to being an arbiter of dreams. He stopped wondering if he would make the show and began deciding who would. Which doesn't immunize Arden from the classical show business anxieties, as he revealed one night at dinner at one of Las Vegas's *luxe* Italian restaurants. The dinner had been arranged as the venue of a formal recorded interview, but one of Arden's colleagues took Kaiser aside as soon as he arrived to announce that this would have to be "a social evening," because "Donn is absolutely exhausted." That was a euphemism.

In fact Arden was angry, frustrated and a little scared, and he was drinking too much. He never quite explained the problem, but after two hours of talk it became quite clear. He was caught in a nasty argument involving the managements of the Stardust Hotel and the MGM Grand Hotel, both of whom used Arden to do their shows. The Stardust is owned, at least nominally, by Alan Glick, whose name keeps appearing in the newspapers in connection with the Teamsters Union, the Chicago mob and the like. Glick apparently felt his contract with Arden took precedence over MGM's. Arden did not like being in this fight. "I've spent thirty years in Vegas," he said, "and I've never had such an awful time as the last three days."

He was due at the MGM at nine-thirty for a conference with the management there, but he didn't leave the restaurant until ten. The conversation was tense and fast. At one point Arden flew into a tantrum at his colleague Madam Blue Bell, who handles his chorus lines in the *Lido* shows. He ranted at her and she smiled, as though she had been there before. The point at issue was whether or not it was time to go to their meeting. "It's not the alcohol," Arden said after he had calmed down. "The alcohol helps, but—" Emotion, he explained, that's what it was.

A month later, sitting in his office at the MGM studios in Los Angeles, Arden was again fully in control. This was the formal interview, and Arden was ready for it. "Can I tell you, I have loved every moment I have been in this business." And so forth. Only after hours of conversation did he get beyond stock commentary. It turns out that impresarios have dreams, too.

I should have worked for Ziegfeld. It's like when I was ready for it, my type of show had gone out of New York. There were no more *Girl Crazies* and *Panama Hatties* and that sort of thing, you know? I missed that era.

Wait a minute. Does this sound unhappy? Does Arden think he was born at the wrong time? "No, I happen to feel that I was born at the right time—for me. I'm ready to retire at any time I want to now, and I figure— I did think when I first started, Oh, why wasn't I doing this in the early 'thirties, on the Ziegfeld scale? No, I feel now that I was born at the right time."

But wasn't he just a little gypped, in that he never did big Broadway shows or movies, never got the reputation of a Ziegfeld or even a Gower Champion? Didn't he deserve to be better known?

Well, you know, I've had people discuss me quite often. They've said, "Donn, you are a definite something." They've said, "You're a phenomenon of this era." I'm talking about good people who've told me this, producers or directors or money people or people that I have respect for.

Do you want to know something? I am one guy—now this is amazing—I have never spent a dollar on publicity. Whatever I have received has been given to me. I have sent a few gifts—you know, be it flowers or bottles of champagne or thank-you things like that, but I have not been a guy with do-re-mi. I don't have a press agent. I don't feel I need it. Frankly, I don't want to— I love to be able to go into a restaurant or someplace and be unknown. I wouldn't want to be like—oh, Barbra Streisand or Steve McQueen. Where everybody knows you, you lose your private life. A lot of people do know me, you know, uh, they'll come to me and say, "Are you *the* Donn Arden?" And, you know, what do you answer to that? [A small laugh.] It's when you bring out your credit cards or something, you know. Generally, I like reservations to be put under somebody else's name, even if I'm picking up the check.

Donn Arden likes to act like a star too.

"Everything I'd Ever Hoped"

Diane Bessee is six feet one, blond, a gymnast, and at twenty-one a would-be showgirl. She would love to be in *Hallelujah Hollywood!* She tried out at that audition that Donn Arden held.

I was born in San Francisco. I currently live in L.A. I was a dance major at San Diego State, but I've changed to languages [after transferring to UCLA]. I'm an athlete. I'm on UCLA's women's crew team. I've wanted to come to Las Vegas since I was a little girl. Why? To dance, because I'm very tall, and you can't get into chorus lines in Hollywood-type productions when you're over five seven. I always wanted to be an entertainer. I don't know how to sing, my voice isn't trained, and I've always wanted to dance. I was a gymnast for years and years and years, and a song leader, and I've always wanted to be right up there. I just shine in front of people, that's my favorite spot. I like the physical output as well as the feedback you get when you're performing—the lights, the applause. I just love it. There's nothing to me like those tense moments before you start to perform, how neat it is once you've started and you just forget you're on a stage, you're just part of a big, huge production. I like being part of a group, like a team sport or a chorus line. I feel real cohesive.

The pretty young woman from the provinces who comes to the glittering lights of Las Vegas to seek her fortune—a classic American dreamer, but not necessarily a romantic figure.

How do you feel about the exploitation of women that seems to be such a large part of the Las Vegas show scene? The exploitation of women as sex object?

I don't understand. What are you talking about specifically?

Just the whole sexy overtone to Las Vegas shows, the nudity and so on. Does that offend you?

No it doesn't. People said to me, "What are you going to do when they tell you to take off your leotard?" And I was just— I was without an answer. First of all I don't think it was anybody's business to ask me that. This has come up a couple of times, and it really amazes me and makes me kind of mad. Well, I said, you know, we'll just cross that bridge when we come to it. But yet these are the same people who go to see the shows and think it's so beautiful. I mean what is wrong with the naked body? And I think that in the show when they're presenting them the way they are, that it all combines to make the theme of the show come through, and I think it's beautiful. I really do.

Now the way they did it yesterday in the audition—they said, "O.K., girls, drop your tops." Drop your tops! Most of the girls had said earlier, "Don't worry, they take you in the back and make you drop your tops in back and everything." They were talking among themselves. It didn't happen. And that for a moment was kind of uncomfortable because you didn't know who was out there in the audience. But then you figure well, Who cares?

Now one girl, I don't know if you noticed, in our line, like threw her head back and left—wouldn't drop her top. When we came backstage someone asked her about it, said "Didn't you want to dance?" She said "No, I was just warming up for the dance auditions" [which came immediately after the nude showgirl auditions]. Whether that was an excuse or not I don't know. But it certainly occurred to me to just turn around and walk off too. It certainly did, for about three seconds. Then, well, big deal.

But in terms of the dignity of women, you don't see this as an affront?
I don't know. How do you feel about it? Do you like the shows?

Diane thought show business as a lot like gymnastics or crew—a competition, something to win.

I don't usually lose very much. I haven't lost too much in my life, as far as running for something, or athletically. I've always been right on top. So I think maybe when I do lose it's even harder for me to take [a laugh], cause I'm used to being a winner. In competition, athletic competition, it's very important for me to win. Maybe that's what compels me so much. Sometimes when I'm running I think, Now, if you just run an extra mile, just think, when you're racing next year it'll just be all that much easier to get that last sprint. So I do think about winning a lot. I want to be a winner.

Have you ever figured out why that is important to you?
Well, I know why it started. When we were young, my brother was the center of our family, because he was male, and my mother was trying to make him more manly because she was afraid that being around the girls all the time that he wasn't going to be— Without a father and such. So he was always very much paid attention to, and I of course was very envious of that. So I wanted to excel in everything to get attention. So of course I started with school. He was sort of a ho-hum C student and I was right up there, but they say girls are always smarter. So I wanted to outbeat him. So I would outrun him and outpush-up him and outpull-up him and everything else, just to get some attention. So I think that started my athletic drive to win. Because everybody does love a winner, don't they? [A laugh.]
We never had any money. I didn't have a father, and I would just like to do some nice things for my family, send the rest of them through school, and get me through school. I know how hard it is without money. And for me, the things that I'm interested in—dancing, or modeling or something like that—is going to make the most amount of money in the shortest time. And I can take that money and say, "Oh, good, I can go to the 1980 Olympics," and not worry about it. Just things like that that I want to do take money.

What happened to your father?

He left my mother. He and my mother were divorced when I was two, or a year and a half. I don't know where he is. Never saw him.

Diane's decision to try out for Arden's new *Lido* show was a lark. It began with her old dream—Diane as showgirl. Her visit to Las Vegas had intensified the dream, especially when she saw *Hallelujah Hollywood!*

My eyes just boggled, because there was so much to see and so much to watch. It was what I wanted to be doing. I don't know what I can say about what I felt. It was just everything I'd ever hoped, all the sparkle and all the glitter. I just loved it.

Diane thought show business was in her blood. "My mother was a cocktail waitress, and when I was young in San Francisco she worked at Sausalito, and we were forever going to live jazz performances." She went often to Lake Tahoe to see Frank Sinatra. "He's just my star of all stars." She decided to come to Las Vegas during a college vacation just to look around, assuming that she would go back to school and get a degree, but looking ahead to the time after graduation when she seriously hoped to get a place in a chorus line. She was staying with an aunt, and saw an ad in the paper for Arden's audition.

I was just kind of a quiet observer at the audition, listening to some of the girls. Some of the girls were crying backstage, and some of 'em were swearing. Some of 'em were saying "I've been five foot ten all my life and I know I'm five ten—and I'm too short?"

So it was really very interesting. All of a sudden, when I was herded into this little group, I knew right away that something was funny. They weren't just picking girls who were five foot eight and giving them a fair shake. They were interested in some look.

We were all standing there warming up. I had thought we were just going to walk for them—walk, walk, walk. So I said, "What are you girls warming up for? All we're going to do is walk." And they didn't really know what they were doing, but they said, "They're looking at us right now!" I said, "Oooh, right this minute?" [She laughs.] But they were. I guess they look at you from the very beginning.

I didn't look like most of the girls. They were all about twenty-three-ish, the ones I talked to, but they all looked a lot older than that to me, a lot older.

Eventually, most of the women who tried out for showgirl roles were cut by Arden and his assistants. Some of those who were dropped had been dancing in the *Lido* show that was coming to a close. This produced a lot of backstage angst, and some tears.

It was so funny, they were crying because— They had beautiful breasts, but they were crying because their breasts were too low. "My breasts aren't too low!" [Diane mimics one of them with tears in her voice.] They were trying to comb their hair and get their dignity back. There were two girls back there when I was starting to come out into the theater and they said, "Wait for us." They didn't want to walk out alone, even though the only people that were in the theater were a couple of the male dancers and a couple of the chorus girls who had already been rejected for whatever reason. They didn't want to go out— I mean, both those girls put their sunglasses on and made me wait for them, which I didn't mind doing. They were just really— Well, rejection isn't easy to take. I understand that. But they were really depressed and just feeling rejected about it.

Diane told this story with considerable aplomb—and without mentioning the fact that she too was found unacceptable for the chorus line. She was dropped after she dropped her top. Arden had seen that she did not dance very gracefully, but Diane's size and California-girl good looks appealed to him. He assumed she could be taught to dance. But when he and his assistants saw her breasts they perceived an insurmountable problem. They were much too small for Diane's large frame, and not well shaped.

Oh, they said that I am not full-enough breasted. But see, some showgirls are really flat, so it doesn't really matter. A couple of the girls said, "Diane, you should go over to *Hallelujah Hollywood!* They hire." Well I could have gotten into the *Hallelujah Hollywood!* show most likely.

It is hard to imagine Diane discouraged by one small setback. In fact, she insisted, she didn't see it as a setback at all, since she wasn't prepared to take a job in a chorus line at the time anyway. She had to finish school first, and conquer other worlds.

I'm Miss Patriotic, I'm a person that— You know, I'm not typical. I cry when The Star Spangled Banner plays. I really can't explain it. Or I get chills when I see a flag. I'm just very patriotic. And I love America, I think it's great. Of course I haven't traveled to some of the other countries. But I'm just an All-American girl, I really am.

In fact, maybe I live unrealistically, but I never enjoyed reading newspapers or watching the news, because there's so much crime, so much this and that, and war—blahh! A couple of weeks ago my godmother said, "You know, we're going to have a depression here in five years, and I want you to start saving your silver. We can all drive to the farm"— she bought some property up the Sacramento River—"and we'll be working." And I'm going: "Come off it! [She laughs.] You've got to be kidding!"

But sometimes I have moments, half an hour at a time, I'll be thinking, Well, maybe that's true, maybe I'll be farming in five years. Who knows what I'll be doing? So I go off and on—mostly off. Mostly I don't think about the country's future affecting me, because I just have this supreme faith in America that we will always be together, and just doing fine, and not at war.

If things go well for you, where will you be in ten years?

I'll be married with twelve kids [she laughs] running around the house, lots of dogs. I'll be president of the PTA, taking my kids to ballet school and flute practice or whatever they chose to do. I'll be a housewife. Uh, ten years, how old will I be? [She pauses.] Well, maybe not that many kids. [Another laugh.] Actually, when I'm thirty-one I'll probably be married a few years, maybe thinking about children, probably still working.

If I do get bored with the shows— Actually, what I'd like to do is come up here for two years, give myself a time limit and spend two years. That way if I thought I was getting bored I could say, Well, you've only got another six months to finish it up. Save my money, then go from there. Actually I'd like to become a model. Hate to say that, but I'm being honest. So many girls said, "I'd like to be a model," and it makes me sick. But I would. I'm very photogenic, and that's by no fault of my own, you know. That's just how it is. The way my face looks on a flat piece of paper [she touches her face with enormous long fingers] is just right. And make a lot of money. I think I'd like that world.

"The Attention That You Get"

Arthur Stevens, twenty-seven and black, self-confident and handsome, also tried out for the *Lido* show, as a singer. After he sang for Arden the first time he was invited back for a second audition three days later. Then Arden told Stevens he had no job for him.

You'll have to forgive me if I seem a little edgy, it's because I'm a little pissed off. I don't mind going through it, it's an experience in itself, getting up there. But when you come out here, you don't have any money, so you call up: "Hey, Mom, give me some money"—you know. I've invested $140 to come back the second time to be told, in essence, "We just can't take blacks in our show." I mean that's what he [Arden] is saying.

Arden had talked privately to Stevens and another black singer after both had auditioned for the second time, and both had sung well. He tried to explain why he couldn't hire them for this show, but mentioned others he would be working on, and asked them to get in touch with him at the MGM studio in Los Angeles, Arden's home base.

I'm very perceptive with people, and I know when someone is not being direct with me. He told us something about he was thinking of a situation to work us into the show. I thought as soon as he used that word "situation" he was thinking in some kind of stereotype, and I asked him directly. He excused us, but I said, "Pardon me, just be honest with me, was it because of my blackness?"

"Nooo," he says. O.K., when a person comes on like that he's very defensive. He was very surprised, shocked, perplexed that I had all of a sudden come on to him like this, because he jumped up, he kind of rose up and took off his glasses and said, "Noooo"—because it is a very touchy subject, discrimination. But what I demand of anyone is to be honest with me and direct. I don't like to beat around the bush, because that's an insult to my intelligence. He said, "You got to understand. If we were doing the show Porgy and Bess I'm not going to hire a white guy to do Porgy." So I knew where the guy was coming from. But he told me to get in touch with him at MGM in Hollywood. I better write that down. Arden was his name?*

---

* Until the Civil Rights Act of 1964 Las Vegas was a segregated town. Blacks still are not integrated routinely into the big shows, though black faces are no longer rare either. Several black entertainers are successful in Las Vegas, including Sammy Davis, Jr., Bill Cosby and Diana Ross. It seemed to us that both the Las Vegas establishment and the mass of visitors to the city included fewer non-whites than the society at large, but perhaps a representative number for Middle America, which is substantially more white than the total population.

Stevens is the adopted son (adopted at age seven) of a woman who runs a catering business in Los Angeles, and who has taken life seriously for herself and her children. Stevens went to college, worked for a time in a big insurance company, bought a Cadillac when he was twenty-three, but eventually got into a fight with the company about its hiring practices and was fired. He had always dreamt of singing, and he turned to that, studying voice seriously and looking for work in nightclubs and neighborhood bars.

I've done some work professionally, but nothing big. I've had some bands of my own, rock bands, but I want to get out of that into solo singing. I think I'm a much better performer as a soloist than I am in a group situation. All that energy, all that desire—the ego, I guess that is what it is, the desire to be seen, get attention.

You know, I was born a person, and I want to stay a person. I don't want to be labeled. Like when you get into a corporate situation, you are almost forced to give up your sense of identity to the corporate identity, you know? Now you are part of the company. It takes away something from you, as a person, and you become part of a system. That's what this whole country is anyway, a system based on the value of the dollar bill, and that's it. It's the most important thing in the system, and that's sad.

I always wanted to be in show business since I was very small, simply because of the attention that you get. I was adopted when I was seven years old. I didn't know my mother until I was seven. I'd been through two or three foster homes, where I'd been through situations like if I did something wrong I was locked in a closet for an entire day, without food or water. I guess I was trying, unconsciously, to block this out of my mind as I grew older, but as I got older I couldn't figure out why I had this paranoia about darkness when I was alone.

So my mom wanted to expose us to quote unquote white middle class values. If a school or an area became forty or fifty percent black, we moved. If a church became fifty percent black, we moved. We'd go to the all-white Christian church, which I'll never understand it. She just wanted to give us *the best;* the white middle class thing was the way it was supposed to be.

So as part of that she wanted to expose us to a lot of things. We came to Vegas when I was fourteen, fifteen to watch the gambling, watch the shows, to watch black artists, and say, Aha! he's black, and he's on stage. He's black and he's making it. Whoa, this is what I want to do." You know? I want to have that freedom, I want to have that kind of protection, I also want to have that kind of influence on people. Being in show business is not simply a financial trip for me, it is a way for me to express myself to people in mass, and at the same time enjoy it and make a lot of money. I will use my work as a means to an end, to communicate with people, through my songs, through writing. I write a little bit. I don't consider myself just a singer. I consider myself an interpreter of songs.

That was how I really got interested in show business. Plus the glamour. You can't put that down.

Arthur Stevens sensed that his mother rescued an entire human existence when she adopted him. "I'm doing pretty well, pretty lucky for a person who came from nowhere," he said. His own experience has made him something of a philosopher on the inequality of dreams. For instance:

I used to work with kids at the Boys' Club—boys, because I could relate to them. I really loved it. I found a lot of children there that had so much talent. One little boy, a little Mexican boy, wanted to be a writer. Well, he didn't want to be a writer; he was interested in writing. He came to me and showed me some stuff. This guy was about ten years old, came from a family with thirteen kids, poor parents, one was unemployed, and he brought stuff to me and I said, *"Wow!"* If I had any money I would just put this kid in a situation where he could just deal with that talent. But in time that kid is going to lose insight into that ability to write, because— Well, for one thing, his parents aren't going to encourage him, because they're going to be so busy trying to keep up, paying the bills. The other thing is that his peer group is doing other things. They'll say, "You wanna be a writer?" They'll be going out carrying switchblades, shit like this, you know.

But Stevens had no doubts about his own dreams.

I believe that by the time I'm thirty years old I'll be on my way to having a lot of money. Not because that is my number one goal in life but simply because I know that I will direct my energies into that area, just pursuing my personal instincts. I know that I'm capable of doing a lot with my knowledge, my ability to communicate with people and to attract people. As a result of that it just seems, um, inevitable that things will turn out.

The Lido Show for which Arthur Stevens tried out had a cast of
50. At the time of his audition the cast was entirely white.

"The Greatest Thing I Ever Did"

Joanie Pond is well into her thirties now. She has put on a little
too much weight, her skin has loosened a little at crucial junctures,
but she still looks fine. Her friends call her "Big Six." She's six feet
tall and large all over. She could pass for Diane Bessee's older sister,
and she has already played out Diane's dream—done it, and retired.

She was a dancing nude in Arden's *Lido* show for seven years.
She got the job—according to the story she likes to tell on this subject—
by finding the guy in charge of the *Lido* chorus line in his office
and instructing him to "fire one of those fat broads you have in your
show and hire me." Three days later she was dancing in the nude.
That's show business.

It was the greatest thing I ever did. Being on stage, being in front, it
was a fabulous opportunity to partake of show business. I wish everybody
in their lifetime had the chance. I feel every human being wants to be
on stage. I don't care if you're the life of the party or what you are, we
all want to be the center of attention. And some of us have the qualities
that allow us to do it in show business.

But now you've done it—satisfied the urge?
Yes. Yes. [A pause.] Actually I satisfied the urge about a year after
I was there. It became a job, although I enjoyed it, except towards the
tail end.

Why did you finally leave?
I was getting cranky and ornery. I'd had enough of show business.
It's a very cloistered life. You don't ever really deal with the public. You're
up there with tits and feathers and asses. Makeup. Rush downstairs to
get on stage. You don't even have an intelligent conversation. I used
to try and read, study, in the dressing room. You can't really do it. You
have ten fast minutes between numbers.

There's a great turnover of girls. Some get disillusioned when they
get in it. They don't realize— They think there's more glamour to it than
there is. There's not that much glamour. It is glamorous to the public
eye. It isn't backstage. They're really disappointed. They don't feel they
fit.

I started out for $197 a week for six night, three shows on Saturday.

The money isn't that good. That was in 'sixty-nine. When I left it was $247. Now it's $287.

I know what star material is, and I'm not star material. A lot of girls don't know that, and they aren't willing to face it either. They all think they're stars. A lot of them are vain that way. I think there's something lacking somewhere to make them not see.

"We're Trying to Develop a System of Prestige"

There is an important distinction in American life between insiders and outsiders. It gives America a unique kind of class structure.

Insiders are a small minority of the population who fill the positions of power and influence in the society. Indeed, that is probably a good definition of an insider; anyone who fills a position of influence becomes one automatically. Insiders live in the America that appears in the newspapers and on the network news.

That puts them outside the world inhabited by most of the Americans in this book. Those who occupy the middle ground are not insiders. For them the network news is another form of entertainment, not a mirror of their own lives. These Americans are not competitors for status and power in the insiders' America. That is alien territory, beyond their ken.

Middle America has a status system of its own, and it is remarkably straightforward. High status belongs to those who self-evidently are important people (celebrities), or to those who have enough money to buy special treatment.

This is an area that the inventors of Las Vegas understood. In Las Vegas the status system is as clean and neat as a stack of new dollar bills. There are few if any artificial obstacles to the accomplishment of high status; one gets what one pays for.

But in a competitive atmosphere, a proprietor who is hoping to dispense status has to know what it is that the market will regard approvingly. Gene Levin thinks he knows. Levin is an interior designer, the director of design and planning for the Dunes Hotel in Las Vegas. He is about forty-five, and favors bright solid-color silk shirts. He wears a large piece of sculptured silver on a pinkie ring:

We're trying to develop a system of prestige out of our rooms. It's one of the few ways we can say, "We respect you as being a bigger player [i.e., gambler, or spender] than just the average guy." Now there's no place else we can do that except in the room where they're going to live. And that's the reason for some of the ultra ultra things that we want to put into our rooms.

I'm doing a suite now for another hotel, I'm putting a six-place Jacuzzi tub, for six people, in the living room. I can't really see guests necessarily using this, but what will run through the guest's mind, and the fact that will hit all of his friends that are here, and all of his friends back in Dubuque, he can say to 'em, "I was in a room—you wouldn't believe this—but I had a six-foot-round bathtub in my living room!" And that's really what it's all about. We find the expenditure there is really minimal to what we're gaining from that kind of guest. I'm doing some suites here that have pool tables in the suites. The chances of anybody shooting pool in their room is really minimal, but the fact that they will tell their friends at Caesar's Palace or another competitor, "Well, you think you got a room? Let me tell you about my room. I got a *pool table* in my room, what you got in *your* room?" That's what it's all about.

We have people that could not get into their local country club and who could not necessarily get a seat at Twenty-One [the New York restaurant] if Twenty-One was booked who are catered to here and who will get any seat they want at any show they want any time they want— and I'm sure that is part of their desire to be here. Because it's a whole different status system here.

What Levin meant was, status for sale. But it is not "a whole different status system." It is the only system in which most Americans participate, because most Americans feel so far removed from the status system established by old families and old money that they don't even recognize it. Status loses its complexity and its subtlety in a world that equates it with money, and that appeals to a lot of people.

However, there is a problem created by the democracy of affluence that can make a mess of this formula. In any status system, the most appealing aspect of high status is its exclusivity. But in a status system based only on the ability to pay, exclusivity cannot be arbitrarily maintained at a certain level—the top keeps getting higher.

Art and Janice Robertson of Toronto, Ohio, heard from already in Chapter 6, have watched the exclusivity of Las Vegas all but disappear during the fifteen years they have been visiting there. (It's the only place they've been on a holiday since their honeymoon.) They described the changes one afternoon while sitting in the noisy cocktail lounge of the Holiday Inn in the Strip—decidedly not a classy joint. Janice was wearing a tee shirt and shorts, and she was not made up. Art wore a sport shirt that strained to get around his enormous girth.

Janice: We're a little disappointed in the changes that have been taking place here. We started coming here, what, in 1964? When the Strip was still the Strip. If you had money, that's where you stayed, on the Strip. Everyone was dressed to the teeth all the time on the Strip. No tee shirts and cutaways, like here. Now you can get here on a package deal, everybody comes, and it's changed.

Art: It's not as exclusive as it used to be.

Janice: It used to be really someplace—and that's the way you were treated, like you were someplace. But we still like to come.

Art: Like ten or fifteen years ago, if you went to a show, everyone had on a jacket, tie. Women had on beautiful dresses. But now if you go to a show, it's the way we're dressed right now.

Another thing. I hate to even bring this up. I am not prejudiced—I hope I'm not. But there are more blacks here than there ever were. And I really don't mean that to sound prejudiced. But, uh, I guess I still have that one old way. I talk to 'em, sit down and have a drink with 'em, but I still don't want one living next to me.

In Las Vegas argot the verb to tip has become "to toke." One night a bellman from the Sands Hotel explained the social structure in a phrase: "You are what you toke." Exactly.

A man of seventy who owns a clothing store in Los Angeles elaborated:

We went up to Tahoe one time and it was out of the season. I didn't make no reservations. We get up there, the guy tells me he don't have a room. He says maybe two or three hours. I slip the guy some money and ten minutes later I had a room. This is the way it is.

We just came back from a cruise, we went up to Alaska, and even on the ship you've got to slip everybody. The day you get on the ship you start slipping them money. Then they take care of you. Then you can get anything. That's the way of life. You want something, you've got to pay for it.

One of the more improbable figures we found in Las Vegas was Jess Kirk, a graduate of Harvard College, class of 1937. Kirk is the maitre d' at Circus Maximus, the huge nightclub in Caesar's Palace Hotel. He had meant to go to medical school, but he got married instead, had trouble finding a job, and ended up a waiter in the old Cocoanut Grove in Boston—before the fire, he notes. Later he worked at the Copacabana in New York, then in the early 1950s he moved to Las Vegas.

Kirk has the courtly Southern manners of a Hollywood senator and a mellifluous voice that treats the English language gently, if elaborately.

Tipping is a fact of life which has been here for these many years, and no doubt will continue forever. The affluent ones in the world like the tipping system especially, because they can come in, and they tip, and they know they can get what they want, there's no question. It's part of their pride, they come in, pay a little extra to get a little extra. They feel that way. I think many people in the world prefer to tip, they want to tip. They would resent it if they couldn't pay a little extra and feel they were treated a little better.

Do people come to Las Vegas to buy a little status for a few days?
True, true, true. The biggest status symbol in the world, I do believe. Just the fact that you have a center booth in this show room or center ringside, your trip is made. Put you in a seat where you can see perfectly well and you're not happy, because you didn't get recognized as the most important man in the room. Course it makes it difficult when you have about fifty parties, all of them the most important men in the room. Takes a little doing. When we opened Caesar's Palace I had two bosses to seat [the hotel's two original owners], and I had one center ringside table. So I moved it over and I had two center ringside tables. I have never deviated from that since. Status. I couldn't put one above the other. One of them would have been an enemy forevermore.

Status reduced to ringside tables—so simple! But why not? We are talking, after all, about America's greatest invention, a huge class of prosperous citizens who in traditional or feudal societies would have been counted among the peasants. There is no hint of nobility here, and none of the pretense of it either. Middle America is the folk grown fat and comfortable, unimpeded by any traditional social structures. Mobility has triumphed over all constraints—first the mobility of unhappy peoples who could transplant themselves to America, and now the mobility of those immigrants and their heirs within the new society they helped define.

"The Gods of the Earth"

The status afforded by a seat at the ringside table is fine, but it is hardly the last word. In fact the kind of status one can buy is a substitute for the last word, which is true celebrity. There is nothing that stirs American adrenaline like a certifiable celebrity.

Mr. and Mrs. Arnie Zweig are former New Yorkers who moved years ago to Las Vegas, where they now run a successful car rental franchise. They talked about celebrity:

Arnie Zweig: We live in an area where these people [celebrities] live. We're not impressed. Robert Goulet lives three houses from me. Pat Cooper lives just down the block. They don't impress us. They're nice people. They're like you and I and Joe Blow down the street. But the people who come here to Las Vegas are very starstruck. They're very conscious of celebrities.

Mrs. Zweig: They go to Caesar's Palace and they see Joe Louis walking around. They crowd around Redd Foxx or Telly Savalas.

Arnie Zweig: What the hell, I shook hands with Joe DiMaggio once, and I'll never forget it.

What the hell, Robert Goulet may not provide much excitement, but you don't forget shaking hands with Joe DiMaggio.

David Lowell Rich is a movie director, most of whose work is done for television. He looks like a high school principal, or perhaps a lawyer. He looks as conventional and conservative as he claims to be. Reluctantly, after the tape recorder was turned off, Rich acknowledged that he was forty-seven. (He is in a young people's business, he explained; someone could misunderstand.)

No one of us is immune from it, no one of us. I don't care who you are. I was in the commissary at Universal not too long ago and Cary Grant walked in. Now I've never worked with Mr. Grant, but I grew up on Cary Grant, and I tell you I thought he was the be-all and end-all.

There's a superstar quality about him. And I couldn't help myself. My eyes followed him all the way. And why?

Well, it's stronger now I think than it's ever been, and that's because of television. People who sit and watch television are so disarmed. They're so relaxed that when there's a star with whom they have a kind of communion in their own living room, sitting in their shorts or pajamas or whatever you will, there is that sense of intimacy which makes the star kind of family. So there is a feeling of "I know you" when the star walks by.

But at the same time there is that closeness there is a vast gulf between them, the audience and the star, because they in their minds think, This person has something marvelous, glamorous, wonderful. The fact that a star's life is made up of very early calls and sitting in makeup and learning lines—that never occurs, because if they're good—and they are good if they're stars—they are capable of transmitting a kind of aura which is very pleasing to be in.

It's warming to be around that, because they are the giants of our age. That's like being among the top political figures of the world. They carry a kind of power with them, and with that power a kind of aura which is satisfying to those of us who don't have it. They're the gods of the earth.

First Hollywood, then television have shaped the American public into the greatest mass audience in man's history. Someday the Chinese or the Indians will surpass us, but a Super Bowl game can still draw more human beings of the same nationality into the same experience than any other spectacle on earth. The celebrities created by movies and television are part of Americans' shared cultural experience. We have Archie Bunker and Reggie Jackson in common—an important part of our nationality.

Americans love to talk about the famous, the glamorous, the rich— simply the *known,* the *recognized.* Persons widely regarded as unique and special, the celebrities can play an important role in Americans' fantasy lives. David Lowell Rich talked about that in terms of the people he sees hanging around movie sets:

It's the desire for immortality, basically. Get on film, get on something that will last, I think. Or a desire for more notoriety—"Know me, recognize me, here I am, don't ignore me!" That's a desperate point of view. And it's a human point of view. So the child who comes up in front of the camera and makes a face, sticks a tongue out and all that—it's not being nasty or mean, it's trying to be noticed. We in life are too often ignored by everybody around us.

In Middle American terms, a good celebrity is exalted but not out of reach. Robert Goulet is not out of reach, but he just isn't exalted, and Arnie Zweig knows it. But Joe DiMaggio—obviously.

Our celebrities tend to come from Middle America. *People* magazine rarely puts a representative of the traditional American aristocracy on its cover; it chooses stars. And stars start out as kids next door. Arnie Zweig, who won't forget shaking hands with DiMaggio, is about the same age as Joe DiMaggio, and grew up in a similar way. He just couldn't make the peg to third quite as well, and curve balls fooled him. Archie Bunker personifies this phenomenon; he became a celebrity because he *was* the guy next door.

This is probably no coincidence. People tend to make celebrities out of those whose shoes they can imagine filling. Otherwise it's no fun.

David Lowell Rich is right; stars are the gods of the earth. For many Americans, celebrity has higher value than power or influence, because to them celebrity seems accessible, but power and influence do not. Curiously, many celebrities seem to feel the same way. Without restraint on their part, we might have had a lot more Ronald Reagans.

Al Rosen's celebrity came in an era when recognition meant far less, but was still real. Al Rosen played third base for the Cleveland Indians. His biggest year was 1953, when he led the American League in home runs (43) and runs batted in (145), and was chosen the league's Most Valuable Player. Sometimes there were more than 75,000 people in Municipal Stadium, Cleveland, shouting his name.

Nobody sitting in the stands ever struck out. They only hit home runs. So it gives 'em a vicarious thrill when that happens. It also gives 'em an outlet when their hero strikes out, because that sort of lets 'em down a little bit. That's why you find the bigger the hero in sports, the more vociferous fans will be when he's not doing well. Because he is all their hopes and their dreams, and when he attains those hopes and dreams for them, it's great, and when he doesn't, it's a letdown for 'em.

Wayne Newton is one of the most popular entertainers in Las Vegas, a singer whose greatest talent is pleasing an audience. Women of all ages lose their sense of perspective over Newton at every performance.

I realized a long time ago that the true adulation of the "fan" is an interesting phenomenon in that you represent to them their fantasies. And when you tumble from that pedestal for whatever reason—and I don't say this unkindly, it's just life—when you tumble from that pedestal, these people will be the most vicious and the hardest on you. Not because you tumbled, but because you took them with you. It gives these people a side of life that they wouldn't have ordinarily. You know, the letters that they write you, and the big part that you play in their life.

Jess Kirk, the Harvard graduate who presides over the show room at Caesar's Palace Hotel, has been watching the public and its stars for many years:

All the single girls in the world want to come here and have the big stars meet—*them!* They want to meet the big stars, but they want the big stars to see them. Can you imagine the following that Tom Jones has? Sinatra has? Girls from all over earth, not just in this country, come specially when these people are working—absolutely convincing themselves that Sinatra will see them, and want them. There are people who will come and see Sinatra, or Tom Jones, or any of the big stars, come see them two shows a night, seven days a week, and sit there just entranced. They love it, and fight to be close to them. "He's got to see me!" It's true. Some young, beautiful girls, some fat, frumpy old girls, but all of them—"Sinatra has to see me!"

I guess every girl has her dream prince, and her dream prince is quite often an entertainer in these United States. They absolutely worship them. They used to come into the Copacabana [in New York, where Kirk once worked], younger girls, when I was there twenty-five, thirty years ago. They would just sit there and adore him [Frank Sinatra]. That was their life. They'd look at him for four or five days, come every night he'd perform, every show. Unbelievable. Never got tired of it.

It's the strangest thing about the women who come to see these stars. It seems to be just a life's ambition, a life's desire to come and sit close to a star, and maybe possibly get backstage and meet, touch them, touch their hand, have a picture taken with them, anything like that. And they'll go to any extreme limit to get there. Sometimes they'll fight with the security guards physically to try to get backstage. They end up the week totally exhausted, but happiest in the world, from having been here to participate. These people feel like they actually know the stars. They know them, they're personal friends, they belong. It enriches their lives forevermore. They never forget it.

There are people who call me from Florida, from California, from Texas, when Tom Jones is here. They call during the show and ask me, "How is he doing? Is he doing a good show now? I couldn't make it this time. And could you hold the phone there just a minute so I could hear him? Whooooo." These fans are sincere.

Jess Kirk also sees the other side of this relationship, a different world altogether:

Buddy Hackett hates himself—well, the world, whatever. Last night, on the phone, he didn't get his order from room service. I tried to soothe him. This was during the second show seating. He had some Chinese food. It didn't come out to suit him. He called the entertainment director [of the hotel] to complain he didn't get the kind of fried rice he wanted. He called him at home. Well, I guess the entertainment director didn't give him too much sympathy, and then he called me, to cry about it. I said I did as much as I could, for pity's sake. He said, "I don't think I can go on."

So I said, "These people who have come to see you—think how you'd disappoint them. You can't possibly let them down. You can't do it. How could you do such a thing to your public? They don't know anything about your food—they don't know anything. They just know they came to see Buddy Hackett, and they're here, here to see you. How could you possibly in your conscience let them down?"

Well, he ended up crying on that phone. Crying. "Oh, I made a mistake."

So many of these entertainers, you have to psych them up.

Sonny is a bellhop in a large hotel, but he once had bigger dreams. The movies, for example:

I was in *Blackboard Jungle,* some other things. It didn't last very long. Everybody wants to see themselves on the silver screen. Everybody wants to see what they really look like. They wonder, Are those people real?

My most famous thing I wanted to be was a dancer. I wanted to get in show business and be like a Fred Astaire, a Gene Kelly. In order to get in show business I had to do other things, like little theater. I did a lot of things. I did a movie with Elvis Presley. But everything I was in I got cut out.

Then I was on the billboards for the Sands Hotel. They took my picture, they put me on the billboards. It was the greatest thing in the world for me, for the morale, you know? You ride down in Los Angeles and see yourself on the billboards, you stop short and say, "There!" A lot of people came up to me and said they recognized me. In fact a couple that comes to the hotel all the time said they almost smashed up, got killed on the freeway, when they saw me. They stopped short and seen Sonny up there. It makes you feel good when they come and they say "Yeah, yeah, I seen you up on the billboard." A big guy comes in from Chicago and says, "I seen you on the billboard in Chicago." I said, "You recognized me?" He said, "Yeah."

"Afterwards I Always Tell Them They Were Terrific"

That big guy from Chicago made Sonny the bellhop feel good by making him feel noteworthy, special. That big guy from Chicago knew something important about dealing with people—something Americans love.

Americans appreciate personal touches. Sometimes that means literal, personal touching. Usually it means that whoever is taking your time or your money has conveyed the impression that he or she shares your sense of your own importance and uniqueness. This is what Gene Levin thinks he is doing when he designs hotel suites that have six-seat Jacuzzi bathtubs in the living room.

Not every American can be a celebrity, a sad truth that most of us learn to accept. But there seem to be very few Americans who are not impressed by celebrity treatment. This proposition is fundamental to the most popular one-man act in Las Vegas, the Wayne Newton show.

Most of the show business figures who play Las Vegas appear for two, four or six weeks a year; Newton performs thirty-two weeks a year, never to empty seats. For this he earns millions of dollars and a permanently hoarse voice.

Newton does not entertain the way Donn Arden understands the word. He is not a great singer, not a great musician, not a great comedian. But he is a superb entertainer of another sort. He entertains with flattery—he wins them over. This is Newton's own explanation:

There's an old cliché that's as old as time. Corny as it might sound, it's one that I have honestly lived by. And that is, it's difficult to dislike someone who likes you.

So Newton makes his maximum effort not at singing or playing or joking, but at flattering and attracting. It is an exhausting effort. A typical Newton show begins with a musical number by his big band, a driving, rhythmic number to which Newton makes a dramatic first appearance dressed all in ruffles or velvet or something else grand. He is tall and handsome and is supposed to have great power over women, so some of the women in the room begin to squeal the instant he appears. Newton beams out on the audience and begins to clap and dance—prance, really—around the stage. Without saying a word, he gets most of the crowd clapping along with him. He starts singing now, "It's Gonna Be a Bright, Sunshiny Day," working on eye contact with the audience all the time. Several women in the front row have reached up toward him, and Newton has taken their hands. Why settle for eye contact? By the third song he has leaned down to kiss two of these ladies, not just pecks on the cheek either, but serious kisses, to the delight of the crowd. Later he'll come back and shake hands with those ladies' escorts, joke with them, tell them he couldn't imagine taking them on man-to-man. The charming cuckolder.

Flattery is crucial. Newton's very first words to a big crowd one night are these: "Oh! We got *people* this time. What a room! You are such a good group. If you only knew what we had to go through the first show!" He returns to this sentiment again and again, as he does in every show, clearly convincing the audience that they really were in on something special.

This routine culminates with the introduction to the biggest musical number of the night, an introduction that invariably goes like this:

"Now I want to do for you a medley, a medley I save for very special audiences and very special moments." Then he goes into the medley.

It turns out to be an elaborate production number, eventually involving the orchestra's disappearance via elevated stage into the depths below the theater and an actual rainstorm before our very eyes. The water splashes lightly onto the front tables.

Later Newton explained his con:

Your first two songs are absolute throwaways. You could walk out with your closing number that usually kills 'em—or at least is designed to do that, that's what you pray for—and open with that and it wouldn't work, only because they're not listening. They're looking at you. They're deciding, "Do I like the suit that he's wearing? Are his pants too short? Is he heavier or thinner than I thought he would be?" I mean, they're going through all the human emotions that people go through when they first meet. You walk into a room, most of the time you miss people's names because you're not listening to the name, you're looking at 'em. So it really just is simple psychology, isn't it? They must develop a like or dislike for you somewhere along the way, because that's why they'll come back. Not because you're a great singer and not because you're a great instrumentalist. They'll come back because they feel like they've met a friend. They go there because they want to take part of that performer with them. They want to feel like when they leave that room that they know him a little.

Making friends means proving you're a nice guy. So when a drunk lady in back interrupts the show to shout, "Mr. Newton, Mr. Newton!" he stops everything, smiles and asks for the house lights so he can see who is talking. "Mr. Newton, sing 'Happy Birthday' to my sister Caroline," the drunk woman pleads. So Newton turns to the orchestra leader, and they're soon doing "Happy Birthday, Caroline."

And throughout every show the patter: You're a great audience, what a special show, what wonderful people, how'd we get so lucky. The final bit of flattery is to play about twenty minutes longer than the show is scheduled to last, sometimes even more. Why not? We don't get audiences like this very often—only twice a night, six or seven days a week. But it works. Everyone leaves liking Wayne Newton. The two of us left liking Wayne Newton.

When he talked about this in his dressing room, sipping a beer between shows, wrapped in a robe and reeking of cologne after the requisite shower, Newton said the reason it worked was simple. He understood what people were looking for.

Partly, he said, they were reacting to the strains of their daily lives. He recalled the 1973 gasoline shortages, the only event in recent times that has seriously damaged business in Las Vegas:

They were concerned, and they stayed home, and then finally there was "Ah, the hell with it, the hell with it. I've busted my butt, I've worked hard all year, and I am going to have some fun. Whatever happens happens. Because we've elected people and hired people and paid our taxes" —this is truly the feeling you get—"and if they can't handle it, I don't know what I'm gonna do about it, but I'm not going to sit around and suffer much longer."

Then, said Newton, there were the smaller problems of simply getting into his show:

If it's a dinner show they show up at five P.M. and they stand in line with the security guards watching the line. That's intimidating enough, isn't it? They finally get up to the door, and then they have to deal with the maitre d'. They deal with him on where they're seated. Now the lady's spent a lot of money on a new dress, usually a day in the beauty parlor, and a baby sitter for the kids in many instances. And the old man's usually gone for a few bucks at the tables or the slot machines. They're not in the best of moods. Then they get seated in the room, and let's face it; there are good seats, and there are bad, and most of the seats are not great seats. Then they're served drinks and they're served food and the comic comes on, usually while they're still eating. It can make it a pretty impossible job to entertain them.

On the other hand, you must realize they've gone through this for one purpose, to be entertained. Not to have their political beliefs challenged, not to have their religious beliefs challenged. Right? They come here, have gone through this, to forget the problems we all live with day in and day out.

In other words, everything that has pushed an audience in Newton's direction is part of mass life in mass America, the great American shared burden. No one likes the sensation of sharing so much with his fellows, and Wayne Newton sets out to convince his audience that their arrival at his show is a sign that they can now begin to feel special. Usually, he succeeds.

This talent we are trying to describe here—the ability to reinforce every person's feeling that he is *special*—is really just the classic skill of the courtesan. But modern America has no courtesans. Modern America has hookers.

The hooker is a Great American Dream herself, of course. She is forbidden fruit—sin and lust incarnate. Is the male American Dream to pay for it or not to pay for it? A little of both, probably—to *agree* to pay for it, then to be told afterwards that this was so special, there will be no charge.

Dee lives in an expensive high-rise apartment house in a compound protected by private guards. She agreed to talk about her world on a day off from work. She was loafing around the apartment in a bikini bottom and brief pullover, smoking a joint. She has smoky dark hair, a carefully nourished tan, an abundant figure and an easy, if tentative, smile. As she talked, traces of her Appalachian origins crept into Dee's speech.

A lot of people don't understand that fucking isn't sex. I don't make my living in bed. I make my living talking.

I don't know if I'm the best. I really don't *do* anything. Here I am and here he comes off the airplane. You become a talker, you become everything. When I meet a gentleman there are vibrations there. I've never had any trouble talking. I like talking to people about anything. I get almost stimulated by talking, and that's what I do, I talk to them.

My problem is making them relax, be comfortable with someone they don't even know. To do it, I've got to make them feel that whatever they do, I will never laugh at them. I will never put them down. I will make them feel the best I possibly can. I will make them feel like a man.

I pick up vibrations from people very easily. I think I've become a lot more perceptive. Like I can tell when a guy doesn't like me. I will bow out gracefully, I will not try hard to hustle him or push myself on him.

Not that she inevitably sympathizes with every client:

A lot of American men are such egomaniacs it's just unbelievable. [A laugh, and a new light for her joint.] They think they have a really nice, firm body. They think they have a body that's going to turn a woman on. They like to brag about how much money they've got, drop names. They'd rather spend money on you than give it to you. The guys who say, "Don't worry about a thing," I automatically worry. I say, "Uh-oh. This guy is going to pay up front." You just handle each guy accordingly. I can convince any guy I'm the best he's ever been with. It's really funny.

A lot of them fantasize about having two women at the same time. Just laying back and being pampered to death. Saying, "Do this, do that," not having to say please. I just make men feel good. All over feel good. Feel good sexually. Because they're not getting that at home. Either the wife doesn't give head or they can't talk about sex. He can't say anything during sex. He feels withdrawn. Maybe he might like to talk. It stimulates him. But telling the wife— No, he doesn't know how she's going to take it. If she takes it wrong, it's going to knock him down. He might not be able to handle it. So he doesn't say anything. So here I am.

What about her own life? What depresses her?

Working. I don't want to work. I don't like it. I stay at it because I don't really know if I could do anything else. Oh, I know I could. But it's just a matter of knowing where I belong. I haven't really found where I belong. I think in the back of my mind I don't know if I'm ever going to get out of here. I really don't know. But I know I can't keep working forever. Eventually it'll get to me. I don't know when. Working makes me think of a lot of things in my past and it hurts.

Where do you think you'll be ten years from now?
Wherever it is, I'm going to be happy. Doing my thing. I'd like to be with a man and know I'm making a man happy.

You've been in the business nine years. Are American men getting more comfortable with sex?
Yes. They're willing to try anything. I try to talk them into something new. Something they'll remember. You make suggestions. You give them a lot of options and see what they pick up on [at escalating rates]. Like

I said, conversation is the key. Afterwards I always tell them they were terrific. Got me nice and hot. I tell them they were somebody special. They like that. Hey, dreams are what it's all about. It's kind of like I'm not selling my body. I'm helping them to like themselves.

16

AMERICAN VOICES

Americans talk good, as a lot of them might put it. This is not a judgment on sentence structure or grammar, but on content and candor. Plain talk, saying what you mean, speaking your mind, getting it off your chest—these are American values, not honored in many other cultures. All sorts of people talked openly and candidly with us, sometimes about personal things that were no apparent business of ours. Without the willingness of Americans to talk, we would have had no book.

The next few sections contain the talk of some of the good talkers we met. These conversations appealed to us partly because they do show what good American talk can be like, and also because they echo so many Middle Americans' dreams and fears. So these sections are sort of a sampler, a tasting of the evidence.

"There's No Hard Times in the United States"

Of all the Middle Americans who have a place in this book, Don Hedrick is surely the most unlikely. Until we met him in his turn-of-the-century saloon in Goodsprings, Nevada, it had never seemed likely that a retired outlaw motorcyclist would turn up here. First impressions reinforced the doubts. Here was a small, nearly round man with a huge stomach, a huge black beard, a wild shock of black hair, wearing a blue tee shirt decorated with a portrait of Mickey Mouse. But no kid—fifty years old at least. Autographed photographs of two porn movie queens hung on the wall behind the old mahogany bar.

But this turned out to be a man as American as—oh, Battista
Locatelli, for example. Hedrick had fallen in love with motorcycles—
"motorsickles" as far as he is concerned—at an early age, rather the
way some young girls fall in love with horses. This had put a funny
tint on the rest of his life. But it was only a tint. He said so himself.
Sure, he knew some of the Hell's Angels. He even had his own outlaw
gang at one time, but people just don't understand what that's all
about:

It's a freedom thing. You don't try to keep clean and have silk shirts
and this sort of thing. You ride to have fun. If you want to stop someplace
and lay down you don't have to worry about nice clean clothes. Why
put on a clean pair of Levi's to go motorsickle riding?

Hey, people loved us. They like to watch gangs, like Jesse James.
Anything like that. It's a thing people like. Not every man, but most men
would like to be doing the same thing. But they can't cut loose from
society to do what they want to do. They have jobs, this sort of thing,
where they have to look straight. It's a thrill thing. They like to watch
us. We were uninhibited. What we might do in public is what the other
citizens would do in private and try to hide. Outlaws never try to hide
what they do.

Riding a motorsickle is a thrill. There's a danger involved in it. It's a
freedom thing. You're out in the air. That's why the helmet law bothers
us. You're closed in [with a helmet]. We ride a motorsickle because
we're out in the air with the wind blowing on us. You never see an outlaw
with a windshield on [his motorcycle]. He wants the wind blowing in his
face. It's hard to explain. It's like a guy who flies an airplane. When he
gets up in that airplane he's in a different world.

Hedrick isn't an outlaw now. He is a burgher of Goodsprings,
the biggest town in Nevada nearly a century ago when the mines
were working, now pretty well dead. Hedrick runs the bar as a community facility and tourist attraction. He drives the town's ambulance.
His establishment looks like the bars in Gabby Hayes movies.

Adjoining the saloon is Hedrick's private motorcycle shop. This
is a man who has an acute sense of the rightness and wrongness of
things—a very American sense that is, too. Tom Wolfe once called
it "marginal difference"— the distinction between any old penny loafer
and a Bass Weejun, for example. For black kids on city playgrounds

the right thing is a Chuck Taylor basketball shoe, not just a sneaker. For Don Hedrick the right thing—the only thing—is a Harley-Davidson motorcycle.

There is only one motorsickle. The Harley is the old original motorsickle. It's the American-made motorsickle. It's the Iron Horse, the Milwaukee vibrator, it's the classic thing. I say today Harley is only a tradition. [Hedrick is furious that the company has been taken over by AMF, a multinational corporation that started out making bowling equipment, which imports *Japanese* nuts and bolts to put into Harley-Davidsons.] Maybe all the other motorsickles that are made are better engineered than Harley and this sort of thing. But Harleys have three things: They look like a motorsickle, they sound like a motorsickle and they sit like a motorsickle. You sit down *in* a Harley instead of sitting up on top. As far as engineering-wise, the other ones are good. Fast, dependable, all that. But they just don't sound, look and sit like a Harley.

Motorsickles aren't cheap; they've always been expensive. Then the Japanese made a cheap inexpensive motorsickle that made all the Sunday motorsicklists possible. But if they're a real motorsickle rider they'll end up with a Harley. It's the Cadillac of motorsickles. It's a big hog.

I found a 1966 Harley-Davidson, full dress, everything on it, just the way it came from the factory. Never had a nut or bolt taken off. Every 'sixty-six nut and bolt was there. I tried to buy it from the guy. I finally had to pay him eighteen hundred dollars to get it. And it was completely wore out. Engine, transmission, everything was shot. But I wanted it because it had all the original bolts and nuts. I wanted that one to build another motorsickle. I have to completely rebuild it. Tear it down to the frame and start with the frame and build back up. Everything will be just like new or better. And when I get through with this it'll run me as much as a new Harley-Davidson would, $4500. But I'll have what I consider a good motorsickle. Not an AMF with all those Japanese parts and that sort of stuff.

Now I've got a kicker and the electric start on mine because I'm getting old. Mine is a 1966 swinging arm frame, with a 'sixty-six FLH engine in it, with a 1972 superglide rear fender, rear struts and rear shocks which keeps that fender from going way down. The front end is two inches over stock with the triple clamps chromed and the sportster headlight on it. Stock Harley handlebars, and *black.* What's prettier than black and chrome? That's all, that's all.

All the motorcycles on the road are just one sign of how Don
Hedrick's world has changed. When he was a young man, working
as a meat cutter and riding his motorcycle whenever he could, life
was a struggle. It doesn't look that way now.

People have got money. It's ridiculous. Everybody's talking about hard
times but there's no hard times in the United States. People have money.
They've got so much money they don't know what to do with it. I've
got a son who's twenty-eight years old, married and with kids, the same
occupation that I had, a meat cutter, and he owns his own home, he
owns a new car, he owns a new motorcycle and takes vacations and
all this. When I was his age as a meat cutter I couldn't do it.

We didn't meet Mrs. Hedrick, the mother of his three sons and
a daughter, but we did hear Don's view on women in general.

Women still want to be told what to do. They want to be loved and
treated nice, but they still want a man to tell them what to do. I don't
know what words to use on it, but they still want the man to run the
house and run their lives and so forth. With the exception of the few
who don't want a man—that's fine. But that's not the average. This wom-
en's lib thing, I've talked to very few women who even like it, even agree
with it. They say that it's ruining things for them. They've got men telling
them now, "Hey, go on out and go your own way."
A man has to dominate. If it ever changed, this country would be in
a real mess, I think. Not that I don't think women are smart. The smart
women are like my wife. She's worked all of her life. She's capable of
making more money than she needs to take care of herself. She doesn't
need me financially, but she needs me because I am her husband. She
don't want to be out in the world by herself.

And do you need her?
Oh definitely, definitely. No one can be alone. No one can do anything
alone. Any man or woman says they don't need anybody, that's ridiculous.
Ridiculous.

Did Hedrick ever cast a vote?

I vote, I vote.

Think it makes any difference?
Oh, yeah, yeah. I've said a lot of times I don't pay too much attention

to politics, national politics and this. Maybe I get into local—that might have some bearing to myself. I say that if everybody was like me, then probably there wouldn't be any United States. Maybe it's fortunate, for I can live and not have any ulcers cause I don't worry about those things. You know, I don't understand it anyway. It's too deep; my mentality won't handle it. I don't have the education for it.

What's too deep?

Oh, I don't really understand all about how our government works. I don't understand, you know, the thing like, we vote for a President, but actually I understand that really it's not the vote, it's the electoral college thing that does it. I don't understand all this. And I'm not going to read to find out about it, because I'm not going to get too much in my head that I can't handle.

What about a thing like the helmet law—is that an intrusion?

The thing is on the helmet law, I don't like to be told I have to wear a helmet. I don't like to be told I can't go ride my motorsickle and kill myself if I want to. I agree with it for young kids, sixteen or eighteen, twenty-one. Because they don't have the knowledge yet to decide what they want to do.

What kind of outlaw are you? You're coming across like some kind of Peoria, Illinois, conservative. [He grew up in that area.]

No, no, I've seen too much. They don't know how to handle it. My kids wouldn't agree with me but that's beside the point. Until they're old enough to learn a few things, I think they should be told. I believe in telling kids what to do. My dad told me what to do.

It's a shame young people have to raise kids. Old people couldn't handle it. I couldn't handle it. My grandkids, I like to see 'em and that's it. But I wouldn't want to have to raise them. It's too much.

What's the toughest part about raising kids?

Hoping they turn out right. Your stomach turning over. Turning flip-flops every time they get into trouble. Worrying about 'em. What's going to happen to 'em. My oldest one just turned thirty-one, and I'm just now beginning to be able to relax. He's just beginning to settle down, accept responsibility. He's got two children. I can breathe now with him. He got married when he was eighteen. It's taken thirteen years.

He behaved worse than you did at the same age?

Yeah, yeah. Definitely. It's a different type of world now. More things to get into. Drugs. Everything. I have no great objection to drugs. I mean, I object to hard drugs, but I object to alcohol more, and I'm a bar owner.

I don't believe marijuana should be legalized, because we've already got one big problem, why add another one? If there was some way to do away with alcohol and replace it with marijuana, I'd say fine.

This entire conversation was a surprise, but the best came last. We had been talking in the car driving to Goodsprings about religion in America, which may have prompted Lowell to ask Hedrick if he believed in God.

Yeah.

Do you go to church?
No. I have. But I don't attend church regularly. The last time I was in a little church was this morning. We buried a motorsickle rider. Accident. We had memorial services for him.

What has organized religion done wrong?
I'll give you what happened to me. About 1956, somewhere around in there, I got involved with the Lutheran religion. My oldest boy was having a lot of problems in public school. Fights, this sort of thing. He got into a big fight, six or eight guys. So they asked me if I would put him in a private school. A friend of my wife's was Lutheran, so we put him in a Lutheran school. So I got involved in the church. Two or three years. I was involved very deeply. Not just going to church. Very deeply. I was on the board. We were building a new church. The thing came up when they were building the new church—what kind of seats were they going to put into it? And I was tithing. Anything I do I go all the way or I don't do it. I wasn't even riding motorsickles at the time. They were going to buy seats and stuff for this new church, and they had to have big, thick, heavy padded seats. I objected. I told 'em, "You don't need these thick padded seats for people to come. They're not supposed to go to sleep in church. They're supposed to be there to listen and to think a little." "Oh no," they said. "We've got to have these seats." I said, "That's it. I'm not going for any more of this. This isn't what me and a lot of people are putting money in for. I just can't handle it." I just dropped out of it. I never went to church since. I think religion is fine, but I don't think all of this fanciness is needed.

"A Home in the Suburbs, Two Cars in the Garage, and a Big Dog in the Back Yard"

Bob Goldberg was joking when he offered that definition of the great American dream—sort of. At age twenty-nine, he long ago passed that plateau. He could probably afford an elephant in the back yard if he wanted one. His interests lie not in American dreams, but in what he perceives to be the dominant American reality—that the society he lives in offers boundless opportunities. Failure is not the fault of the system, and success is not one of its products. The system is simply there, like Everest, to be conquered by people with intelligence and ambition.

I'll try to be serious. There's financial success, tangible satisfaction, the opportunity for advancement in a career. The opportunity to get something you want. I think that I have enough courage and common sense to tell my daughters when they grow up that if you want something and want it badly enough, then you have to go out and work for it if you *really* want it. You have to be a little bit lucky. That helps. Sometimes you have to be in the right place at the right time. But luck, by itself, is not going to make that dream come true. It takes hard work, dedication, knowledge and persistence.

The earnestness in Bob Goldberg's voice—the confidence that life repays one's investments in a relatively predictable way—struck us both as uncannily similar to the tone of Don Hedrick's conversation, though the two of them have nothing ostensibly in common. Except their nationality, of course.

Hedrick's personal source of well-being was a saloon in a ghost town. When Goldberg talked about himself, he was one step away from a vice presidency of the General Motors of the liquor industry, Seagram's. (The firm's sales convention had brought him to Las Vegas.) Goldberg got that far in the six years since he had quit his previous job as a disc jockey and jack-of-all-trades at a Chicago radio station and become a liquor salesman.

I was doing almost everything. I was doing a little disc jockey work. I was writing copy for commercials. I was doing news. I was sweeping up the control room at night. I was working in the control room. You knew the opportunity for financial advancement wasn't there, and in retrospect I think that deep down I wasn't really happy with what I was doing. I couldn't really invest my life, my future in that career. So I got married, went on my honeymoon, didn't have a job. It was pleasant coming back without a job. I applied for a job with Seagram's because they are number one. I wanted to work for number one. That's something that made me comfortable. I like working hard. I like doing my best. I'm very competitive. I demand the best of myself. I push myself. I want to be good. I want to be constantly better.

Goldberg's ambition is not one of the malevolent strains. He's simply devoting all his efforts and resources to going as far as he can with Seagram's, trying to understand his own talents and limitations at the same time. The end result has been a thoroughly American mix of dedication to his job, almost to the exclusion of anything else, and the sense that whatever sacrifices he, his wife and two daughters are making in the process are both right and necessary.

I enjoy what I'm doing very much. I'm in a job which has removed me to a large degree from direct sales and has given me much more administrative responsibility. It's been tough for a guy who likes to sell and be one on one with people, but I always wanted to be in this area. It's very satisfying to help make things happen. To develop a plan, formulate a plan, to put it into motion, to execute it and bring it to fruition.

Does that mean you wouldn't want to be president of the company?

No, that doesn't mean I wouldn't want to be president of the company. That, obviously, offers a tremendous amount of responsibility, authority, obviously financial benefits. But my immediate goal, my five-year goal, and I don't really set those goals, is to advance. But still staying close to the field, sales.

What are the important things in your life outside of business?

Not necessarily in order, money is obviously important. My family is the most important. My family consists of my wife and my two daughters. Those three girls are number one in my life. My happiness and their happiness. But it doesn't, necessarily, revolve around money. Because I know a lot of people who make a lot of money, more money than I do, perhaps more than I ever will. But I don't consider them to be happy individuals. I'll tell you, at this point in my life, because of the intense attitude I have towards business, because of my goals, I have immersed myself into my job. I'm trying to become the best that I can, the best that anyone has been in my job. That, to me, is ultimately of great satisfaction to me personally. When I go to bed at night, put my head down on the pillow, I have to live with myself. When I get up the next morning and look in that mirror to shave, I have to live with myself. And to know that I've done the best I can and have been fair and honest with other people. And myself. That's the most gratifying thing to me at this point in my life. My outside interests are very few.

How much time do you spend working?
Probably all my waking hours. It's constantly on my mind. Physically, I like to put in about a twelve-hour day, five days a week. Weekends belong to my family. Five days a week is more than fair to my company. Two days a week I want to give to my family. I want to be with them while they're growing up.

Ever read a book, go to a concert?
Yes I do. Yes I do. I enjoy movies very much. I enjoy going to sporting events very much. Reading, I don't spend a lot of time reading. I think it's probably a lack of patience. And time as well. Taking the necessary time to get myself into a book, into a novel, newspapers, magazines. Sporting events I like very much. I can relate to that easily. It's competition. I'm a keen competitor in what I do, and I can relate to that very easily.

Sports on TV, Saturday night out with the wife ("sometimes just the two of us, sometimes with friends"), a trip somewhere new each summer—Goldberg's life is not showy. He lives in a suburb he likes ("We feel very secure there"), takes care of the cars and the lawn, pokes around with the kids, and works hard. No surprises.

Can you say anything about the things that give you pause, the things that scare you? Either now or the things that might come up later?
There's two categories. There's my personal concerns. And I say concerns rather than fears, because what you say, we're getting into semantics and it doesn't set too well with me. The word "fear." The first area of concern is at the personal level. The second is at the business level. Personally first. My ultimate happiness is the happiness of my family. Their health. Their good health. Uhh [long pause]. And you notice, I didn't talk about dollars, economics. Sure I want to make money. It's one of the many reasons people work. I want to make more money, as most people do, but it's really not my ultimate concern. It's not a pressing concern. I want to be happy in what I'm doing as long as I'm doing it. I want my family to be happy, I want my wife to be satisfied. In whatever she's doing. Right now she's in the process of raising two small children. Ultimately, I want them to be free to make their choice of whatever they want to do. With their lives. I want them to be free to do what *they* want to do. To be fair with themselves and others.

What real concerns do I have with my personal life? That, obviously, well—old age even though I'm only twenty-nine years old. I don't greatly understand or appreciate the way older people are treated in this country. It bothers me greatly. It upsets me that they're treated as second-class citizens. But from the business viewpoint, obviously my future within the company. The future of my company itself. Where is it going? In what direction? Will it reach its ultimate goal? If it does, will I be there? If it doesn't, will I be the recipient of whatever negative effects occur? I have often told people I sleep with Seagram's, but I'm not married to them. I'm looking to do the best I can at whatever I'm doing. To do the best damn job I can possibly do. And also make it as financially rewarding as possible. I *will* give my all. I was told, when I was first starting to work as a young boy, by my brother, that whatever you're doing, do a fair day's work for a day's pay. And that's what I'm doing. They're [Seagram's] not perfect, but the company is composed of people and people are not perfect. I'm very dedicated to the company, but ultimately I have to look out for myself. Ultimately, if I have an opportunity that will afford me greater responsibility, greater authority and greater opportunity to learn, to excel in my industry, to make more money for my family, I would strongly consider it.

What about the nation's future?

I have concerns about where our world's going. Where it's heading. The economy, race relations, crime, the energy crisis, morals, American morals, where they are going, where they are leading to, how it will affect my children. I don't worry on a day-to-day basis, to be very honest, but those things concern me. I'm very conscious of them, but I'm not worried about them. Not that I'm a historian, but I have perhaps a naïve feeling that this country will survive, this world will survive. Perhaps in spite of itself. Every generation has had problems, maybe ours are more complicated. But somehow we'll survive. Hopefully for the better. I think it's certainly a possibility that the country of America could go into a nosedive within our lifetime. Maybe it's my optimistic attitude, but I think the American people, when the chips do get down, come to grips with the situation, make a firm, good effort to overcome.

There is no touchier problem for Middle Americans to talk about than race. Some simply deny there is a problem, others suggest that whatever problems minorities face, they are largely self-inflicted. Again and again we heard the statement that the opportunities are there for those who will seize them. But Goldberg avoided the simple formulas. He has thought about race, and he has decided that much of Middle America is not mean-spirited or actively racist. A lot of people have simply chosen to keep the issue of race—like many other social problems—as far from their daily lives as possible:

There's a certain dark corner, crevice, that exists in every human being's soul, consciousness. It's made up of prejudice. I'm not a sociologist or a philosopher, but I think to a certain degree it may be inborn. Some of it may be developed by peers and by family. I think it's always existed, exists today and will exist in the future. I think one of the big differences with prejudice today in our so-called very sophisticated American society is that people do not outwardly express it to the degree they did years ago. I'm sure that the prejudices that have existed in the past towards blacks or any other minority always exist to a large degree. Today, they're not talked about as much. Perhaps they're expressed by the way people run their lives. What I'm talking about might be the migration Americans have made to the suburbs. They're looking for the best for their families. To live a nice life without being bothered by the uncomfortable aspects of our society. They want to get away from those problems. They want to get away from certain minority groups for valid or invalid reasons. I think the migration to the suburbs is part of that. There's a certain amount of fear and insecurity that exists in all of us. Some people exhibit that fear more than others, but I think it's there in everyone. It's the degree that's different.

Bob Goldberg is Jewish. He doesn't go regularly to synagogue, but like so many Americans, his Jewishness—his ethnic connection— is a primary point of reference, a special quality that helps establish who he is. Goldberg thinks his Jewishness also helps him sense the frustrations of other people who feel victimized:

I don't think prejudice exists only toward black people. It can cross beyond race and ethnic background. It can also cover financial and economic discrepancies among people. Poor people might be prejudiced towards wealthy people and vice versa. I think it's there. I still think it can affect people in terms of their own advancement in a career and in the situation of their own personal life. One of the things that sits on my mind while we sit here and talk about fears—and I use the word "fear" because I think that the possibility is very real that what happened in Germany in the 1930s could happen in this country. It would be a terrible tragedy obviously, but it could happen. Because you're dealing with people. It's not something I think about on a day-to-day basis, but as we talk, yes, I've thought about it several times. Some of it has to do with the fact I married a Jewish girl of German extraction. They fled after the republic collapsed. I don't see anything on a day-to-day basis, anything tangible, anything outward. Maybe it's a little paranoia.

Do you think about the future of Judaism?

Yes I do. I'm concerned about the future of Judaism. I see a lot of intermarriage, which doesn't bother me really, but it upsets me in the sense that a lot of Jewish people who marry a gentile person lose contact with their Judaism.

Among the things that Bob Goldberg does worry about on a day-to-day basis are the unpredictable tastes of the people to whom he is trying to sell liquor.

What's the relationship between ego and consumer goods?

There is a relationship because everyone has a self-image. Products that he consumes help in some way to satisfy his ego. In the case of distilled spirits, which I sell, it's something that can not only satisfy him physically, physiologically, it can satisfy his ego. He is using something with a quality image, something he has aspired to.

What does prestige mean in American society?

It means a lot to a lot of different people. Perhaps to some people it means something they will never really be. Perhaps it means the grass is always greener on the other side of the street. It means quality to some people. It means the ultimate goal to other people.

The conversation eventually made its way toward a discussion of the great American inclination to equate price and quality. If it's expensive, it's good. But that standard is not applied with great constancy, particularly in the liquor business. Goldberg described the tendency of Americans to be one person in private and to at least try to be someone more impressive in public. Many people drink cheaper brands at home than they do in a bar or restaurant.

There is something about the American consumer, that he is associating in a literal sense price with quality. In the long run, the quality must be there, the actual quality itself, but initially the consumer does associate price with quality. It's expensive, it has quality. I think it's very evident today by the great growth of the premium and super-premium products. These are the products that are experiencing the greatest amount of growth. It's brands like Crown Royal, Chivas Regal, Jack Daniel's, Wild Turkey, Tanqueray, and Beefeater. A lot of people, maybe all people, like to buy the best. If they're going out to dinner and they can afford it, they like to go to a fine restaurant. It might not have the best-quality food, but it's expensive.

Is this a little bit crazy? Does it make sense to sell a product for nine dollars that cost less than two dollars to manufacture? Does it suggest something disquieting about the society that people make purchasing decisions on some irrational sense of social status?

Goldberg's answer here cannot be adequately conveyed simply by repeating the words. He started out on a well-beaten path, reciting one of the old chestnuts of the liquor business. But suddenly—the signal is the word "sure"—Goldberg dropped that and told the truth. The old chestnut began with some commentary on high liquor taxes:

Depending on the state, tax can go over fifty percent of the purchase price. The product itself is not terribly expensive. But when you age products—and with the exception of vodkas and gins, most products are aged—that costs money. Obviously there's overhead, the support expenses, advertising, merchandising, my salary. *Sure* I think it's crazy. Sure I question why a Cadillac costs fifteen thousand dollars and a Chevrolet costs six thousand, and when you knock on the hood of the car, they both sound tinny. And they both have the same tires. And five years from now they're both in the junkyard or the trade-in lot. But I think that's part of the American system today.

That it is, and people like Bob Goldberg don't worry much about it. There are kids to be raised, long hours to work, accomplishments to be accomplished. Some craziness goes with the territory.

"Really, Deep Down, I Think We're Satisfied"

Madison Heights, Michigan, is a suburb where skill as a driveway auto mechanic assures more prestige among the neighbors than a crushing backhand or knowledge of vintage wines. The accents are rural South, Appalachian or second-generation ethnic. It is a city like Gary, Indiana, or Parma, Ohio, where people have been coming since the 1930s pursuing the holy grail of blue-collar America, "a good-payin' job."

Madison Heights is not one of the new sprawling suburbs that typify Middle America. It is older and more compact. There is a palpable sense of impending change in the community, but it is difficult to say whether it promises decay or revival. Some of the modest tract homes have been meticulously cared for and expanded. Others, with boards on the windows, are tilting ominously toward slums. The population is virtually all white and blue collar.

Madison Heights achieved Middle American status through the power of cash money. The people who live there may be auto workers and truck drivers, but their paychecks and fringe benefits qualify them to stand with the salesmen and accountants in the newer suburbs nearby.

The auto workers who live in Madison Heights provide a classic example of America's blue-collar bourgeoisie. Thanks primarily to his (or her) aggressive, well-run union, an auto worker starts out with fully paid hospitalization insurance, dental and optical coverage. He is paid for three weeks of vacation and fourteen holidays. He can retire after thirty years of service, regardless of his age, with one of the few generous pensions available in all of private industry. If he is laid off, under normal circumstances he can collect 95 percent of his usual take-home pay under a supplemental unemployment benefit plan. And if he works a full year with a reasonable amount of overtime, his earnings will be near $20,000. Perhaps all this helps explain why the votes of auto workers have helped elect a chain of Republican governors in Michigan during the last twenty years.

"The old issues don't work with our people any more," concedes a political organizer for the United Auto Workers. "We've gotten them most of what they wanted, and now they want to protect it."

Caution and concern about holding a piece of Middle America distinguish people like Frank Ziemba, forty-six, a member of the UAW, from the Americans who grew up expecting a comfortable life as their due. Ziemba describes himself as a "workingman" from a family of workingmen, but he also places himself squarely in the middle class. He and his wife, Shirley, have a daughter, nineteen, and son, seventeen, neither of whom plans to attend college. A gentle, shy, soft-spoken man, Ziemba wears his hair in a 1950s pompadour and notes wryly that he and his wife are one of just two couples in their neighborhood who haven't gotten divorced.

Where do you work?

The Chrysler Corporation Mound Road engine plant in Detroit. I'm on the third shift. That's the midnight shift. My shift starts at eleven P.M. and works till seven, a straight eight hours with a paid lunch. I enjoy the shift. I run a grinding machine, it grinds the main bearings on the crankshaft. It's work, but I enjoy it. I've been there six years, and on the midnight shift close to three years now. I like the coolness of the evenings, and there isn't that much going on like during the day shift and the afternoon shift. There's more pressure during days and afternoons. I just enjoy it better. I feel more relaxed.

Doesn't it bother you that you don't live hours like everyone else?

No, it don't. It don't at all. In fact I sleep more comfortably and my wife sleeps more comfortably without me. [Hearty laugh.] We get along fine.

Does your wife work?

She's got a part-time job. She works for a sprinkling and irrigation company. She does office work, secretary work. Right now she does payroll and practically everything. Anything to do with office work.

Can I ask you roughly what you gross in a year.

Mound Road engine, where I work, we're generally sometimes busy. Like last year I was putting in, like out of fifty-two weeks, I must have put in at least twenty-five to thirty Sundays. This year it's slowed down some, and I haven't been working any Sundays at all. But I've still been working six days a week. In 1975 to '76, I grossed about $21,000. Last year was about the same. This year, I'll probably gross about eighteen thousand. My wife will make about four thousand. It's only part-time, and it's seasonal work.

I've had numerous jobs in my lifetime, I spent seven years at the Ford Motor Company River Rouge assembly. There I had a pretty rough job. I was a solder grinder working in a solder booth where you have to wear a hood and have the air pumped in to you. Anything that was soldered, you had to smooth it down. You couldn't do that in the open. It had to be in a special booth. It was a dirty job, but you get used to a job, and you're on the line and you've got to do it, so you do it.

Isn't one of the attractions of working as an hourly worker in an auto plant that when you punch out, you don't have to worry about how the job is going when you're not there?

Right. Like I said, I've got six years at Mound Road and two and a half years were on supervision. Supervision was all right, but in 1975 I got laid off [as did thousands of other auto workers] and then I got called back and they asked me to go back on supervision. I was more relaxed on the job I got called back on, which was on the midnight shift and all. There's less responsibility and I'd rather just do what I'm doing.

Ziemba, a trim man, six feet tall, who is obsessive about maintaining his home, tends to brood about what he regards as the touch-and-go nature of his life: the sense that however well he's doing, the family is only one unexpected crisis away from hardship.

What's your sense of how you're doing? Are you comfortable?

Well, no. Today no one is really comfortable. Everybody tries to get ahead, but the way it is in today's life you just don't seem to make it. No matter how hard you try. Something will come up. The refrigerator will go out. Or a washer and dryer. Then you're out a couple hundred bucks. It's hard. That's why the wife works.

Do you have a sense you're better off than your folks were?

It wasn't easy for him either, but I think so. But you see the families that get ahead have to be brought up that way. My dad, see, he wasn't a college graduate. If he was, maybe I would have been brought up that way. But he wasn't. He was always a workingman. I'll try and make my son go to college, but it's hard. He figures twelve years of school is enough. My daughter feels the same way. That's the way it is in our family. Other families are different. They press their kids. But they want to do what they want to do. [Long pause.] That's the way I was brought up and I guess that's the way I bring up my children.

If somebody had told you when you were fifteen that someday you'd be making $21,000 a year would you have believed them?

No, I don't think so. But I'm working at a plant that's busy, and it's a good company. I have to live in a bracket where there's at least fifteen thousand a year. Otherwise I couldn't get by.

Fifteen thousand a year used to be a good wage.

Right. But today you have to have it. A family of four, if you're not making that you're hurting. If you want the better things in life—a new car, a color television, better furniture—you have to have that. But hey, well, let's just say I'm happy. Let's put it that way. I'm happy the way I live, my lifestyle. No complaints. If I wanted to push myself, I could probably take up a course or something. But the way my lifestyle is, I enjoy it. The way I am. *I'm happy.*

This last assertion of happiness may seem to contradict Ziemba's earlier observation that "today no one is really comfortable." In fact, the ambivalence in his views is typical. On one hand, things are no longer getting better (government statistics show that Middle Americans' purchasing power has not appreciably increased since 1969). If Ziemba is in that frame of mind, or if he is asked a question in a way that elicits that sort of opinion, he might sound crabby, even a little bitter. But pursue the question further, pin him down as to his own assessment of his own situation, and suddenly he is *happy.*

Ziemba's wife, Shirley, is a pleasant woman with an easy, captivating smile. She chose to stay out of the discussion until subjects like religion and the family came up. (Later, Ziemba said that his wife was wary of this interview. She thought Lowell was trying to sell them something.) When she and her husband did discuss their family, a familiar Middle American attitude emerged. Much as they loved their children, they were looking forward to the day when both kids were independent, on their own. That would make the Ziembas independent again too.

Shirley: I could have gone to work when the kids were young. But they would have been waiting when I got home. Now they're older, I can do it.

What are you going to do when the kids are gone?
Frank: I imagine we'll probably do more traveling. Things we've never had a chance to do. Like we've never been to Hawaii. Or Southern California. Anything out that far. Once both kids have graduated and have their own jobs, it will give us more free time so we can go on our own. That's one thing we've never had. Our vacation's always been with our children. The boy's still in school, so he still comes with us. Once he graduates and gets on his own, I don't think he'll still want to come. I think he'll want to go his own way.

Ziemba said that in a way that suggested he was counting on the son to go his own way. He wanted that vacation alone with his wife.

Both of the Ziembas are devout Catholics, but their children survived an orthodox childhood in the church without becoming regular churchgoers. Shirley hoped that as they get older they would return to active membership.

Frank: I'm a Catholic. I go to church every Sunday. I'm comfortable with the church. The changes upset my wife a little but they don't bother me very much. The kids at the present time aren't involved. They were when they were younger.

Shirley: It's strange. When I went to Catholic school, we went to church every day. With my kids, I figure after a certain age you can't drag them any more.

Frank Ziemba's own world strikes him as a lot more tranquil than the world that comes to him on the television news and in the newspaper, both of which he follows assiduously. Turmoil in Iran, civil war in Nicaragua, terrorism in Italy, blend into a generalized sense of foreboding for Ziemba. Though his life is pleasant, he would not be surprised to see everything else go to hell in the proverbial handbasket at any moment:

It's always been on the borderline as far as I'm concerned. It's always been touch and go. One day, somebody's going to make a mistake and we're going to have another world war. That's the way I look at it. It's hanging there. Always hanging there. It could break out at any time. Let's just say I don't want to be President. I think Carter is probably not as happy as he thought he would be. It's a hell of a world we're living in, really.

What would he do to change it? Frank's immediate reply was to do something drastic about economic conditions:

Well, with inflation the way it is, if I was President I'd stop everything. It's getting out of hand. I'd make a freeze. Freeze the wages, freeze the prices, just right down the line freeze everything. It's getting out of hand, just getting out of hand. People are paying ten thousand dollars for a car. To me it's just ridiculous. I only paid $13,500 for this home when it was new. [Today it would fetch about $35,000.] People are paying that for a new car. It's just unreal.

Mrs. Ziemba was concerned about declining morals. She seemed genuinely baffled by the soaring divorce rate as she ticked off the divorces in their own neighborhood, shaking her head:

I don't know, it seems like the morals are dropping. A lot of people, if something goes wrong, they just get a divorce. It didn't used to be that way. I really don't know. There is only us and one other couple in the neighborhood who aren't divorced. Mothers with the kids, grandparents with the kids. New husbands. New wives. It isn't the way it used to be.

But for all the dark shadows, strange goings-on, ominous feelings of foreboding, when asked about their own lives, Mr. and Mrs. Frank Ziemba of Madison Heights, Michigan, ended up like this:

Frank: I'm happy. [Turning to his wife] Are you happy?
Shirley: I'm very happy. I think I've got everything. Really. I'd love to have more. More of whatever people seem to have. A bigger house. But when I look at other people, I don't see all that much happiness. We haven't had any problems with our kids. You think you want this or you want that, but really, deep down, I think we're satisfied.

17

POLITICS AND MONEY

"The Average American Smells a Rat, But They Don't Know the Dimensions of It"

There isn't much about politics in this book, because there isn't much spontaneous talk about politics in Middle America. Partly this is because people's immediate lives fill their thoughts and conversation. Partly it is because many Americans believe that their options and priorities count for little when they come in conflict with what "they" want. "They" are the people who make things happen, people only vaguely perceived from the middle ground. The term seems to have religious connotations; it helps explain the unexplainable.

In our conversations "they" ordered the busing of a father's children from suburban Louisville to a downtown ghetto school. "They" shot the Kennedys, Martin Luther King and George Wallace. "They" were blamed for the price of gasoline, the rise and fall of Richard Nixon, fluoride in the water and smog in the air. They got us into the Vietnam war, then refused to win it. They invent schemes for unnecessary defense spending and plot to make us helpless before the communists. Their influence pervades business, government, media and church. Perhaps most important, they are using Middle America's money to subsidize both the rich and the poor.

We knew that "they" belonged in this book, but it wasn't clear how they would get here until Lowell met Bob Pierson. Their chance encounter exemplified the pleasures we had in rounding up something other than the usual suspects to talk about America. Pierson is the lead alto saxophone player in the house orchestra at Caesar's Palace in Las Vegas, but he is also a widely read self-taught political historian who has tried to make a science of "their" role in American life.

Pierson is remembered in Detroit as a mythical sax player who had drifted in and out of the city's once-thriving jazz clubs but left an enduring impression as a musician of consequence. One day he had simply vanished, off on the road to play with big bands or to back up big-name entertainers like Paul Anka.

Then, early one morning in a struggling Las Vegas jazz club, there he was, playing jazz for union scale because he loved to do it.

He was surrounded with a nest of different saxophones and a flute, and the sounds he made were soaring, confident. The flute playing was sensual, almost arrogant. Pierson played jazz standards mostly, nothing exotic, but the crispness of his solos and the warm precision of his imagination had the small but knowledgeable crowd repeatedly on its feet.

So there Lowell stood in a smoky nightclub as dawn approached, talking with this great sweating bear of a man about Detroit, music, his travels. Lowell explained that he was working on a book about Middle America, and suddenly Pierson didn't want to talk about music any more. He wanted to talk politics.

Pierson was something of a scholar. For more than twenty years he has been reading, two and three books at a time, most of them on history and politics. He has read the collected papers of presidents, treatises by European socialists, accounts of war and peace by Russian historians, military histories by students of warfare of half a dozen nationalities. He has waded through diplomatic memoirs and the biographies of American capitalists. Books borrowed, bought and purloined have become his consuming interest outside of music.

As he has read, Pierson has accumulated grievances about the country he lives in:

I kept wondering why people were killing each other. The more I read, the more I became convinced there had to be some kind of renaissance in this country or the whole thing would become a garbage pail. All we do is change heads [of state], the body remains the same.

Married, now in his late forties, the father of two children, Pierson has run for the state legislature in Nevada twice on the quasi-anarchist Libertarian ticket. He was less interested in winning, he said, than in trying to alert the citizenry that the political process is not what it may seem.

Who really runs the country?

I'd say over the years, the Rockefellers, the Mellons, the old, wealthy gentile families. There's the Lehman brothers and, maybe, men like Howard Hughes. You can go on and on. And we have a supercharged military to back up anything they want to do. Defend the oil people, the seven sisters [the biggest international oil firms], no matter what. This is international money, the multinational conglomerates are pulling the strings. Along with the other lobbies. It's an unholy situation. It's like Anglicized Nazism. We've got socialism for the rich. And we're playing around with a kind of serfdom.

The great lie is that inflation is caused by higher wages. That's all bullshit. It's caused because we mortgaged our goddamn ass for armament. We've built more of it since the Second World War than the rest of the world combined since the beginning of history. Once you've got a country hooked on your arms, it's like having them hooked on heroin. The Russians are even better at it than we are. Now who's a threat to World peace?

But who controls the country, who owns it?

I try to separate facts from opinions. The average American smells a rat, but they don't know the dimensions of it. That isn't the only reason for the problems in our society, but it's one of the big ones. I just don't feel there's any honest leadership at all. The only one I would have given you two cents for was John Kennedy. He came from the power elite that runs this country, but I felt that I could trust him, and the other Kennedys with all their faults. I wasn't looking for the messiah. I know better.

I think the only mistake the Kennedys made was that even though they were of that ilk, they didn't realize who they were threatening and they got their heads blown off. This country's got nine intelligence agencies that we know of. What's going to happen when you go around making statements that you're going to cut the oil depletion allowance, cut the CIA in a thousand pieces. Bobby Kennedy had his vendetta against Hoffa. Well, I don't believe in miracles.

Pierson thought it was typical in American history to discover conspiratorial explanations for events years after they occurred:

For example, about two years ago I did a lot of reading on the Spanish-American War. Even George Kennan, who was the dean of our ambassadors, admits there was a deal made in the Cabinet. That's as far as he'll go. But the war was over in Cuba and we acquired Puerto Rico and the Philippines. When you look back on it, Patty Hearst's grandfather was the coordinator of all the forces that wanted the Spaniards out of there. Included were what was left of the aristocracy of the South, oddly enough, who hated the Spanish for freeing slaves before the Civil War. That was one thing, along with the people of the North who were going to make a buck, et cetera. Since his newspapers were a big thing, Hearst was the one who promoted this thing. Remember the Maine.

I think it was all premeditated, because, my God, every Spanish ship of the line was sixty years old. They were wooden. We built the great white fleet to take them. What the hell, Wall Street made the decision on the First World War. The Second World War, we were more prepared for it than Germany was. We were the sole armorer of the Japanese during the 'thirties. I just don't buy all these accidental things that are always happening to us. They go back into antiquity. Back 4500 years ago, they authenticate the fact that there was collusion and conspiracy between nations where the average—pardon the expression—schmuck didn't know anything about it.

I see the situation as being basically the same. I don't call people stupid. "Ignorant" would be the best word to describe it. They're turned off by it. They don't want to hear anything about it. I say politics, it isn't just politics, it's history. They get mad at me. Like the old maxim, What's past is prologue. I mean that's just a fact. If you don't want to pay attention then you're going to be in a lot of trouble.

If you're right, why are so many Middle Americans relatively happy?

I know. I'm certainly well aware of that. But what comes home is the situation when I went over to buy a piece of furniture. It was like 'sixty-eight. The woman I was talking with said something about the war and I let off a volley of invective towards what it was. I don't think that ninety-five percent of the people know how the war in Indochina got started. She brought on the fact that in mid-America, Iowa or Kansas, the nineteen-year-old son of a friend of theirs had just gotten killed. They couldn't come to grips with that. They were doing well. Well, if that's the price you want to pay, then you're going to pay it. Unfortunately, the rest of us pay it too.

I'd certainly like to make people aware that a lot of these people running around talking about the Lord, or whatever they're talking about, are nothing more than ancient predators. They may come in a nice business suit with a lovely smile, but I'm not fooled by that. I think that's the only big mistake John Kennedy made. He didn't know just because he was one of them. He didn't know. He should have.

Do you have a secret ambition?

I'd like to be a senator. But if you do it right, it won't work. Everybody I like gets shot.

Pierson's interest in political matters makes him wildly atypical of Middle America, but a central element of his point of view is so typical as to be nearly universal. That is Pierson's implicit certainty that the powerful are different than people like him, and are moved by considerations that seem alien to him. Pierson has reacted to this perception by becoming deeply involved personally in studying and practicing politics. Most Middle Americans react to it by ignoring politics and political issues, or reserving only a small compartment of their consciousness for them.

The postwar boom in America created a curious circumstance. Whereas in the 1930s Franklin D. Roosevelt's New Deal seemed vividly relevant to the daily lives of the bulk of Americans, the spread of prosperity and of suburban living increasingly separated an ever-growing segment of the population from personal exposure to the issues that animated national politics. While the political process seemed mired in narrow or irrelevant issues, the new American society produced conflicts and problems of intense interest to Middle Americans that the politicians either ignored or were helpless to deal with.

For example, the spread of drugs through the culture is a source of alarm and agony for many Middle Americans; this is a phenomenon with a life of its own, one that seems to many to be responsible for a profound discontinuity in American life. The politicians have made fitful attempts to *do something* about drugs—Richard Nixon even created a Gestapo-like federal police force to try to dry up the drug trade—but without palpable effect. Perhaps sensing their powerlessness, most politicians avoid the subject altogether.

Politicians have failed to control interest rates on borrowed money, though nothing has done more to alter the accessibility of a home of one's own—a fundamental American dream—than higher interest rates. (Statistically, the average American income has kept up with the cost of the average American house, but the doubling of interest rates over the past twenty years has substantially increased the burden of monthly mortgage payments, even allowing for inflation.)

Judicial decisions have transformed many aspects of American life and created turmoil (or at least the perception of turmoil) in the lives of millions of citizens. Judges, not politicians, integrated America's races, often with extreme remedies like school busing. Judges, not politicians, sanctioned many of the liberalizing trends in the society, by legalizing abortion for example. During the last generation, judicial decisions have probably had more direct impact on the lives of Middle Americans than all the acts of Congress and proclamations of presidents, except perhaps for those proclamations that gave us the war in Vietnam. Yet the judges seem utterly out of reach to Middle Americans, and the politicians offer no prospect of bringing them under control.

Control, in fact, is just what the political process has *not* offered to Middle Americans. Perhaps the best single example of this has been the fate of the public schools. Because of court decisions, increasingly influential federal policies and—in many areas—the new militancy of organized teachers, the public schools have passed beyond the control of the communities they serve. At the same time, schools are conveyors of the aspects of the youth culture, particularly drugs, that most alarm parents. And if all this were not enough, Middle Americans have now been given abundant evidence that their kids can pass through the schools without learning very much. But despite all their shortcomings, the schools continue to extract from the populace—usually through the ubiquitous property tax—large amounts of cash.

The positive accomplishments of the political process during the last twenty years or so have generally benefited the Americans who fall below the Middle American category that is our subject here. One exception is the Medicare law, which has set off a subtle revolution in the way Americans deal with old people by substantially reducing the dependence of elderly citizens on their children. But most of the programs of "big government" are either taken for granted (like Social Security) or aimed at the poor or disadvantaged. And in the perception of Middle America, most of them don't seem to work. At least they don't eliminate the poor and the disadvantaged, despite their apparent ability to devour vast quantities of revenue.

So it seems no surprise that politics as currently practiced fails to capture the imagination or even the interest of so many Americans. Politicians bewail the failure of half the population to exercise its vote, but they might just as well express delight and amazement that so many—fully half!—do vote (in presidential elections, anyhow; about a third vote in congressional elections). Lacking the belief that politics will ever do much for them personally, Americans must generate a good deal of abstract enthusiasm to participate in the process as much as they do.

In recent years the only politicians who have really been able to make the electricity start to flow in Middle America have been political outlaws, those who—by design or happenstance—find themselves outside the traditional system. George Wallace, for example, or Bella Abzug, Howard Jarvis, Jerry Brown. Jimmy Carter started off with a bit of this too; at least he exploited the notion that since the traditional politicians had messed everything up so badly, perhaps something new was needed.

Any prognosis about the future of American politics seems perilous, given the potential instability of the present situation. If any movement or individual succeeded in mobilizing the indifferent masses, there is no telling where that might lead.

"The Number One Motivating Force"

The field in which politicians have most vividly demonstrated their inability to impose control is economics. Americans have come to accept the idea that the federal government should be responsible for the state of the national economy, but a succession of presidents have revealed a persistent incompetence in this area. Stagnation, inflation and recession are now a normal, repetitive sequence of events— a sequence that can infuriate Americans while it reminds them of their political leaders' failures.*

---

* This repetitive cycle has less real impact on the lives of middle class Americans than might be expected, since the overwhelming majority of them seem to be protected against the consequences of both inflation and recession. Inflation raises both incomes and expenditures, but in recent times the two generally have kept pace, particularly for the better-off Americans who are our subject here. Recessions, too, tend to hit the lower end of the economic scale much harder than the middle class, especially when a recession leads to layoffs. But the psychological impact on the middle class of inflation and recession is obviously strong.

In America in the late 1970s, the only political issues that touch the lives of all citizens are those involving money. During 1978, the politicians and the pundits concluded that inflation was one subject that people really cared about, so it quickly became their principal preoccupation. (As a result, a new recession—a product of sterner anti-inflationary policies—was a distinct possibility at the beginning of 1979, when this book went to the printer.)

The politicians' rush to do something about inflation was understandable. In Middle America, money is of paramount importance. Al Rosen, the president of the New York Yankees, explained it:

Money is the number one motivating force in most people's lives. And I say "most people" only because I'm sure there are some scientists who couldn't care less if they ever made a dime as long as they came up with another polio cure or something like that.

In other words, if there is somebody who doesn't put money ahead of everything else, he must be some kind of mad scientist. This is a commonplace sentiment, sometimes hedged ritualistically with "money-can't-buy-everything" reservations, and shared by most of the Americans we talked with.

No dream is more basic or more powerful than the American dream of great wealth. In its pursuit we succumb to all variety of schemes and ruses. Most Americans seem to share an awe for those of their countrymen who do strike it rich. Few complain that the tax code is so generous to the wealthy, or that what purports to be the world's fairest society imposes taxes on inherited wealth that are among the lowest in the industrial world. Americans make mythic figures of their Fords and Rockefellers.

Ironically, the clearest expressions of American egalitarianism involve money. We tend to equate net worth with human worth, a formula that allows each of us to imagine acquiring all the fame that— well, that money can buy. Thus the bellhop in a Las Vegas hotel who measured a man's social standing entirely by the size of his tips. Thus Muhammad Ali's heartfelt belief that he really has been "The Greatest." If he wasn't, why would people pay him more for forty-five minutes' work than the presidents of large corporations can earn in ten years? "Money talks" is not an expression that the Pilgrims brought with them from England. It is an American sentiment.

Money is America's standard unit of measurement. So, for example, in this book we define Middle America in money terms. We define it as that category of the population between the richest 5 percent and the poorest 40 percent or so. This gives us a group of at least 110 million people.

The available statistics on the money earnings of Americans are frustratingly imprecise. A figure for the national median income, for example, would probably impress the residents of Bellows Falls, Vermont, or Yazoo City, Mississippi, as high, but would make a New Yorker or a San Franciscan wonder how people are getting by. Local variations are enormous. To cite a typical one, the average family buying a home for the first time in San Francisco in 1977 earned $26,000 a year and paid $72,000 for the house. A comparable family in Portland, Oregon, earned about $16,900 and paid $35,500 for the house.* Yet both families share the same economic status in their communities, and both are demonstrably members of the middle class.

Such variations make it difficult to find much meaning in the crude national statistics. They offer at best a rough guide. In early 1979 the median income of the average family (about 3.35 persons) was approximately $18,500. This means as many families made more than $18,500 as made less. The average family income was somewhat higher. If that average family actually existed, one could say it would do quite nicely living in Portland, but have a rough time in San Francisco. But of course that family does not exist.

Statistics published by the Bureau of the Census do offer more meaningful figures than the national averages. For example, they show that the average income of families that include at least one adult who holds a full-time, year-round job was about $24,000 at the beginning of 1979. (About 60 percent of all families fall into that category.) The average family headed by an adult between the ages of thirty-five and fifty-four earned roughly that amount too. Families in large metropolitan areas earn about a quarter more than those in small towns, and a third more than those in rural areas.

A rough rule of thumb accepted by many demographers is that a family earning at least three times the official "poverty level" qualifies

* The statistics were compiled by the U.S. League of Savings Associations.

for middle class status. In 1977 the government's poverty level was $6191 for a "non-farm" family of four. Three times that—$18,500—should provide some significant discretionary income, allowing for a few luxuries, a vacation trip, a second car—some of the privileges of the modern bourgeoisie. Three times the poverty level also virtually coincides with the median income nationally, suggesting again that 40 to 50 percent of the total population falls below our Middle America.

The distribution of income characteristic of the late 1970s has not changed significantly since Richard Nixon was first elected President. The boom of the 1960s effectively completed the postwar transformation of American society, establishing the great middle class as the largest element in the society. The percentage of Americans left out of the new mainstream has remained constant ever since.

Of course the gross numbers have changed a lot since 1969, thanks to inflation. During the 1970s prices and incomes have risen about 75 percent. Because both rose together, real buying power has remained virtually the same for ten years.

Inflation has become commonplace, and a lot of Americans have come to count on it. But it is no less disquieting for that. Inflation scares people. If it's true that we measure our human worth by our net worth—and that's what Americans tend to do—then inflation is an uncontrollable, alien force that can eat away not only at bank accounts but at self-esteem.

Tony Jackson has been watching inflation for years, both taking advantage of it and worrying about it. Jackson is forty-nine, a country boy from outside Charlotte, North Carolina, who has spent most of his adult life working in credit unions, the new banking institutions for America's new middle class. He is a smallish, roundish man with a high forehead and curly hair. Now he is the director of a credit union with 15,000 members, all of them school employees in Fairfax County, Virginia:

I've been recommendin' people who almost can't afford a home to buy it. Why pay rent? Because the inflation of a house, the appreciation of value will bail them out in the long run. Of course if we have a drop in the real estate market a lot of people are going to get hurt. I think in the past people have learned from the situation. They've seen this happen time and time again, and they've just about got around to thinkin', Well,

I'm not going to make the same mistake again. So they don't mind going in debt, because they know tomorrow that debt will be insignificant. And they're gamblin' that this thing's gonna keep on rollin'.

I think inflation's by design, I really do. I think they're deliberately doin' it [the government]. They're deliberately doin' it because that's just about the only way they can justify the debt they've created. If we had deflation of the dollar, the government would find itself owing the same amount of money. They're going to owe $300 billion regardless of what the dollar's worth or revenue's worth. This inflation bails the government out from their past follies, you see.

I think really that if inflation doesn't stop, there's gonna be a day of reckoning. I don't feel that you can control inflation. Once it gets out of hand, it's unstoppable. We've seen it happen around the world. Why can't it happen in the United States?

I don't deny that the United States has resources, tremendous resources. I can't imagine the United States ever bein' a bankrupt country. In land and resources we have— We could back up anything we print. However, the dollar bill is only a medium of exchange, and it's only as good as the other man says it is.

Tony Jackson jumped back and forth this way between gloom and optimism during a long conversation. He reads the business pages and a number of private business forecasts; he watches the janitors, bus drivers and schoolteachers who belong to his credit union plot their private economic futures; and he is clearly confused, though he doesn't want to put it that way.

His members are actually saving a lot as a hedge against inflation, yet they are saving dollars of declining value, which could be used to acquire assets that are less vulnerable to inflation than greenbacks. Yes, he sees the contradiction, but equally he insists that is what is happening. (Many banks report the same phenomenon.) But some people are plunging into expensive homes on the theory that today's onerous debt will be lightened by the future's inevitable inflation. Johnson hedges his conversation with periodic references to the possibility of future downturns in the real estate market or deflation of the dollar, but these were ritualistic remarks. During the conversation, he revealed that he himself had recently bought an expensive new house, doubling his mortgage payment to $500 a month.

Johnson also explained how matters of personal finance have found their way into the great American buffet in these inflationary times:

There is a tendency today to go bankrupt. Bankruptcies are occurring more than they used to. A lot of people think it's better just to go bankrupt and not worry about it. It doesn't have a stigma attached to it—just like divorce. Society bein' what it is, you know, it's no longer a black mark against you.

I recommend bankruptcy in a lot of cases. Person comes in, and I can see he's got no way out, no way out. Medical costs—that alone is the biggest cause of bankruptcy. An illness in the family and they just absolutely cannot pay those bills. It just puts them in a hole they can't get out of. And I believe they should go bankrupt, definitely. People that could possibly for five, six years sweat it out, I've told 'em, "Don't do it; it's not worth it. You may think you're savin' pride and all that, but your pride is the fact that you didn't put yourself in this position, and so there ain't nothin' to be ashamed of. That's why the bankruptcy law was created."

Most bankruptcy in middle class America is not brought on by the classic confrontation between excessive obligations and inadequate resources. Millions of Middle Americans routinely carry debts that are larger than their assets. That's now the American way. As a result, private debt in the United States totals about one trillion dollars. Middle American bankruptcy typically is provoked by excessive *payments* every month, a question of monthly incomings failing to keep up with contractual outgoings.

This is part of the new American psychology of money, a subject too little studied or understood. In a society of mortgage loans, revolving credit plans, credit cards, credit unions and so forth, money loses its absolute, concrete value. People show scant concern for the ultimate value of things or money; they concentrate instead on getting by from month to month.

Paul Renner has learned something about the psychology of money by spending a lifetime in small-town banks. He is now the president of the Gettysburg National Bank in Gettysburg, Pennsylvania, and he has the square-faced demeanor and three-piece suits that fit that job. Renner grew up nearby in south-central Pennsylvania, an area of farms and small manufacturing enterprises. He never got to college, but over the years he has gained an education:

People read about inflation, the devaluation of the dollar and so forth, and yet to them the real things is the grocery basket—that's probably what we hear the most complaint about. The people are funny, you know. You've got any number of people who will raise all kinds of heck and havoc about the price of a loaf of bread or a quart of milk, and won't think nothing of walking up to a bar and ordering a double scotch and they don't even ask the price. There are just some things that are more sensitive, when you raise prices on them.

The price of new cars has about doubled during the 1970s, but according to Renner the buying public has absorbed this easily, not least because banks now offer forty-two- and forty-eight-month loans to finance car purchases, whereas they once lent money to buy a car for just thirty-six months. "Unfortunately, people relate to payments, not necessarily to principal. It's what you can afford."

Renner had another story about the psychology of money:

We have people who will come into the bank and they will borrow money for a new car. Now they could go to the savings department and draw the money out and pay cash for the new car, but there's two reasons why they don't. First of all, they know that if they take it out of the savings account they won't put it back, but if they make a loan they will pay that off. Now there's an interest rate difference between what the bank is paying on those savings and what it's charging for the loan, but they are willing to pay that difference—and I'm not so sure they're wrong, don't you see. They've got a reserve that they don't have to ask anyone for, it's theirs. Part of the reason they're going the loan route is a lack of discipline that many of us have. If we're not obligated we don't do it. So what they do is borrow money to save their savings, and I don't think it's all wrong.

Renner acknowledged something that Tony Johnson refused to admit, though he bought himself a new house on the assumption it was true: Inflation can help people as well as agonize them:

We've seen tremendous increases in the value of real estate, particularly in the rural sections. We've seen farms double, triple, even quadruple in price. And inflation here has in some ways been a blessing. It's something like our national debt: Where do we balance the ledger? Or do we ever?

For example, we can talk about a farmer who hasn't been able successfully to justify his operations, because of his costs, but who has been able to survive and stay with it because inflation has been his benefactor. He has been able to have lending power and to keep going because the value of his capital goods—his land—has increased so rapidly. It's kept him going, even to the point where eventually he can sell out for a tremendous price and is able to put some kind of savings back and retire. And just on the basis of farm economics this farmer could never have cut it were it not for inflation. Now I'm not an advocate of inflation, but there is some good with the bad, just like anything else.

Because inflation is a political issue that touches every American's life, it poses special dangers for politicians. The world's best economists fail satisfactorily to explain inflation, so it is not surprising that ordinary citizens are baffled by it. "They don't understand it," as Tony Johnson put it, "but they blame the government for it."

Inflation gives Americans something to worry about, something to complain about, something to vote about. The windy analysts who perceived in Proposition 13 and other manifestations of the "tax revolt" of the late 1970s some elaborate expression of displeasure with "big government" were missing the point. More precisely, they were putting their concerns and their ways of thinking into the heads of Middle Americans who actually share neither. Dramatic reductions in taxes represent an answer to the effects of inflation, and surely appeal to Middle America for that reason.

In the late 1970s it appears that many middle class Americans are beginning to think of the political process as a tool they may be able to use to assert their rights—particularly their economic rights— as a class. Proposition 13 and the commotion it set off smack of a kind of class warfare. This doesn't have to be the racism attributed by some to Californians who supported Proposition 13, or others who joined the "tax revolt" in different ways. One can be relatively pure of heart and still succumb to the temptation to cast a vote that offers the tangible prospect of immediate cash reward.

In fact, Middle Americans have long been effective in using politics to achieve narrow objectives to preserve their immediate interests. This effectiveness has foiled most efforts to place public housing or other subsidized shelter for poor people in middle class neighborhoods, for example. In community after community, the burghers have risen up to block such proposals. The new tax fever set off by Proposition

13 suggests that the stage on which the middle class can struggle for its "rights" can now be enlarged.

In a generation the social and economic structure of America has been transformed, with enormous political consequences. FDR offered a New Deal to a substantial majority of Americans, members of the great industrial working class and the rural poor. The beneficiaries of the New Deal had disadvantage in common. Now the natural majority of Americans is privileged by the standards of the 1930s. It is much easier to muster 51 percent of the votes on behalf of the haves than for the have-nots. Perhaps we are entering a time when Middle Americans will realize that "they" are really "us," or could be.

18

BAD NEWS

The decline of civic pride symbolized by the great American apathy toward politics is one example of the bad news we found in Middle America. There is plenty more, and some of it follows in the next three sections.

Part of the national defense mechanism—a clause in the unwritten insurance policy that protects American optimism—is a general agreement not to dwell on bad news, and to accept the deals the culture makes with itself. So, for example, if we want to build a society based on the automobile, we must also accept 50,000 dead on the highways every year—in large measure because we have established alcohol as the society's principal social lubricant, and can find no way to separate cars from alcohol. The cultural definition of freedom includes the freedom to keep and shoot off guns, so there are 150 million guns in private hands in America, and guns now kill more than 13,000 of us every year.

American values: We spend four times as much on tobacco as on books; twice as much on booze as on all religious and charitable activities; more on toilet articles and preparations than on our parks. Bad values? Bad question, one we generally don't ask. Democracy speaks for itself. There may be anomalies, but they are the result of *freedom* (as in "Gino's Gives You Freedom of Choice").

Ordinary Americans tend to be fatalists about their society's foibles and failures. The Puritan strains once so important in American ideology have been diluted.

We have decided to be fatalists too, in the sense that we are devoting very little space to things Middle Americans don't often think or talk about—like bad news. There is no moral lesson in this movie. We have ducked a lot of hard questions. For example, do the customers of the great American buffet have much prospect of discovering their own human creativity or the limits of their moral or intellectual powers? We tried once or twice to ask a question like that, and got funny looks instead of answers.

However, we kept running into reminders that there is room for moral questions and moral lessons in contemporary America, and some of those reminders deserve noting here.

Troubles

Professor Craig Walton, a compact, muscular man who bubbles with nervous energy, is an eager social critic. He enjoys outraging his students at the University of Nevada. Sometimes students walk out of his classes:

When I get to racism in my moral issues class—people quit. It's extremely difficult to get people to think about it or talk about it. It's all worked out now in a lot of people's minds—that yes, there's going to be a certain amount of public posturing that tells us we shouldn't have these opinions, but fuck it, we do have them, and we know we're right. "Look at those people in the ghettos; you've seen 'em on television"— and that's the end of it. There is no perceived cost in being a racist. On the contrary, there is a scary amount of willingness to talk about it.

Ruby Duncan is an enormous woman, built like a defensive tackle, but with a lovely face and a very appealing manner. She has big eyes and a quick smile, and it is hard not to like her. She is poor and black—not one of the Americans this book is about. She too came to Las Vegas to seek her fortune:

I came from the backwoods of Louisiana, and I came to Las Vegas about twenty-three years ago. We had been hearing about this great big rich world, that you could really just come out and get a job and make money and eventually be prosperous. Well, when I got here I found out it was a fraction different. Getting a job wasn't quite that easy, and once I did get a job it wasn't the type of money that I guess some people were talkin' about. But it was much more money than they would make in Louisiana, because I was workin' at a drugstore in Tallulah, Louisiana, makin' like nine dollars and fifty cent a week, and from eight o'clock in the morning till eight o'clock in the evening, and when I got here you could at least make nine dollar and fifty cent a day.

Did you come alone?

Well, uh, yes, I come along with two children. And then after getting here and being here for a while, I guess I had more children, so I'm the mother of seven children.

The story of Ruby Duncan's life in the big city is a long odyssey of the American underclass. "All of a certain some bad things happened, and I had to go on welfare," she recalled. She tried to go back to work, but injured herself in a fall, and went back to welfare. She told the long story with a keen sense of detail—how she slipped on a greasy spot in the restaurant kitchen where she worked while rushing to bring the boss himself the grapefruit he always had for breakfast. She always fixed his grapefruit. "I guess I must have fixed a very good grapefruit." The fall injured her back, which has never been the same.

But Ms. Duncan is too engaged with life, too bright and energetic, to end up just another welfare mother. She soon found herself an organizer of welfare recipients and a spokesman for the city's poor. She terrorized Las Vegas's establishment by leading a march of welfare mothers and children down the city's Strip, past the gaudy monuments to conspicuous consumption that gave the city its reputation. Bravado like that made Ruby Duncan something of a national figure. Now she flies to Washington regularly to testify before Congress and other government agencies.

Would she compare the world she sees in the hotels and casinos to her own community about five miles away, a neighborhood of unpainted bungalows and liquor stores that looks a lot like Watts in Los Angeles?

Whether you know it or not, this area of town has nothing to offer. Over there you can just look at people and tell that they're just creamy rich, and then you comes over here and here's a family don't have $125 to pay its rent or sixteen dollars to pay its light bill. I really feel that there is too much richness for some people, and not enough for other people to survive. Eventually something has got to happen for some of this richness to be shared with people that really need it.

Can a poor kid growing up on welfare today take seriously the civics book lessons about the land of the free, the land of opportunity, everybody can be President—that kind of stuff?
No. I mean that's really silly.

In 1976, according to a survey of 145,000 American students, only one-third of the seventeen-year-olds questioned could explain correctly how a candidate for President of the United States is nominated. Just four years earlier, in a similar survey, half the seventeen-year-olds could offer a correct explanation.

On the other hand, young people have become much more conscious of the rights of persons accused of crime. In a survey of thirteen-year-olds the question was asked, "Are police allowed to keep an arrested person in jail until they collect the evidence against him, however long that takes?" In 1970, 41 percent of the thirteen-year-olds answered yes, 53 percent said no. By 1976, only 24 percent said yes, and 73 percent knew the right answer.

"Explanations for this change can only be suppositions," commented the National Assessment of Educational Progress, which conducted the surveys. "One hypothesis might be that the rising number of television shows about police and lawyers had contributed to thirteen-year-old improvement in this area."

Americans consume more alcohol than any other people on earth. In 1977, 2.7 gallons of straight alcohol (200 proof) were consumed in the United States for every citizen sixteen years old or older.

But according to the National Clearing House for Alcohol Information, a third of the country's over-sixteen population doesn't drink, leaving about 100 million drinkers. On average, then, every drinker consumes each *week* a quart of distilled spirits, ten cans of beer and half a bottle of wine. But of course many moderate drinkers consume much less than that, so many others consume much more.

There are said to be 10 million alcoholics in the United States. The total economic cost of alcohol abuse is reckoned to be about $43 billion a year—about $290 per adult in the entire population. This includes workdays and productivity lost because of drinking, the cost of auto accidents caused by drinking, etc.

Per capita consumption of alcohol is up by a third since 1960, and is growing steadily.

According to a survey reported by the Department of Health, Education and Welfare, 13 percent of American men between the ages of twenty and seventy-four and 23 percent of the women in the same age group were found to be "obese" by actual skin-fold measurements that determined the amount of excess fatty tissue in their bodies. About a fourth of all adult males and half the adult females consider themselves overweight, the same survey found.

Tony Addabo is just forty, a successful contractor who recently opened a new resort hotel built by his firm and owned by a partnership of which he is a senior member. Though he had no previous experience as a hotelier, he did have boundless self-confidence, and he decided to run the place by himself. Was this an interesting experience, starting up a new hotel?

Well, it starts to put seeds into your mind that stink, quite frankly.

We wanted people working here that were youthful, willing to work, and who would support the environment that we're trying to put together. We went through fourteen thousand applications, but we did the best we could do. We had ten or fifteen people selecting the employees. It inundated us. We spent a lot of time with these employees. We put together a handbook with a lot of neat things; we advocated benefits for the employees that had never been done around here before. We spent an awful lot of money up front; we even spent money on some training. And when the doors were opened, the thing that really took me back more than anything was the amount of theft within this house [i.e., the hotel] that started taking place—before we opened and after we opened. Everybody had an angle. *Every*body had an angle. Well, there's some exceptions, I'm sure, but the majority. This really destroys your mind. Did me.

Because it was twenty-four hours a day, the stuff was walking out of the back of the house, the side of the house. We had maids taking from the supplies and from the rooms, and they're going up on the roof— you have to leave the door open for the fire marshal—and throwing stuff off the building into pickups down below [fifteen stories!] where

their husbands or boyfriends were waiting. We had the instruments of
the band that was here stolen off the stage. The food was going out
the door as fast as it was coming in. Chairs—anything and everything.
It just plants a seed in your head that says, "Really, what the hell are
you beating your head against the wall for? Why did you go down to
that bank and sign a $24 million mortgage?"

During the course of a year, merchandise worth $10 million is
stolen from Macy's main store on Herald Square in New York. The
merchants of metropolitan Detroit estimate that their aggregate losses
to shoplifters add up to more than $450,000 a day. "Shoplifting may
be our most serious problem," a Miami department store executive
told the New York *Times.* "We have caught priests, lawyers, doctors,
teachers, pilots. You name it, and we've caught them."

A spokesman for the Famous-Barr Company in St. Louis, the
city's largest store, told the *Times* that his firm had come to a discourag-
ing conclusion about why shoplifting losses have continued to increase
despite elaborate new security measures. Apparently, employees of
the store who received special training to detect the cleverest shoplifters
have used their new knowledge to steal from the store themselves.

Department stores estimate that the costs of losses and of maintaining their own security forces add as much as 10 percent to the retail
prices of the goods they sell.

Enough of that. We have no intention—and no ability—to resolve
these troubles, but they seemed worth mentioning.

Old

There is one group of Middle Americans that lives apart from
the rest, less happy, less hopeful, less enthusiastic: the old. Time has
expired on their dreams. They are often left out.

Of course, old is what a great many Americans are trying desper-
ately not to be, regardless of their actual age. So, old is bad for many
not because they have calculated the advantages and disadvantages
and reached this verdict but simply by instinct. If the goal is to run
with the Pepsi generation, to stay young, think young and feel young,
then old *must* be bad.

There is an eerie consciousness of this among young Middle Americans who are still decades away from old age themselves. Many of the people we met brought up the perils of old age spontaneously, without being asked. We found a lot of guilt about the way the elderly are treated in this country. And a high percentage of the unhappy people we met were themselves old.

For example, an elderly couple from Pittsburgh who were waiting in a hotel lobby to be assigned a room. They declined to give their names, and at first declined to talk into a tape recorder, but after a few minutes of conversation they didn't seem to notice when it was turned on. They are plain-looking people, he without much hair, she with a boxy figure and those familiar plastic-rimmed eyeglasses that sweep up and away from the nose like wings.

What kind of shape is the country in?
  Terrible, terrible.

What's it going to be like in ten years?
  She: Everybody's going to be on dole, welfare. It's going to be like England.
  He: That's right. The government's going to have to support all the people who aren't working.
  She: For example, in our little community we have a dairy store; they serve lunches. This colored boy started working there as a cleanup boy. He said "Uh, uh, this is too hard work for me. I'm going back on welfare." He was about twenty years old. That's the way they feel. They can make more on welfare than they can working. Doesn't seem right.

Looking back over your lifetime, what was the best period in American life that you experienced?
  He: When I was about seventeen years old, and you could buy something with a dollar bill. [Does he really mean "When I was young and just starting out?"] The government didn't take everything off you.

We're interested in dreams—what people are hoping for.
  She: We're a little too old to have many dreams about the future, you know? We're both retired. All we want to do is be comfortable and have our money be good. Good enough to live on. That's our hope.
  He: In other words, to go on a vacation we have to save all year long. Just to go on a vacation. They give you a fifteen-dollar raise on Social Security and the rent goes up thirty-five or forty dollars a month.

How has life in your community changed over the years?
  She: Oh, tremendously. Dope in junior high. It's gotten very bad.
  He: The generation coming up—you can't trust anybody. Prices are going up sky high, but your income is standard and that's where it stays.
  I feel sorry for the kids today. Like I say, years ago you could give a kid fifty cents and he'd have a good time. Today they want a five-dollar bill or a ten, or better. And they buy those hot dogs and Pepsi-Cola and that's it. It takes them a five-dollar bill just to get a Pepsi or something. Years ago for half a dollar you could go to a show, things of that sort.

Do you think the younger generation today has good standards?
  No, absolutely not.
  She: Yes, some of them do. Now you take our nephews—
  He: But they're exceptional kids.
  She: Well, I'll grant you that.

What do you think went wrong?
  He: The parents are letting them run free.
  She: They're too permissive, they need more paddling.

  There was a perfunctory quality to that conversation, as though these two tired and old people had better things to do than tell some stranger the facts of life. And that was what they were talking about—facts of life, their sad and rather lonely and now almost-ended lives. They had no children of their own, which may have exaggerated their sense of disconnection with the younger generations.

  But the tone of that exchange was not unusual in our conversations with old people. It recurred in the observations of a man from Los Angeles who runs a chain of men's stores, a much more comfortable fellow than that couple from Pittsburgh. He too declined to give his name, but he liked talking. Small, white-haired, trim, looking all of his sixty-five years, he sat by a swimming pool and explained.

  I have two grandchildren. I don't know what's going to happen. I don't think I'll be here to see it, but it's got me worried.
  The prices on everything is up. Most of the people can't afford it. You go into a market in Los Angeles, you walk out with a little bag for about fourteen dollars. Most of the people are on relief. They don't want to work. We have fellows working for us who as soon as they leave us they try to get on unemployment. They're making more on unemployment. They don't have to work.

It's no good worrying about it. There's nothing you can do. You take in Los Angeles—the apartments, the rents. If you get a year lease you're lucky. To even get a lease. As soon as your lease is up, the guy raises your rent. You can't get out. There's nothing better.

You see in the paper the different things that are happening. I'm originally from Philadelphia, but I've been in Los Angeles so long I'm like a native. But I go back to Philadelphia and I'm shocked to see the way things are back there. Ninety percent or eighty percent is colored back there now. You're afraid to walk around the street. But we're afraid to walk anywhere. Even Los Angeles. They don't walk at night.

I can't understand kids. I don't know whether it's family or it's dope, all this marijuana and this stuff. I'm scared of what's going to happen later on. You see some of these kids and you figure these kids are going to run the country someday. I don't know.

I'm glad I was born in my generation. I know that I never did or would never do to my father and mother what these kids do today. They have no respect for them. They don't care.

John Licini is about the same age as that unhappy clothing dealer, but he has found a different way to cope. Licini is a professional gambler—a real professional gambler, which means he does not gamble his own money, he works for the house. He started out in Detroit in the 1930s, then moved to Florida, working in gambling at times and in places where this could get a man a prison sentence. Then the state of Nevada allowed John Licini to practice his trade openly and legally, which he has been doing for a generation. He is tall and elegant.

It's a different civilization today. I don't know whether it's good or bad. As you know, you read in the newspapers—morals are different, the whole thing. To you, being part of this generation, maybe that's the normal way. To me, being older, I'd say it's very difficult for me to accept it. I have changed, because if you don't change you're going to get lost, right? And I think that the only thing in this world that is constant is change, and if you resist that change you have to go backwards.

Do you worry now about your grandchildren, their world?

No, I don't think so. I have four children and six grandchildren. I don't worry. My wife might, but I don't, because I'm part of this, you know, where she isn't. She can get excited over a headline or what she sees on the news or whatever's being discussed in the way of what the students are doing, the younger generation. But I don't. I feel it's a way of life. And it might be good, it might be bad, but it eventually will be good, I think. Nothing continues if it's bad. Good always continues. It'll always come to the top. Might take a little longer, but they'll find it.

The religions are changing, everything's changing. I'm a Catholic, right? The religion has changed in the last five years to where my wife says, "Hold on, I sometimes wonder if I'm in the Catholic Church." But not the youngster. They're dealing to the youngster, allowing guitars to be played, allowing 'em to kind of make entertainment of the mass, rather than to have that solemn Latin-type dignified mass. My wife don't like it, but she's— She's going the other way, the kids are coming up, and that's what they're looking for.

They're dealing to the kids, as the old gambler put it: a slogan for our times.

But the times do not entirely cooperate with that spirit. The number of old people is growing steadily, and the average age of the population is rising. Americans are not good at coping with the old, but the institution of Medicare—federally financed health care for the elderly—has created a new way to deal with the problem. We now farm out our old—institutionalize them in nursing homes and other facilities that Medicare helps pay for. This has been one of America's great growth industries. In 1964, 2.7 per cent of Americans were institutionalized; now the figure is about 5 per cent.

In a culture preoccupied with youth, being old isn't much fun. Traditional cultures eased this stage of life with veneration, but we offer little of that in America. Instead, an old person's daily life is filled with reminders that the principal preoccupations of the society exclude him or her almost by definition. At the same time, old people often suffer the most from the frenetic changes that are typical of the society, from changes in the value of a dollar to transformations of entire neighborhoods.

Not surprisingly, America has put old age on the buffet table too. People with enough money can buy their way out of the usual dilemmas of the elderly—or try to—by uprooting themselves and transplanting to Florida or Arizona or Southern California, to a "retirement" community where they will be surrounded by people like them. This is a relatively new dream, a dream for the ultimately mobile society: Let's work hard and save money so that when we reach retirement we can leave family and friends and have a chance to start afresh in the sun, the easy life at last.

Outside Looking In

There is bad news in our definition of Middle America. We have defined at least 100 million Americans out of it. The category is enormous, but so is the number of Americans who don't qualify, and who look up at the Middle Americans with awe or envy.

Kaiser met two of them one afternoon—two young women who were wandering through the Cecil B. De Mille splendor of the MGM Grand Hotel. It was midafternoon, so the seemingly endless lines waiting for admission to the two giant nightclubs were not yet in place. The gaming tables spread across an area bigger than two football fields, never empty, were busy but not frantic. The jai alai fronton was dark, the movie theater not yet open. One could, however, have his picture taken with a live lion, eat at any of half a dozen restaurants, swim, play the miles of slot machines, drink, buy a fur coat or an "original art work," book a flying tour of the Grand Canyon, contract with a hooker. The two women looked at all this with the open expressions of utter strangers, visitors from a distant planet.

"Who do you think these people are?" Kaiser asked one of them.

"Fools." She laughed. "Probably gyp-offs. Embezzlers. Shit, I don't know."

"I don't know because I never met anyone like them," offered her friend. "You probably have."

Yes, Kaiser said, he had, and the conversation grew more animated.

"How do they talk? Do they talk like us?" one of them asked. Her friend was thinking:

What they don't realize is, if it wasn't for people like us, they wouldn't be up there on the ladders. Here they're makin' thirty and forty thousand dollars a year and I make forty-five hundred. You know? And here I am paying taxes out my ass and they're gripin' cause they have to pay a little bit of tax.

Money's not all that important. It's important to have enough. It's important to have just a little bit more than enough. Maybe say at least forty dollars that you could say is mine, that I could do what I want with from payday to payday. But when you don't even have fifty cents to say, "Oh, I can go get an ice cream cone this afternoon—"

Her friend interrupted:

There's no extras, you know. And here your kid wants— "Hey, Mom, can I have a dime to go get an ice." "Baby, I ain't got it." "Why, Mama? All's you have to do is go to the bank and write a check." My boy wanted a wallet and some money. So I got him a wallet and some play money. He said, "Mommy, you forgot the checks." He wanted some checks. I'm just waitin' for him to discover credit cards. I can't even get a credit card. My husband could not get a credit card. Because we don't make enough money. You know, we filed for this Bank Americard and that Master Charge, so that maybe we could—if something happened—we could go home and not worry about it. Pay it off, you know. Well, dream on.

Annie Frazer is twenty-two, from Oklahoma, married to an American Indian and the mother of two children. Jane Jeffers is twenty-five, from a tiny town in northwest Florida, married to a black man and also the mother of two. Both women are white, both are Air Force enlisted personnel. They were on thirty days' temporary duty at Nellis Air Force Base without their families.

What kind of world will your kids have?
Annie: I don't know. Ain't gonna be— I know my boy, even though he's smart for his age, like he knew his colors when he was two years old and that's doing good for two years old, and at the age of four he can draw people and he puts pupils in the eyes and nostrils in the nose and that's really good, his nursery teacher commented on it. But even if he grows up to be a scientist or somethin', I mean, what the fuck's he going to do when he's out in the world? It's going to be so many people pushing that he's going to be makin' what we're makin'. Living from day to day, hand to hand, worrying where every little penny is going to be. It ain't right. It's not right.
Jane: That's the way we live.

Who's making out well? Who's on easy street?
Jane: I would like to meet someone who actually was, someone who's got all the money they need. I've never met anybody like that, who's got everything they need. Who's got all the money they need. I never

met anybody like that. I don't know how they've gotten it.

Annie: I ain't figured out how these people drive these brand-new cars around yet. I know me and my old man together, we scrape in a little over fifteen hundred dollars a month. We still ain't got enough money to pour piss out of a boot if the directions are written on the heel. Because we got bills. I mean the electric bill, for instance, gas bills coming in, and you rent a place cause you can't afford to buy homes nowadays. You have to have a few months' deposit and rent yourself out for the rest of your life. Shit. So we rent places, you know? And your landlady charges a hundred dollars' deposit for this, you know, and goes around bitching all the time.

Jane: And then they sell it out from underneath you and make you leave.

Annie: I'll tell you what, I was renting a trailer, rented it for a whole year, lived there. We went home on leave, came back in April. Note on my kitchen table. "We sold the place. Will you be out by the tenth." Ha, ha. What could we do? There's nothin' you can do. "We gave you two weeks written notice."

Repeatedly in the conversation the two women came back to their inability to understand the conspicuous consumption going on around them. They visited the Middle American parade as spectators, and what they saw both amused and mystified them. It also brought flashes of sadness and envy.

Annie: We've been makin' fun of people all day.

Jane: Like that lady in the $150 dress and a fifty-dollar purse. Probably got three hundred in it. [They laugh.]

Annie: Charges $150 an hour—I don't know. We was looking at a hotel menu. What was that, breast of chicken for $9.50?

Jane: When you can buy a whole chicken for two dollars.

Annie: Two bucks. Even make dumplings if you wanted to. And egg noodles.

These two women will probably never understand how much they have in common with their Middle American counterparts. For example, both were uneasy about what their children pick up from television, casual attitudes toward violence and sex. Annie said her family had even tried not watching their set for three weeks when one of the children announced that when he grew up he was going to buy a gun and shoot "that lady at the store." They tried playing games like tiddlywinks and doing things like fingerpainting, but eventually the set flickered back on. Annie reflected:

I'll tell you what. I got a girlfriend and she's married to a man quite a bit older than she is, and he's got two older daughters, age eighteen and nineteen. One of 'em has lived with four or five dudes and works in a massage parlor. One of 'em's a heroin addict. What can he do? It's how you raise your kids, I think, from the foundation, you know. And what it takes is both parents to work. You really have to be particular who you get to watch your kids. Like I put mine for a while in the base nursery, which is really nice, but they kept raising the price on me. So I got this other lady to watch them, and she's really good with the kids. What can you say? And there's so many weird people today, really weird people. Homosexuality is really, really on the screen, you know; everybody's talking about it and stuff. And I was raised, that's just wrong. Sex is wrong anyway, unless you're married. That's just the way I was raised, and I hope that's the way my kids will be raised.

Both women said religion was important to them. "Praise the Lord!" Jane exclaimed when the subject first came up.

Do you go to church regularly?
Jane: Not regularly, but I praise God regularly.

How do you handle religion with your kids?
Jane: I have just begun. I have a long road ahead of me. I don't intend to do it alone. I am depending on a pastor and a Sunday school teacher, and I have started going with them.

Annie: We have church at our house. Four or five couples come over, and read stories out of the Bible. And we tell 'em what they are and stuff. Because my husband, he won't go to church ever since we started gettin' bills for tithes. [She laughs.] We feel like if we're going to give money to the church, it should be what we feel like we should give, what we want to give.

Jane [addressing Annie]: Are you Catholic?

Annie: No, we're Baptists.

Jane: I never heard of Baptists sending bills like that.

Annie: Religion is getting weaker now. Everything's O.K. in the society now, you know? Nudist colonies—"Hey, that's all right, that's fantastic"—hookers on the street, advertisin' it on television. Society is acceptin' these things. Churches are gettin' weak. Used to be they'd preach hell's fire all the time.

Jane: I don't think the spirit that God left here when Jesus arose and left is gonna accept things as being all right. If you are truly saved he's gonna let you know what's right, what's wrong. And you're gonna have the strength within yourself, through the spirit, to overcome the devil.

Annie: I've got to the point where I just don't give a fuck what goes on in democratic society and what the government does, cause they're gonna screw you anyway. I mean, we can vote, but how do you know they ain't changin' the ballots around? All those trustworthy people up there.

What happened to make you so cynical about it?

Annie: Cynical about the government? Every day, living with it, working for it, doing as it tells you to. Shit, you know those people up there ain't straight. You know it. They're gripin' about young people like us not voting when it's time for us to vote. Hell, who wants to vote, you know? There's just no reason to. Because they're going to have it their way. How do you know the CIA don't put in who they want and knock off who they don't want?

Annie and Jane both felt it was clear enough that the government did not have their interests at heart:

Annie: I mean, I can see where you're supposed to open your arms to for all the immigrants that's comin' over. But man. Like when we ended the Vietnam war and shipped all these refugees over here into Elgin Air Force Base, my old man worked thirty-six hours around the clock putting in telephones for them to use free of charge when Americans had to pay for it—while they've got their gold sitting in boxes with guys sittin' on top of it with M-sixteens guarding it. Going to the commissary, I had eighteen bucks to feed me, my two kids and my husband for two weeks till he got paid again—buying beans and macaroni and flour, you know, stuff to make it really last. And here come these so-called reverted enemies that we took in and all this stuff, just loadin' their baskets full and showin' that little pink card. "I'm a refugee," you know. "Bye-bye. Charge it to good old Uncle Sam." They help out—America helps out—everybody but their own people.

Jane: Seventy-five percent of the world's population is fed by the United States.

Annie: And here we have to pay outrageous prices for food, worrying about not havin' enough food to last. I think about it a lot. We get into a lot of arguments at the shop about it. Like I was raised up on a farm. O.K., now we had an acre garden. And we had to put in a spring garden, a summer garden, and a fall and winter garden to last us. And I canned and I helped Mamma freeze food and we slaughtered pigs. I still remember Grandpa stringin' up the pig in a tree, you know, and slicin' its guts out. We'd cook and boil our lard right there and store it away for the winter and stuff. Cause we were so damn poor, we were so damn poor, we were livin' in a log cabin, and Grandpa was too proud to ask for welfare. Which was good. And he'd been electrocuted. He was a carpenter, and he was up on top of the roof and the electricity was supposed to be off. His hammer hit it and he was electrocuted—had big old burn marks all over him. He was, you know, really bad off. But we worked. And my grandfather still lives on the farm. My mom and dad still live on the farm. And I wish that if we could afford the land, and pay for it, that's where I'd raise my kids. I really would.

Jane: I don't hope for anything.

Annie: Just live on a day-to-day basis.

Jane: I don't wish for anything, because I know anything I wish for—

Annie: Will make you sad and depressed.

Jane: It depresses you cause you can't get it.

Annie: So why should you, you know, waste your life bein' depressed. Might as well just live life. That's the way we are, you know. Me and my old man, we're happy. Goin' out down the highway and pickin' up pop bottles to get spare change. We're happy. Just the way it is. What I worry about most is like— I know when me and my old man start fighting about finances—ain't got money to get this, ain't got money to get that—my kids get uptight. And that's not right for a four-year-old and a two-year-old to get uptight cause their parents are arguing. I never heard my parents argue. You just live and try to see the bright side of everything. Even though it's hard sometimes.

19

FOUR LAST DREAMERS

"You've Got to Have Something to Look Forward To"

Cliff and Mariella Owston live in Garden City, Kansas, where he is in the real estate business and she works in a bank. They sold their farm in 1969 to move into town, a decision they are proud of. They sometimes take vacation trips with Ed and Joanne (Jo) Lewis, who still have their farm in Ulysses, Kansas, though they are thinking about selling it. All four are at or near their fiftieth year.

Kansas farm people—Norman Rockwell Americans, the original decent folks, the backbone of the nation—these four qualify for all the clichés. They grew up in the dust bowl of the 1930s, when the farm life in Kansas was hard. Ed Lewis remembers the fortuneteller at the county fair in 1935 or '36 who told his dad he would make his fortune someday by irrigating the Kansas plain. This was some years before the first irrigation wells, and it seemed a fanciful prediction. Then in 1937 the Lewises were driven off their place and all the way to Nebraska by the drought. But they came back during the war and started digging irrigation wells and canals, and by the 1950s Lewis's dad had a prosperous farm.

The speed with which life around them has changed amazes these four Kansans. Here they were in August, gallivanting around Las Vegas, hardly even thinking about the farm work at home that made the Augusts of their youth so busy—a typical example, they thought, of the transformed world they lived in. The four of them sat with us one night at a performance of *Hallelujah Hollywood!* and we resumed talking the next day in the Owstons' hotel room. They had not expected to be cross-examined on their views of the world during this vacation trip, but they took to the exercise enthusiastically, and talked for a long time.

When Ed Lewis began farming a section of land (640 acres) on his own in 1950, he started up with a $1900 loan from the bank. Today, he and Cliff agreed, it would take $190,000 to set up farming operations on the same size farm. They are all much better off than they expected to be, but all four referred to themselves as "working people" during the course of a long conversation. And when they described the hours they once put in working the land, the description seemed apt. This is Cliff on his decision to give up farming:

I quit in 'sixty-nine. We belonged to what they call the "farm management." You know, they figured your books and advised you on the operation of the farm and one thing and another. When the farm management cleared my records for the year, they figured I spent 360 days to operate. And I told Mariella [his wife], "I blew that five days somewhere, I don't know where!" [A laugh.] But I decided that if I had to work that hard, and what I had left at the end of the year after I'd paid taxes and expenses and one thing and other, for my salary I think it amounted to about eighteen cents an hour for 360 eight-hour days—

Mariella [interrupting]: And he really did work that many days.

Cliff: Well, I don't know if I really—

Mariella: Where did we go then?

Cliff: Well, we didn't go anywhere. Cut one day and went to town there—

Mariella: Got a haircut! [She laughs.]

So Cliff went into the insurance business, then into real estate, and he's pleased.

Ed Lewis is still farming his land, obviously making a comfortable go of it, and now he has help with the work. He was a little guilty about being on vacation in August: "Our son is takin' care of the farming. We're right in the busy season gettin' ready to plant wheat. I ought to be home."

The fact that they could be off on a holiday in August was a vivid example of how the world has changed for the Lewises and the Owstons. They talked about other changes, too:

Cliff: I wonder about the young people at home. Can they afford the two, three cars, $56,000 houses and the boats and the campers that they've got? I don't know how. They're startin' where Mom and Dad spent thirty years to get.

Mariella [who works in the bank]: Let me tell you— No, most of 'em can't afford it.

Cliff: I don't know about that, but they've *all* got it. They've got it. It's just sittin' out there. Even our kids.

Ed: We were on Conant Springs over the Fourth, and we met a couple that had been to California, and they came back through Las Vegas. And, uh—where was it they were from, hon?

Jo: Missouri.

Ed: Springfield, Missouri. And we asked him what he done, and he said [Ed is laughing], "I'm unemployed." [More laughter.] They left their kids with the grandparents and made this trip. They'd been gone two weeks. She worked in a telephone office. They came through Las Vegas and talked about seein' all the shows and stuff. Now, evidently he was drawin' unemployment, takin' a vacation. [A laugh.] How mixed up can our society git? The government, I suppose, has a lot to do with it.

Cliff introduced this subject, but he wanted to take the discussion in a different direction. He didn't mean to suggest that today's kids were somehow worse than previous generations:

As far as the young people are concerned, I was eight years on the unified school board there in Garden City. It's the largest school district in Kansas, area-wise. And any time you put one of these boys or girls, these kids, students, whatever you want to call them, young people, to the point where they had either to produce, or that was it—on their own, nobody to tail 'em up—I would say there was eighty percent of these kids who when it got to that point, they came through with flying colors. But as long as they didn't have to do it, and somebody was there to back 'em up—Mom, Dad, you know—they wouldn't do it. But when they was right out there, it was just kinda like throwin' 'em in a lake and tellin' 'em to swim back to shore. Eighty percent of 'em would make it, now I'll tell you for sure. So I think these kids can handle it. They can handle it just as Mom and Dad do, I guess, really.

Later the question arose about their grandchildren's generation, and what sort of world they might make or inherit. Cliff again wanted to make his point:

As far as the generations are concerned, they're always goin' to hell, every one of 'em. Every generation has gone to hell ever since when, and let's hope that's what they'll continue to do. [He laughs.] But I can't help but think that it'll continue to be as good to the future generations as it is to the ones now. Of course, everything is going to be different. My dad, I can remember, when I was a kid, he was always talkin' about "They're gonna farm with an airplane someday." Well, basically, there is things that we do with an airplane; it's part of farm operations. I've said too, hell, twenty-five years from now the kids won't even drive cars; they'll all fly helicopters. I may not be too far off.

Each generation thinks it's the toughest one there ever was, because that's the one they're in. I know our kids think so—"Oh, God, it's tough," you know. Well, their kids will think it's worse than Dad ever had it. I always remember this little old cartoon I saw. This father and little son was walkin' out in the snow and the father says to the boy who is walkin' along behind him, "It's not near as bad as it was when I was a kid. When I was a kid the snow was clear up to my chin." And that little kid was up to his chin in snow, you know?

What have these kids got to look forward to? Well, of course, Ben Franklin wanted to close the patent office way back when he was a young fella, because he thought everything there would be in the world was already invented. So, I don't know what these kids are thinking about. I mean, they may be thinking about pullin' a plow with a jet plane. Hell, I don't know. But they'll have a dream. You've got to have something to look forward to.

Ed Lewis was much less confident:

I just think, What are our grandkids— What kind of dream can they catch a hold of, that they can go ahead and develop? It's gonna be pretty rough gettin' through the society that they've got to go through. Our oldest grandchild is a little granddaughter. She's seven, she'll be in second grade next year, and what's worryin' me more than anything is the drugs that they're gonna have to go through. Now our kids were just at the age where—just before the drugs came in. See, they got through high school and kind of developed their patterns without any drugs. That's the biggest worry I think I've got is what my grandchildren are gonna go through with the drug problem and everything they have.

Ed had been thinking a lot about the next generation of his family lately, as he explained:

I've been debating with my son. He's twenty-eight. Married, they live on the farm too. He's been, you know, wantin' to get into farmin'. But he can go out and start to work at any gas plant around there—we're right in the middle of the gas field; it's the largest in the world—he can go and start workin' there at about seven dollars an hour with nothin' but his two hands, is all it takes—and his head. And I can't begin to make that much with around a $100,000 worth of equipment.

I'll never forget my dad askin' me, he says, "Ed," he says, "what do you want to tie yourself down for all your life, practically, payin' for this farm?" I said, "Well, Dad, what did you buy land for?" "Well, I bought it for you kids, something for you kids to have." I said, "Well, Dad, we've got three kids, that's what we bought our farm for, was so when we go, we can leave our kids a little endowment."

But Ed Lewis saw that issue differently now. The connection from generation to generation didn't seem as strong as it did. This is something we heard from many Americans.

Since then I kind of changed thinking—that a person in business builds up a business, then he will sell it when he's ready to want to retire; he'll sell that business on a contract or something, and collect the money over a period of years for his retirement. The farm, I'm thinking, maybe I might use for the same thing. If I could sell the farm over a twenty- or twenty-five-year contract, collect the interest, besides some principal, we could live pretty good and quit worryin' about the price of wheat goin' up or down.

Ed didn't say how his three children felt about this idea.

There is a limit to how far ahead a man can see or plan his life, Ed and Cliff agreed. During the course of the conversation both of them told stories about life's surprises. First Ed's:

Several years ago there was a boy at home had a bulldozer and backhoe and he was goin' broke. And he went out to Las Vegas to work with that equipment. And the next thing you knew, he had two or three bulldozers and two or three backhoes. Next thing you knew he was rollin' pretty good, decided to take up flyin'. Always wanted to learn how to fly an airplane. Well, he was a student, flyin' one day, crashed, and that was the last of that dream.

Cliff's story was more personal:

My attitude on life, I think, is probably different than anyone here, for one reason. In 1955 they gave me six months to live, three months on my feet and three months in bed, or have open heart surgery. And there wasn't but five seconds to decide which way. So I'm kind of bullet proof; I don't scare too easy. I've had more than twenty years [since he had that operation]. So my attitude towards life—as far as tomorrow— is probably different than anybody's here, because—uh—I've had a good one! [A laugh.]

They talked quite a lot about how they as Kansans felt about the country's big cities, their ghettos and their problems. "The laws ought to be more strict," Mariella Owston said. "I don't think it's right they let those people go in there and loot." She also thought immigration explained some of it. "Why don't they keep the immigration down like they used to?"

Wasn't it the other way around? Didn't we used to have floods of immigrants early in the century? "Well, I just don't like it," Mariella said. Did she see any connection between her life and the lives of people in New York, Chicago, Philadelphia? "I've never been there!" she said with a laugh. Ed Lewis joined the discussion:

As far as some respects, there's quite a bit that would be the same. Well, we can't compare ourselves with the ghetto in New York, but I think probably the average people, average working class, the average businessman is experiencing the same thing we are. I know there's probably businesses in New York that are going broke every day, and there's some of 'em that's makin' money—and it's the same all over the United States.

When you get into a world deal, what's hard for us to realize, these people in other countries have faced this years ago. [By "this" Ed appears to mean present-day conditions in Kansas.] Now Spain—we was lucky enough here a few years ago, the four of us, to take a trip to Spain. And I thought at that time, Gosh, see these little cars. I mean, that's all that's there; you didn't see anything bigger than, uh, a Mustang. That's a big car. Chevy Impala I think was the biggest car we saw there. Gas was a dollar-something a gallon at that time, and that's been four or five years ago. You see more of it here now every day. The compact car—because of gas consumption we're forced into it.

Our state of Kansas is what, close to the size of Spain, not too much different. It's four hundred miles to the capital from home, and in one of them little compact cars [he laughs] I'd hate to think about drivin' it, but I suppose I could. The record shows that big cars are what's in demand, but we might as well face it, they ain't going to be in demand very long.

Mariella: When I read about the people in the larger cities back East, I think, what do they have to look forward to? You know, I'd really feel pretty hopeless. And I don't know what I have to look forward to that they don't, but that's how I feel when I read about them. It just seems like it's a hopeless situation.

Cliff: Aw, it's not hopeless.

Jo: Well I think we all have relatives that live in cities, and they're just working people like us. They like the city. We like the country. There are people that like the city. They don't mind at all.

Mariella: I don't think some of them are there by choice.

Cliff: The problem is, I mean, our problems and their problems are related. They're not there by choice, but some of 'em can't get out. And there's poor people right in western Kansas that are in situations, they're not there by their choice.

That discussion did not lead to any consensus or conclusions. Perhaps the subject was too remote. But the four of them found agreement relatively easy on a local matter, the behavior of their public officials in Kansas and government in general. As he mentioned, Cliff was a member of the school board. Ed was still a county commissioner.

Cliff: You take school boards and county commissioners and city commissioners and college trustees, whatever—they do not operate it like they would if it was their own private business. What I'm talkin' about is the dollars and cents they spend. For instance, on the school board, they would argue for hours how to spend five hundred bucks, then in thirty seconds they'd spend five hundred thousand. Ain't nobody knew what they were doin'. But on five hundred bucks: "Yeah, I know about that; that's too much for that little item." But they'd spend five hundred thousand because they couldn't realize in their minds what they were buying, or how many dollars five hundred thousand was, so, "Yeah, yeah," everybody votes aye.

Ed: The thing that worries me as much as anything, every year we've got to make out a county budget, and every year we've got to decide how much. It's not whether to give a raise; it's how much, what percent are we going to give this year—this cost-of-living raise. It's got to stop someday. Just think, in twenty years, if we go ahead and give five to ten percent every year, what is that going to amount to? And who's going to pay for it, except the taxpayer?

The four of them agreed that government was becoming remote. "They take things away from the county, take it to the state, it gets bigger and goes to the national," as Joanne put it. This could even be laughable. Mariella had an example:

Who was it that went to Washington, D.C., last winter on his knees about the energy crisis, our gas situation? And they wanted to know in Washington what we needed gas to heat the irrigation water for. I couldn't believe—

Ed: We'd better explain to Bob here, we don't heat irrigation water!

Mariella: Oh, no! We need the power to get the water out of the ground! They thought we wanted the gas to heat the water!

Cliff: That's how far removed they were from the issue. And yet the individual who asked that question was on a committee that was supposed to be advisin' the President on the energy program.

Ed: So much of it is laws that the legislature has passed that we have to conform to ["we" means his fellow county commissioners]. Our care home, we thought we had to add to it, because there was always a waitin' list. It was a fifty-bed care home. We said, "Well, let's add twenty-five beds." The care home was built in 'sixty-six, and it cost right around $350,000 to build it at the time. What we had to do to bring it up to the new state specifications so that the patients in the home were eligible for Medicare was going to cost $300,000.

Sprinklers—that's something the insurance companies have demanded and got. All it is is an expense. Because in a care home with sprinklers, all you're goin' to have is a bunch of dead, wet, suffocated patients. A little old smoke alarm would work so much better, and they only cost about thirty-five dollars to put in a room. A smoke alarm'd go off from just a little smoke. And by the time one of those sprinklers goes off, if there's a fire the patients are goin' to be dead from smoke inhalation.

We build the addition to the home, and it was a million dollars. We had to put in sprinklers, fire doors, up in the attic was fire walls. The doors on the bathroom we had to replace because they got to swing both ways, it's the regulation.

Mariella: If some of these people that made these regulations could admit they made a mistake and go back and change it. Like they came out last year and said farmers in southwest Kansas had to have these drinking fountains and restroom facilities for their help. That just isn't feasible. Well they finally admitted it and rescinded it.

Ed: Some of these silly laws is costin' the people, the government, billions of dollars every year for these regulations. Just all it is is to keep a bunch of bureaucrats down there with a job.

20

THE END

A huge new Middle America, half the population at least, disproportionately powerful in its influence on popular American culture, is the force that defines American life today, and those millions are essentially a contented lot.

Statistically, at least, this new Middle America has existed since the end of the 1960s, when the great postwar economic boom came to an end. By then American society had already been transformed, though it has taken some years to recognize what has happened. That transformation created a majority of "haves"—a middle class majority, a majority that has acted out the great American dreams and found them realistic, attainable.

The bitter atmosphere of the 1960s disguised this transformation, and thanks to Richard Nixon and Vietnam, the '60s didn't really end until 1974, when Nixon finally gave up. Only then could the country exhale and re-examine itself. Only then could the 1970s acquire a tangible identity.

The America we found several years later was far removed from the tumultuous, painful '60s. Of course that era had left many scars and many changes, but there was an entirely different mood. After 1974 the new Middle America could come into its own, and it did.

Some of the characteristics of this new Middle America are just old American verities, like Jack Gordon's enthusiasm for gadgetry or Sandy Ford's indomitable optimism. Others are specific to this age—for example, Dr. Tippit's search for a "happy" operation, or fourteen-year-old John's complaint that he didn't know what his own father's boyhood had been like.

But the essential nature of this new America is unprecedented; it has given us a new kind of country to live in. We have no experience of a society numerically dominated by the fortunate, the relatively prosperous and the contented, but that is just what we now have. This finding seems to surprise people. It surprised us. But there has actually been dispassionate research that supports our conclusion.

For example, Professor Willard Rodgers of the University of Michigan's Institute for Social Research, probably the world's leading institution for the study of public opinion, has been conducting "soft" polls of popular attitudes for years. Rodgers does surveys on "the subjective quality of life" that have found high satisfaction among middle class Americans. People tend to like their personal lives, family relationships, jobs and neighborhoods. Dissatisfaction increases as the subject under discussion grows more remote—national politics, the future of the economy, the morals of strangers who inhabit other corners of the society, etc. His surveys have prompted "a lot of skepticism" from some colleagues, Rodgers told Lowell, "because people express so much satisfaction and so little dissatisfaction with so many different things."

These generalizations can be carried too far. If Middle America is essentially content, it also contains a lot of grouches. If optimism is typical, deep gloom is not hard to find. Though politics bores the vast majority of Middle Americans, enough of them participate to keep the raft of state afloat.

Our generalizations are also value-free. We are not going to pass judgments on McDonald's hamburgers or the opportunities for creative individuality in America's suburbs. Many social critics are appalled by both, but we are more struck by the nature of the human category at issue. Middle America is a unique historical invention. The new middle classes have risen from something akin to the peasantry of traditional societies, risen quickly in a generation or two to become a mass of unprecedented size, power and wealth. Now they set the tone for an entire civilization—and no pipsqueak of a civilization either.

Middle American instincts have largely wrought the postwar transformation of the country into a suburbanized, automobilized society knit together by television and the interstate highway system. Middle American tastes explain the popular music of the era, the clothing styles, the boom in fast-food restaurants and junk-food concoctions. The great buffet is the richest single marketplace in the history of all human commerce, and capitalists of this and many other nations have competed eagerly to place their products on the buffet table.

The political influence of Middle America is still primarily negative, but this could change quickly, and may be changing already. The negative influence grows from the fact that a clear majority of citizens (and a large majority of voters—since the poor vote even less than the middle class) now believe that the United States works fine the way it is. These are the people who have seen great American dreams come true in their own lives, and who believe the old truths: hard work pays off, anyone can get a share if he or she works hard enough for it, and so forth. These Americans tend to exaggerate the size of their own class and underestimate the number of their fellow citizens who share neither their confidence nor their standard of living. They tend to think of themselves as the real Americans, the typical Americans, and to look on less fortunate citizens as a fringe group. The society at large reinforces this impression by catering almost exclusively to the middle class, and by allowing Middle Americans the opportunity to cut themselves off in suburbia's homogenized enclaves.

All this puts Middle America on the side of the status quo. The status quo may include chronic high unemployment, 40 to 50 percent unemployment among young black men, a huge and unassimilated underclass, deplorable living conditions for millions of people—but none of this directly affects Middle America.

There is more involved here than selfishness. Middle Americans have a keen sense of how much they think has been done by government and the courts to protect the rights and opportunities of less fortunate Americans. The promise of the New Deal has been kept, or so it seems. Welfare payments of various kinds provide food, shelter and medical care to the indigent. There appears to be no basis for feeling guilty about poor people. And besides, what are we supposed to do about them? That is a Middle American rallying cry, one to which there is no glib answer.

There is selfishness, too, and economic conditions in recent years have aggravated it. The fact that the great postwar boom ended a decade ago has only slowly come to the attention of most Middle Americans. Inflation obscured the true state of affairs by providing nearly everyone with a steadily rising income throughout the 1970s. The same inflation nullified the practical benefits of those rising incomes, but this has been less obvious until recently.

Besides inflation, the 1970s brought a new and troubling phenomenon to Middle America's attention: shortages. The Arabs' oil embargo in 1973 set this off; and in the years that followed, Americans experienced all sorts of surprising shortages: of sugar, of coffee, even of water in many western states. In 1979 unexpected shortages of oil and abrupt increases in its cost again jolted the country, though the populace seemed determined not to believe that the shortage was real.

Economic troubles have challenged the essential optimism in Middle America by suggesting that the long history of middle class progress might be coming to an end. This is an alarming thought. The upward curve has been a part of Middle American lives, something to count on, "like death and taxes." The possibility that the curve might now flatten out *permanently* has evoked inconsistent reactions. Many indomitable optimists remain optimistic; some have been shaken; some are scared.

The thought that future progress may not be inevitable lends to a range of new concerns, chief among them the desire to secure what has already been accomplished or acquired. And in many circumstances that instinct can be easily confused with simple selfishness.

This force was certainly at work in California in 1978 when about 30 percent of the adult population voted for Proposition 13. That vote was widely interpreted as a repudiation of "big government," and no doubt there was some of that; but Proposition 13 itself said nothing about the size of the government. It concerned the size of the property tax rate, and the vote for Proposition 13 was first of all a protest against soaring taxes. It was a vote to put several hundred dollars in every homeowner's pocket—a vote to help California homeowners cope with a devastating inflation.

The unexpected boldness of those Californians in voting so decisively (2–1) for Proposition 13 resounded around the country. A great many citizens and politicians suddenly sensed that Proposition 13 lit the path to a new kind of assertive middle class politics. Politicians particularly rushed to get a place at the head of this new parade.

Talking with Middle Americans has given us new appreciation for the difficulties faced by the practitioners of politics. This is a time of satisfaction and drift, a time for looking inward, a time without a national consensus on any great public issue, except perhaps a general agreement that something must be done about inflation. Many of the citizens who are really active in public affairs belong to what the politicians call "one-issue groups" that throw all of their enthusiasm behind a narrow cause: against abortion, for example, or for the Equal Rights Amendment, or against controls on guns. The minority of Americans who regularly vote have lately behaved most erratically, sometimes turning on incumbent officials for no apparent reason, sometimes sticking by them in surprising circumstances.

So what is a politician to do? Where does popularity lie, and how can one get there? Proposition 13 provided the first plausible answers in a long time, and the politicians fled like lemmings in the direction of tax cuts, less government and the like.

This was big news. The pundits reflected on it at great length, the speechmakers spoke on it windily, but all the professional excitement failed to touch the citizenry. In the 1978 elections—held at the height of Proposition 13 fever—just 38 percent of the adult population bothered to cast a vote.

Politics as it is now practiced simply fails to reach the great mass of Americans. People cannot get interested. Either they don't want anything from the government, or they have no faith in the politicians, or they are convinced that nothing they can do would make any difference. There may be a positive element in this situation. At least many millions of Americans still feel competent to run their own lives, take care of their own needs without depending on the government. But there may be an equal number who have given up on politicians in despair.

Where this may lead is a mystery to us. Given the existence of a potentially decisive electoral majority that is currently ignoring politics altogether, the possibilities are numerous.

It appears likely that Middle America will increasingly sense its own power to influence public policy. If relative economic stagnation continues, a politics of middle class self-protection—some will call it selfishness—will probably grow stronger. There is an inherent logic to this, since the middle class now really is a majority of the population.

Much could depend on the values that prevail in Middle America, and it is impossible to say just what they are. The cardinal liberal values that have animated the American experiment came to us from a small revolutionary élite, but their survival now depends on mass acceptance. We found that Middle Americans do care about individual worth, access to opportunity and the fair exercise of authority. But whether they care enough to preserve those values in serious adversity remains to be seen.

Repeatedly in their conversation Americans speak of their confidence that "when things get really tough," or "when the chips are down," the country will pull together in common endeavor for a common good. There is a widespread craving for guidance in Middle America—guidance toward common goals for which all Americans could happily make sacrifices.

And what fate for the American Dream? The answer may depend on who the dreamers will be.

Many Middle Americans worry that their own children will find the basic dreams unattainable. Parents fear that their protected, pampered children—apparently so happy yet also so isolated—won't know how to compete in the "real" world, and won't be able to sustain the social and economic progress that their elders have taken for granted.

These concerns could prove justified. But even if they do, the great American dreams can survive if substantial numbers from the lower strata—the left-out 40 percent—can push themselves upward into Middle America or even beyond. That huge reservoir of humanity contains more than enough energy and talent to keep the spirit of Horatio Alger breathing.

In recent times the American social structure has demonstrated interesting flexibility. During the same postwar years that Middle America has grown into the largest element in the society, the old Anglo-Saxon Protestant élite has lost its grip on many of America's command posts. We have learned that second-generation Italians can make perfectly adequate partners in the giant law firms of Wall Street, and that a Jew can run E. I. duPont de Nemours and Company.

During the 1960s a new social phenomenon appeared—downward mobility. It became commonplace for the children of the American élite to voluntarily relinquish their status to become carpenters or farmers or even bums. Downward mobility may also be in the future of some of Middle America's children.

American society might maintain its present character for years by providing simultaneously for upward mobility from the lower classes and downward mobility from above. This combination could make room for new dreamers and keep new energies flowing even if the economy can no longer sustain the continuing expansion of Middle America.

But that is an optimistic view, and there are certainly other possibilities. The middle classes and particularly the upper middle classes have proven effective at passing their status on from generation to generation. For example, a Harvard Business School survey a few years ago found that the social characteristics of American business leaders had remained remarkably constant throughout the twentieth century. College students are increasingly likely to be the sons or daughters of college graduates, whereas thirty years ago this was the exception.

If the middle class and the élite can preserve for their children the best access to the best opportunities, and if there is insufficient economic growth to expand the upper and middle classes, then American dreams are in serious jeopardy. Conceivably, the enormous growth of Middle America has created not only a new kind of America, but also an unprecedented risk of inertia or even stagnation.

But if Battista Locatelli could fulfill his dreams and learn to fly, too, if Shirley Walker could find a meaning in life and Ed Lewis's dad could irrigate the Kansas plain and make it bloom, if Bob Goldberg could conquer the world before he was thirty and Sandy Ford could raise four children as a widow, then anything can happen. Hold on.

AN AFTERWORD

Las Vegas, Nevada

A fat lady in a halter top and double-knit slacks stopped her younger, red-haired female companion, she with the explosion of curlers not quite hidden under a chiffon kerchief, and pointed at Robert Dolgin.

"Is he a rock star?" she asked earnestly, examining the profusion of long hair and blue denim. "He must be," her friend replied, motoring off to the nickel slot machines.

Actually, Dolgin was operating a booth in the Las Vegas Hilton as one of 2,000 delegates to the annual convention of the National Nutritional Foods Association. He was handing out samples of soybean products.

We asked several of the delegates why the health food industry had chosen as their convention center America's gaudiest salute to excess, but none of them had a comfortable explanation.

Las Vegas could exist only in America. It is a monument to American classlessness and—if the truth be told—tastelessness too. The city casts many spells, creates countless illusions, and appears in radically different form in different Americans' minds' eyes. It can be a glittery red-velvet and whipped-cream venue for a weekend tryst, or a mid-desert stop on the family's cross-country drive in a camper. It is a gambler's haven where millions of dollars can cross the gaming tables in one busy weekend, or a place to invest nickels in slot machines while waiting for a big-name "star"—usually someone whose name was made big on television—to go on stage in the evening.

The setting and architecture of Las Vegas are crucial to its appeal and its success. The setting is a moonscape, a lifeless desert valley surrounded by rough, beautiful, bare mountain peaks on all sides, like nothing most people ordinarily experience. Spread across the valley floor are some of humanity's rarest monuments, the malproportioned, disfigured, bizarre but undeniably dramatic structures that house the most profitable resort hotels in the world. Some have 2,000 rooms or more. Some are tall and angular, others squat and rambling, but all have one attribute in common: a giant electronic sign out front, meant originally to catch and trap passing motorists, but now equally intended to make a good impression—on competitors as well as customers, maybe also on the art historians who must eventually record these signs as works of art, as Tom Wolfe realized years ago.

Some of the signs are fifteen stories high, others are an acre across. All are surrounded by explosions of electric light. Every giant sign stakes out one hotel's territory, and a large territory it is. The major establishments each occupy an area about the size of a big suburban shopping center, with about as much asphalt devoted to parking lots. Theoretically, the client should find so much within those precincts to titillate, amuse and sate that he will never feel a need to venture elsewhere, and particularly not to some competitor's casino, where the serious money is made.

The huge casinos complete this unique environment. They are just inside the front door of every hotel, and to get anywhere within a hotel one usually (at least this was the architect's intention) must pass through or next to the casino floor. The atmosphere here is created by tobacco smoke, mirrored ceilings (one-way mirrors, so company detectives can watch the gambling unseen from above), but mostly by the noise—the crunch of slot machine handles coming down, the jangle of silver dollars bouncing out of slot machines into hyperresonating tin trays, the shouts of manic craps players pleading with dice to behave, the shuffling of cards and clicking of chips.

Altogether the moonscape, the signs, the hot desert sun, the casino noises and smells create an otherworldly impression. To be in Las Vegas is to be *elsewhere*. The feeling this generates is not easy to describe. We concluded it was something like arriving in a free port for the superego, where the captain hands out passes to disembarking passengers authorizing them not to worry about whatever they usually worry about.

Those passes produce a lot of ridiculous and pathetic behavior in Las Vegas. People can lose money they'd never had, do things they'd never dream of doing at home and generally abandon standard definitions of acceptable behavior without evident qualm. We tried to avoid most of that on the theory that it might be relevant to a book about Las Vegas, but really didn't have an important part in a book about the great American dreams.

Another consequence of the Las Vegas environment was more relevant to our project, and more helpful. Americans on a fling in Las Vegas, we found, were willing to talk freely to strangers about many matters, including deeply personal ones. Now this is an American trait anyhow, and we found numerous people outside Las Vegas who shared it, but it seemed to us that the Nevada moonscape was particularly well suited to our inquiry. We spent hours hanging around hotel swimming pools and lobbies, camping grounds and convention halls in Las Vegas just walking up to people and asking them questions. Most of these encounters were polite but fruitless, but many turned into long and interesting conversations.

Las Vegas gave us another advantage, too. It provided a huge sample of Americans from an extraordinary range of backgrounds in a single locale, with a virtually complete turnover (involving perhaps 80,000 people) every few days. The casinos brought one category of humanity, the campgrounds another, the conventions countless more (including people who would never dream of a trip to Las Vegas without the excuse of a convention). An extraordinary percentage of the total sample seemed to fall into our Middle American category, somewhere in that 50-plus percent between the very richest and the mass of poor or nearly poor.

As we said at the outset, we make no claim to have found a scientific sample, or to have conducted a systematic survey. This book represents the accumulated weight of 10,000 different impressions, plus a dash of mischief and a lot of fun.

We had a taste of Robert Dolgin's soybean paste from The Farm, and neither of us liked it. But the banquet of humanity we found in Las Vegas was a treat to be savored.

ACKNOWLEDGMENTS

This book was made possible by the kindness and generosity of hundreds of men and women who agreed to talk with us or helped us find other interesting people. Many of them appear in the book itself, usually under their real names. Many others were squeezed out of the book as we went along, not because they were less interesting, but because we had to be selective and often arbitrary. We are indebted to everyone who helped.

We owe thanks to John Hawkins, a rare literary agent who can actually inspire his authors, to Simon Michael Bessie of Harper & Row, who supported this project with both his confidence and then his considerable gifts as an editor, and to Amy Bonoff, whose thoughtful editing was a great boon. Carl Bernstein gave the manuscript a rigorous reading that much improved the final product.

This project was a strain on two families, both of whom endured our trips to Las Vegas, our weekends over typewriters and a great deal more besides. Amy Lowell and Hannah Kaiser were helpful critics as well as invaluable companions; we thank them especially.